Schools for Conflict or for Peace in Afghanistan

Schools for Conflict or for Peace in Afghanistan

DANA BURDE

Columbia University Press   *New York*

Columbia University Press
Publishers Since 1893
New York   Chichester, West Sussex
cup.columbia.edu
Copyright © 2014 Columbia University Press
All rights reserved
Library of Congress Cataloging-in-Publication Data

Burde, Dana.
Schools for conflict or for peace in Afghanistan / Dana Burde.
pages cm
Includes bibliographical references and index.
ISBN 978-0-231-16928-8 (cloth : alk. paper) — ISBN 978-0-231-53751-3 (ebook)
1. Education—Afghanistan.   2. Schools—Afghanistan.   3. Education and state—
Afghanistan.   4. Nation-building—Afghanistan.   5. Economic assistance, American—
Afghanistan.   6. Humanitarian assistance, American—Afghanistan.   I. Title.

LA1081.B87 2015
370.9581—dc23

2014010612

Columbia University Press books are printed on permanent and durable acid-free paper.
This book is printed on paper with recycled content.
Printed in the United States of America
c 10 9 8 7 6 5 4 3 2 1

COVER ART: "Flower and Bomb" by Ehsan Hossaini, age 8 (Kabul, Afghanistan). This
drawing was submitted to the United Nations Art for Peace Contest in 2012, sponsored by
the United Nations Office for Disarmament Affairs and the Harmony for Peace Foundation
(see www.unartforpeace.org).

References to websites (URLs) were accurate at the time of writing. Neither the author nor
Columbia University Press is responsible for URLs that may have expired or changed since
the manuscript was prepared.

To my husband, Jehanzaib Khan,

and my parents, Ed and Emily Burde

Contents

Acknowledgments

I COULD NOT HAVE COMPLETED THIS BOOK without enormous support from many people and institutions. I began the work when I was a postdoctoral research scholar at the Saltzman Institute of War and Peace Studies (SIWPS) at Columbia University. Kathy Neckerman and the Institute for Social and Economic Research and Policy (ISERP) at Columbia supported my first trip to Afghanistan. My wonderful colleagues at SIWPS—Tanisha Fazal, Page Fortna, Bob Jervis, Pablo Pinto, Tonya Putnam, and Jack Snyder—gave me terrific feedback and provided a stimulating and supportive atmosphere that allowed me to thrive. Devon Curtis and Kelly Greenhill—co-postdocs—also enriched my time at Columbia and helped me design successful plans for my projects. Thanks also to Neil Boothby and Gita Steiner-Khamsi for their encouragement and support early on in this work.

The Spencer Foundation, the United States Institute of Peace, and the Weikart Family Foundation funded my first pilot study in the Panjshir Valley in Afghanistan in 2006, without which the larger study in Ghor Province would not have been possible. Phyllis and Kathy Weikart, Cindy Embry, and Jenny Danko, all of the Weikart Family Foundation, gave tremendous support and a crucial vote of confidence; David Weikart's work and memory have been an inspiration throughout. The Spencer Foundation and the National Science Foundation (NSF) funded the large-scale randomized controlled trial in Afghanistan, and I owe an enormous debt of gratitude to Susan Dauber of the Spencer Foundation for her willingness to take a risk on a project that surely seemed crazy at the time.

Thanks also to Brian Humes at NSF, who saw the merit in collecting data in difficult circumstances. Kathy Neckerman at ISERP went above and beyond in providing insights into the secrets of proposal writing.

Since moving to New York University, I have been fortunate enough to work with another truly lovely group of colleagues, without whose support I would not have been able to complete this book. At the Steinhardt School I owe tremendous thanks to Dean Mary Brabeck, Senior Vice Provost for Global Faculty Development Ron Robin, Vice Dean Beth Weitzman, and my department chair, Jon Zimmerman, all of whom have taken a personal interest in my adventures and offered generous support both institutionally and personally. They supported my research leave in Pakistan in 2012–13 (Goddard Fellowship, New York University Challenge Research Fund, CARE Fellowship, and Fulbright Research Scholar Fellowship), which provided both essential proximity to the data and time to complete the manuscript. I am grateful also to my departmental colleagues, who have been willing to make do in my absence and been patient as I phone in to meetings and advise students from afar. I am particularly indebted to Phil Hosay, Cynthia Miller-Idriss, and Kiki Pop-Eleches, who were also critical in making my research leave possible.

Of course this work could not have been completed without the help of a great number of colleagues in Afghanistan or the tremendous work of my coauthor on the large-scale, mixed-methods, randomized controlled trial, economist Leigh Linden (University of Texas at Austin). I appreciate the help and patience of the Catholic Relief Services (CRS) team in Afghanistan that collaborated with us: Zia Ahmad Ahmadi, Sara Alexander, Epifania Amoo-Adare, Feroz Arian, Keith Aulick, Sara Bowers, Christine Carneal, Michaela Egger, Eric Eversmann, Kevin Hartigan, Paul Hicks, Matthew McGarry, Dominique Morel, Nafi Olomi, Huma Safi, and Aude Saldana. Anita Anastacio and Helen Stannard, from the Partnership for Advancing Community Education in Afghanistan, and Lisa Laumann, from Save the Children, provided additional support. Thanks to Fotini Christia for insights into her study of the National Solidarity Program. Nathan Falkner provided valuable research assistance. Matthew Hoover offered exceptional support as both a research assistant and project manager, and thanks to Saeed Mahmoodi for his unparalleled work as our survey manager.

Acknowledgments

CRS and CARE provided institutional support in the last phase of this study, cohosting me in Kabul in fall 2012. For that trip I owe thanks to Doc Coster, Denzyl Kennedy, and Jennifer Rowell at CARE; Bill Schmitt and Michelle Neukirchen at CRS. And thanks to Nancy Dupree for the tour of the archives at the remarkable new Afghanistan Center at Kabul University.

Many friends and colleagues offered support and insights on the other side of the border, in Pakistan. I owe a tremendous debt to Helen Kirby for hosting my first trip there in 2005 and helping me understand the refugee villages in Balochistan. Amin Aminullah was also instrumental during that visit. At CRS in Pakistan, I thank Jack Byrne, Carolyn Fanelli, Michelle Markey, Joanna Olsen, and Andy Schaefer for their key support at critical moments.

Very dear friends provided transnational support. Without their collective insights and good humor, writing this book would not have been possible. They include Susan Allee, Maureen Agostini, Anita Anastacio, Allison Anderson, Ashley Barr, Charlotte Blomhammar, Sara Bowers Posada, Elise Cappella, Dalton Conley, Staffon Darnolf, Wendy Fisher, Simona Gallotta, Toral Gajarawala, Marcela Goglio, Debby Greenebaum, Susie Greenebaum, Jennifer Hill, Katre Jervis, Carolyn Kissane, Karen Krahulick, Jamie Lew, Mimi Lind, Cathryn Magno, Veronica Mijelshon, Mike Meyer, Yolande Miller-Grandvaux, Erin Murphy-Graham, Kim Perlow, Cybele Raver, Pilar Robledo, Sarah Simons, Tammy Smith, Sherrill Stroschein, Pietro Tilli, Florencia Torche, Kathryn Vittum, Niobe Way, and Davina Weinstein.

A number of friends and colleagues offered invaluable feedback at several phases of the writing. I am deeply grateful to Kevin Hartigan, Lori Heninger, Jennifer Hill, Bob Jervis, Elisabeth King, Jennie Matthew, Joel Middleton, Chris Pagen, Jennifer Rowell, Nerina Rustomji, Melissa Schwartzberg, Jack Snyder, Noah Sobe, Chris Steel, Niobe Way, and Jon Zimmerman. Thanks also to Paul Fishstein and Jason Lyall for their astute comments on chapter 4. I also owe immense thanks to my doctoral students for their research assistance over the years: Amy Kapit, Rachel Wahl, and Ozen Guven. And special thanks to Max Margulies for his phenomenal job of editing and helping me stay on track. Of course any errors are my own.

I would like to thank the "Tight-Knit Critical Thinkers of Quetta"—Hafiz Abdul Basit, Shahzada Rashid Mehmood, and my husband Jehanzaib Khan—for their humor and perseverance, and my brother-in-law Gohar Iqbal for stepping in to help out when most needed. Thanks to my parents Emily and Ed Burde for their unconditional support and concern when I travel to faraway places, and to my brothers, Jim and Mark, and sisters-in-law, Kay and Lisa, for their continued interest in my work. Thanks also to Lynne Weikart, who has inspired me for many years, and to Jim Weikart and Dana Lichty for being so supportive.

In my rush to find cover art, Angela Braid came to the rescue and mobilized her family of artists to help. Deep thanks to Ange Braid, Cath Braid, and Naomi Braid for their coordinated efforts across three continents to find or create just the right cover image. Tremendous thanks also to Anne Marie Marten and Helen Stannard for contributing to this quest for children's art.

Columbia University Press has been a pleasure to work with, making a complicated and stressful process proceed smoothly and painlessly. I am truly grateful to my editor Anne Routon, who was focused and supportive throughout. Thanks also to Whitney Johnson, David Sassian, Roy Thomas for their work, and to the anonymous reviewers of the proposal and manuscript.

Finally, I would like to thank again my husband, Jehanzaib Khan, for his never-ending patience with my long work hours and moments of frustration, and for providing a limitless source of stability and love from which all good things come.

Time Line

Education in Modern Afghan History

1747	Ahmad Shah Durrani founds the Durrani Empire, marking the birth of the modern Afghan state.
1839–42	First Anglo-Afghan War is fought, strengthening the local clergy and tribal leaders.
1878–80	Second Anglo-Afghan War is fought.
1880–1901	Abdur Rahman Khan rules Afghanistan. His reign is characterized by attempts to modernize the country and exert central control over the religious education system.
1893	Durand Line is surveyed, dividing large populations of Pashtuns, as well as other groups, and delineating the frontier between Afghanistan and the British Empire.
1901	Habibullah assumes the throne.
1904	Habibia College, Afghanistan's first modern secondary school, is founded.
1913	The first department of education in Afghanistan established, though it would be another nine years before a minister of education is appointed.
1919–29	Amanullah Khan rules Afghanistan. He institutes many reforms to education, including compulsory and free primary education for certain groups;

ending the clergy's control over mosque schools; and expanding curricula to include nonreligious classes.

1929   Civil war breaks out, in part over opposition to Amanullah's attempts to wrest power from the clergy and intervene in rural family life, but also as a response to financial crises. Amanullah is deposed by Habibullah Kalakani.

1931   Nadir Shah, who seized power from Habibullah Kalakani, enacts a new constitution that undoes most of Amanullah's reforms, defining the state of education in Afghanistan for the next two decades.

1937   Zahir Shah, the last king of Afghanistan, assumes the throne.

1953   Mohammad Daoud Khan becomes prime minister. He expands support to education, enlisting aid from the US.

1956   Teachers College, Columbia University (TC) begins its education development work in Afghanistan by training English teachers for secondary schools. School enrollment climbs considerably.

1966   TC, funded by USAID, expands its education work in Afghanistan to supporting curricula reform and providing textbooks, which it continues to do for the next ten years.

1973   Mohammad Daoud Khan, the former prime minister, seizes power from his cousin Zahir Shah in a coup.

1973   Zulfiqar Ali Bhutto becomes prime minister of Pakistan after previously serving as president for two years.

1977   Zia ul-Haq deposes Zulfiqar Ali Bhutto in a coup in Pakistan and declares martial law. General Zia governs Pakistan for the next eleven years, overseeing the Islamization of Pakistan's education system; ex-

	panding madrassas on the border with Afghanistan; and managing US and Saudi funding for the Afghan mujahideen living in exile in Peshawar.
April 1978	The Afghan communist party seizes power in the Saur Revolution and attempts to secularize education across Afghanistan.
December 24, 1979	USSR invades Afghanistan. During its occupation, the USSR launches aggressive literacy campaigns throughout rural Afghanistan and revises the Afghan curricula to reduce the focus on religious studies.
January 1980	US President Jimmy Carter authorizes additional covert aid to support the Afghan resistance.
1984	Saudi aid to the mujahideen increases, especially for the building and funding of madrassas.
1984	Afghan mujahideen leaders request support from the US government to provide a culturally relevant, religious curriculum to the Afghan refugees.
1986	University of Nebraska at Omaha (UNO), funded by USAID, begins to provide jihadist textbooks to Afghan refugees.
February 1989	USSR completes its withdrawal from Afghanistan.
1992	President Najibullah falls. Eventually Burhanuddin Rabbani becomes president, but civil war is raging.
1992	US/UNO revises jihadist textbooks. However, revisions are minimal and originals remain widely available throughout the Taliban's rule (with images removed).
1994	A group of mujahideen called the Taliban emerges from villages in Kandahar Province and joins in the civil war in Afghanistan.
1996	The Taliban take Kabul, eventually consolidating their control over most of Afghanistan and ending the civil war.

October 7, 2001   US and several allies invade Afghanistan in response to the September 11th terrorist attacks on the United States.

2002   At USAID's urging, Afghanistan redistributes redacted versions of the UNO jihadist textbooks rather than the better-quality "Basic Competency" materials. UNO is awarded an additional education contract to distribute these books.

2006   US military institutes a new field manual outlining operations to support counterinsurgency in Irag, later used in Afghanistan.

2006   In partnership with the Ministry of Education, USAID supports a dramatically successful community-based schools program across Afghanistan, which runs until 2011.

2008   US-government support grows for US-funded stabilization programs.

2013   USAID releases millions of US dollars to support community-based education through the Ministry of Education (MoE) in Kabul ("on-budget").

Schools for Conflict or for Peace in Afghanistan

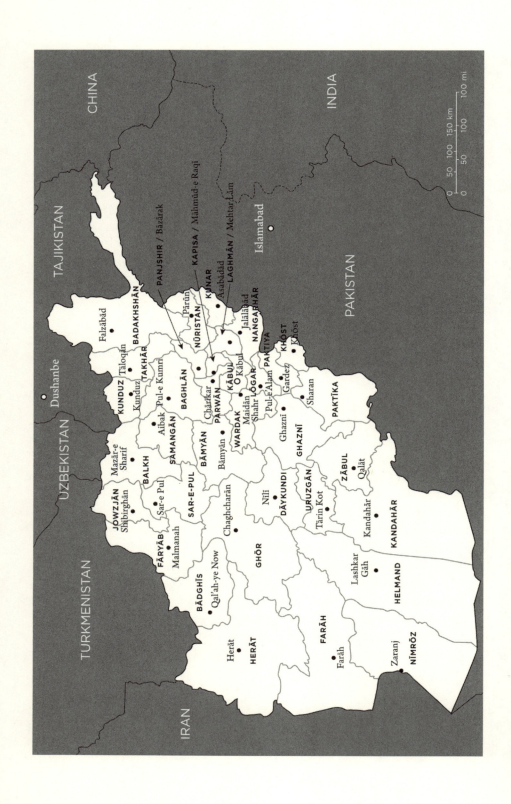

1

Introduction

On my first trip to Pakistan, in spring 2005, I visited several Afghan refugee camps in Balochistan, close to the Afghan border. I was working as a consultant for Save the Children, a US-based international nongovernmental organization that for a decade had been supporting schools for Afghan refugees living in these camps. Save the Children had hired me to assess their education programs, as their work was coming to a close. The camps had been there for many years—most of them since the early 1980s, when the Soviet invasion prompted a mass exodus of refugees from Afghanistan. "Camp" was a misnomer: each was really its own village, with clusters of mud-brick houses that seemed to have grown from the beige sand and earth that surrounded them. In each, I met with students, teachers, administrators, and members of the school management committee to discuss the schools and the interviewees' educational aspirations. One of the boys in Girdi Jungle, the largest camp I visited, spoke clearly and articulately about the importance of education in his life: "It's so important," he said, "that I will go all the way to China to get educated if I have to."

It was my first foray into a highly observant Muslim society, and I knew little about the relationship between Islam and education. The comment struck me as unusually sophisticated for a twelve-year-old boy in

Figure 1.1 Map of Afghanistan Provinces

the fourth grade. Yet I heard the same sentiment, expressed repeatedly and in virtually identical language, the following year when I was collecting survey data from illiterate Afghan villagers living in remote areas of the Panjshir Valley. It was then that I learned that this commitment to education was drawn from a famous hadith, widely known among Muslims around the world.* Afghans of all ethnicities—Pashtuns, Tajiks, Hazaras, Uzbeks—regardless of their level of literacy, learn and recite phrases from the Qur'an and the hadiths.† Most Afghans are deeply committed to educating their boys and girls, both because they believe it is a religious obligation and because they understand that success in the modern world hinges on education. They refer to "education for the soul" and "education for the world" to distinguish these two roles for schooling. Education for the soul refers to religious education and acquisition of knowledge for spiritual development that is intended to ensure an active and fulfilling afterlife. Education for the world—sometimes also called "worldly education"—refers to the study of subjects such as mathematics and science that leads to the acquisition of skills necessary to work and prosper in this world (Burde 2008; Khan 2012).

Many Americans are surprised to learn of the role of education in Islam and the importance Afghans place on learning. They often assume that Afghans find it threatening, preferring to keep their children away from modernizing influences such as schools. The Taliban's notorious refusal to allow girls to attend school during their reign in the 1990s received broad media attention and reinforced this impression. Despite the publicity accorded the many women and girls who flouted the prohibition, at the risk of grave danger to themselves, the Taliban's mandates were thought to reflect a widespread conservatism dominant in rural Afghanistan, particularly among the Pashtun population from which the Taliban emerged.

This perspective was encapsulated in a conversation I had with a US military officer in New York in 2010 about our respective experiences

---

* The hadiths are the collected sayings attributed to the Prophet Muhammad that are studied along with the Qur'an, the main religious text for Muslims.

† Although *Afghan* has been and occasionally is still used to refer specifically to Pashtuns, in keeping with current conventions, I use the term to refer to all citizens of Afghanistan regardless of ethnicity.

working in Afghanistan. He had seldom encountered educators or thought about local schooling during his time there, and was surprised to hear of my research on community-based schools. I noted that many Afghans consider education essential to improving their lives. After reflecting for a moment, he recalled a military meeting he had attended in Kandahar—a predominately Pashtun province—with a group of local Afghan elders. He described how they had been sitting around a table in the thick of intense negotiations when a delivery arrived. The men broke up the meeting and rushed to receive the package. The officer thought it contained something instrumental to their meeting or critically important to their lives. "They were yelling and carrying on with so much excitement, I couldn't imagine what it could be," he told me. "It turned out that in this package there was a delivery of new textbooks for primary school children. One of these old guys explained to me, 'I've been waiting for a textbook to give to my grandson. I wasn't able to go to school. He is now enrolled.' It was funny to see these tough old guys with turbans and big beards jumping up and down, giggling with excitement over children's textbooks."

The enormously popular book *Three Cups of Tea* and its successor *Stones into Schools* went to some lengths to dispel the notion that Afghans— even in conservative rural regions—undervalue education, particularly education for girls. These best sellers recount a US mountaineer's rededication of his life to building schools in Afghanistan and Pakistan. Trekking down from a high peak in northern Pakistan, he loses his way. When he stumbles sick and exhausted into a village, the inhabitants take care of him, nursing him back to health. Upon recovery, the climber promises to return to the village to build a school, since the village children desperately need one. He encounters many setbacks, but keeps his promise and builds not one but many schools in the impoverished region, returning many times over a number of years.

The first book casts the adventurer, Greg Mortenson, in a postcolonial redemption narrative; he brings the gift of modern education to the needy but dignified natives, in return for the gifts they have bestowed upon him—health and native wisdom. In this story, education, particularly for girls, is the promoter of peace that arrives in an act of beneficence. Although the success of these books went far toward countering conventional ideas among Americans as to the status of girls' education among rural Afghans, at the same time they fostered a simplistic narrative of US-Afghan relations—an uplifting account of the role of Americans in the region, who with a few pennies can build schools, educate Afghans, prevent conflict, and foster peace.

Mortenson and his books have been roundly criticized in the media, most notably in a *60 Minutes* broadcast of April 2011, an exposé mainly of financial malfeasance and fictionalization of segments of a story that had been billed as nonfiction. To those living and working in the region, however, the books were equally jarring for their geopolitical inaccuracies and lack of serious attention to education. In particular, there is scant discussion of the schools' curriculum, of teacher training, or of specifics regarding a key issue that the program claims to address—"sustainability," that is, enduring support to education given weak governmental administration. Moreover, the reader is left with the impression that Mortenson is the first—and only—person to promote girls' education in these remote regions of Pakistan and Afghanistan. In fact, local and international NGOs (nongovernmental organizations) have been supporting girls' education in the region for decades, often successfully, and braving all kinds of dangers to do so.[1]

However, neither the conventional wisdom articulated in journalism and stories like Mortenson's nor the more nuanced view promulgated within international humanitarian circles captures correctly the way education is related to conflict or peace. Conventional wisdom, on the one hand, assumes a simple, unidirectional relationship: "more education equals less conflict," as articulated clearly in Mortenson's books. The dominant humanitarian paradigm, on the other hand, favors ostensibly more urgent or less controversial forms of aid, downplaying education aid as only effective once peace has been restored.

Despite this attention to education in the popular press and among practitioners, the vast majority of political scientists and scholars of peace and conflict studies neglect education in their analyses of conflict. Indeed, from 1994 to 2010, only 1 percent of articles in peace and conflict-studies journals and 0.5 percent of articles in international-studies journals addressed educational practice outside North America and Europe (King 2014).[2] Scholarship that explores state-building and peace-building would appear to have a strong motivation to understand education, since the establishment of an educational system that provides equal access to citizens is a key ingredient of democratic state formation. However, education has received limited attention even within these specialized subfields. Scholars studying state-building focus on the way external interventions can stabilize a state after conflict, but education makes only an incidental appearance in their analyses, which emphasize instead institutions related to justice, security, and the economy (Paris 2004; Hehir and Robinson 2007; Paris and Sisk 2009). Typically, conflict-studies and civil-war literature have assumed material interests as drivers of state or individual behavior. Education has been included in this model only occasionally (Mundy and Dryden-Peterson 2011a; King 2014).

There is a small but burgeoning literature within international and comparative education studies that focuses on countries affected by conflict, but most of this examines theoretical links between education and conflict (e.g., Davies 2004; Nelles 2004). While practitioners focus on how education may contribute to peace-building, this work often lacks theoretical analysis or empirical backing. Empirical data on which research on the relationship between education and conflict might be based is especially limited (Mundy and Dryden-Peterson 2011b).

At the same time, the US government has never fully understood the role that education plays in Afghanistan or the importance it holds for most Afghans. US education policy in Afghanistan shifted from promoting "jihad literacy" in the 1980s to "education for stabilization" in the 2000s, and most official support for education was withdrawn in the intervening years. The use of education as a strategic tool—first to inculcate habits of war among the mujahideen in the 1980s and then to support the pacification of communities considered hostile to the US-backed Afghan government—has likely contributed to underlying conditions for conflict.

Historically, in fact, outside actors have taken three flawed approaches to providing aid to education in countries at war, each of which can be counterproductive to efforts to build a sustainable peace. First, education has been neglected. Humanitarians have frequently overlooked the importance education holds for populations affected by conflict, not considering it a basic need that warrants a humanitarian response or perceiving it as political activity in the context of work that is meant to be apolitical. When support to education is included as part of humanitarian aid packages, it is often as an afterthought or in a way that does not consider how it might interact with conditions that lead to conflict. This is beginning to change, in part because strong states have recently enlisted education as key to stabilizing weak states and thus fighting militancy and extremism, but support to education still lags behind other humanitarian initiatives. As I discuss later, without adequate resources dedicated to education for the sake of humanitarian assistance, important pathways to conflict can remain open.

Second, aid to education has been employed to support politically expedient goals that do not necessarily include peace. For example, the US used support to education to enhance its war efforts in Afghanistan in the 1980s. US-funded curricula were designed to teach Afghan children to hate the Soviets and support the mujahideen in their fight against the Soviets and the Soviet-backed Afghan government. Unlike in situations where education is overlooked altogether, this flawed approach is actually intended to spur conflict in the short term, with unpredictable long-term consequences.

Third, even moderately well-funded and politically neutral education programs can go awry if they are implemented unequally or unfairly. US efforts to stabilize Afghanistan in the twenty-first century, subservient to US military strategy, may unintentionally aggravate local grievances by exacerbating inequalities between ethnicities and clans. Uneven support that denies education to some peaceful groups while providing it to groups perceived to be hostile to the government raises intergroup tensions and may reduce faith in the Afghan national and local governments' right and ability to govern. While low levels of governmental legitimacy and high levels of "horizontal inequality" (inequality between groups) may not be sufficient to produce conflict, they increase the likelihood of violence.

In contrast to these approaches, neutral, reasonably good-quality education, supported thoughtfully and systematically and with humanitarian assistance rather than politico-military advantage as the goal, has the potential to mitigate conflict and promote peace. This type of aid to education should be provided uniformly across communities, rather than as a reward to restive communities that exhibit a desired response to an occupying force.

In this book, I provide a systematic analysis of the relationship between education and conflict, tracing how these four different approaches have been applied in Afghanistan as the rationale for aid has shifted from a policy of benign neglect, to an effort to support war, to an effort to mitigate conflict. Using this history as a case study, I explore how foreign intervention in education can contribute either to conflict or to peace. I argue that instead of preventing conflict, US aid to education in Afghanistan has contributed to it—deliberately in the 1980s, with violence-infused, anti-Soviet curricula, and inadvertently in the 2000s, with misguided stabilization programs. In both of these phases, education aid was subordinated to the political goals of strong states and used as a strategic tool—a situation made possible in part by humanitarians' tendency to neglect education's role in conflict. However, I also show how US aid to education can yet support peace. Although this is possible in Afghanistan, I argue that it cannot be achieved simply by building more schools. Rather, expanding access to good quality community-based education is necessary to overcome obstacles to peace. To assess the relative successes and failures of the various endeavors that constitute the case history, I draw from on-the-ground field research in Afghanistan from 2005 to 2013, interviews with education-aid workers in the region, and private archives, as well as two decades of personal experience working on education in countries affected by conflict.

The flawed approaches to aid to education described in this book may in part reflect problems inherent to administering any type of humanitarian assistance. However, as I argue below, the detrimental effects of bad education policy should be of particular concern. Few institutions can have such a pervasive and enduring effect on the individuals with whom they interact as a nation's educational system. At the same time, the focus on education in this book should not be read as questioning the importance of other types of aid. Rather, it is a call to reframe the dominant understanding of the place of education in humanitarian and peace-building efforts.

The Importance of Education

The power of education to transform individuals socially and economically should not be underestimated. That power may, in fact, be more important in less literate societies, where literacy is often described as a light in the dark. In my work, interviewees from countries as varied as

Guatemala, Mali, and Afghanistan have used the metaphor of light to describe the transformation that occurs when one moves from illiteracy to literacy (others report similar data, e.g., Frye 2012). Likewise, desire for the benefits that education can bring is overwhelming—social and economic status accrues to those who are educated. Many researchers remark on the reverence with which education is viewed in developing countries, particularly as compared to the attitudes of Americans toward their own education (e.g., Anderson-Levitt 2003). This may be in part because in societies with fewer educated people, those who are educated have historically experienced significant economic and social rewards.

Education is not only a tool for individual enhancement, it is also a key instrument of the state. Indeed, education plays a singular role in mediating between the state and its citizens. States use schools to create national identity, train a work force, and cultivate a particular form of citizenship. Education develops the human resources that boost the economy. In addition, a well-educated work force leads to a better distribution of wealth, or, in other words, to more equitable economic growth (Hojman 1996; Londono 1996 cited in Thyme 2006:734). A national curriculum inculcates a collective understanding of identity, social norms, and a shared sense of purpose (Heyneman 2003; UNESCO 2004, 2011; Dupuy 2008). In developing countries, schools are typically the most prevalent government institution in rural—and sometimes even urban—areas, outnumbering health clinics, police stations, and post offices. For many children, attending school constitutes their earliest and most frequent contact with the state, as represented by teachers, textbooks, and school buildings (Rose and Greeley 2006). Because of the broad and deep contact citizens have with schooling, education is a critical component of any effort to create social change. Thus, interventions in education that are designed to promote peace—or conflict—can have disproportionately large effects.

Education, Politics, and Conflict in Afghanistan

Education is important in Afghanistan, for all of these reasons, but to dispel the popular myths that say otherwise, it is important first to review education's role in modern Afghan history.[3] Most Afghans do not reject education, though their attitude toward it has been influenced by the fact that education has been manipulated as a key vehicle for inculcating religious adherence and for maintaining the power of those who transmit it. Religion permeates every aspect of Afghan society, and reading or studying the Qur'an is a fundamental element of religious expression and a requirement of Islam. Because the Qur'an is in Arabic, comprehension is a problem for many Afghans, most of whom are native speakers of Pashto or Dari. Still, reading, reciting, and memorizing are critical aspects of religious embodiment (Boyle 2006), and village mullahs (religious leaders) are essential to this process. Afghanistan has always been a rural society; even today, as much as 75 percent of the population lives in villages, most of these with five hundred inhabitants or fewer (Thier 2008). Every village has a mosque, and nearly every mosque has a mullah who calls villagers to prayer, manages the affairs of the village, and runs a small religious school.[4] The mullah is typically the most literate person in the village and often the *only* educated person in the village.[5] In the absence of the state—most villages do not have government schools—mullahs monopolize education through the mosque schools that by the early 1900s were prevalent throughout rural Afghanistan.[6] With this monopoly comes power, respect, a modest income, and a relatively comfortable lifestyle—since mullahs live from villagers' donations and do not need to farm the land, although many maintain small plots of their own. In addition to social standing, mullahs' control over education conveys religious authority, and in a profoundly religious society religious authority can be difficult to challenge.

For this reason, education has often been at the center of power struggles in Afghanistan. Historically, the most comprehensive and destabilizing of these struggles have stemmed not from ethnic, religious, or tribal divisions, but rather from those between urban and rural life, which have often mapped onto conflicts between modernizing and conservative forces (see e.g., Barfield 2010). Rural leaders in Afghanistan have always maintained a following and commanded respect. Tensions between the urban court of the monarchy and rural clergy and tribal leaders were strong even at the country's founding as a distinct empire in the mid-1700s.[7] Control of the limited education that existed at the time was a key tool for influencing these relationships, playing an important role in aligning the religious leaders and tribes for or against the king. For example, in an attempt to ingratiate himself with the clergy at a moment when he required their support, Zaman Shah issued an order in 1793 that "forbade the study of logic as dangerous to the Muslim faith" (Gregorian 1964:114).

The Afghan-Anglo wars of the 1800s strengthened the social position of religious leaders and their monopoly on education by weakening the monarchy's ability to assert itself (Gregorian 1964:260).[8] During this time, even nongovernmental schooling reached only a small percentage of the population—those in large towns and cities—and was characterized by a focus on metaphysics, rote memorization, and the exclusion of scientific knowledge.[9] This education, typically carried out by mullahs either in private homes or village mosques, aimed to promote strict adherence to Islamic law, encourage orthodoxy, and protect against outside influences (Sassani 1961; Gregorian 1969; see also Ekanayake 2004, and Baiza 2013). When Abdur Rahman ascended the throne at the end of the nineteenth century, he reportedly bemoaned that "there was no typewriting or printing press throughout the whole dominion of Afghanistan and education was so neglected that I had to advertise all over the whole country for thirty clerks that could read and write their own language. I could, however, find only three to fulfill these conditions" (Gregorian 1964:304, citing Mir Munshi 1900).

Although Abdur Rahman recognized the importance of education to his administration and took significant steps to reform and neutralize the religious elite, his attempts to modernize and centralize the state failed to take root. Governments in Kabul have since been weak, and the rural population has often objected to impositions from the center that threatened the power of local leaders. Reforms to education have been particularly challenging because of the connection between religion and education and because of historical associations of science with heresy. Mullahs perceived any regulatory changes as threatening the social structure from which they derived their power (Nawid 1999:92). Additionally, attempted reforms spoke to "the imagined fear that the state would undermine fundamental social relations sanctioned by Islam and Pastunwali [Pashtun tribal code]" (Barfield 2010:185). Initiatives designed to modernize the country were commonly perceived as attempts by the center to gain control over the periphery, and efforts to reform education in particular were seen as bids to impose urban secularization on rural society. Such efforts created tension and, depending on the extent of the reforms, produced significant conflict (B. R. Rubin 1995).

Some of the most enduring efforts to modernize Afghanistan by expanding education emerged not from attempts to exert Kabul's authority but from initiatives to make Afghans better Muslims. One key figure, Mahmud Tarzi, argued for the importance of modern learning and its compatibility with Islam. Tarzi was convinced that education was the remedy for the woes of his country—that the key to social and economic development lay in science and learning, and that in the absence of "true knowledge, superstition and tradition reigned supreme" (Gregorian 1964:384). In 1911 he established Afghanistan's first widely circulated newspaper[10] and used this platform to attack "the opinion, held by most of the religious establishment, that science was a product of Kafirs (infidels)" (Gregorian 1964:386). He argued that the clergy used rote memorization of the Qur'an and charges of heresy to hide their own ignorance and quoted extensively from the Qur'an to defend his view that education was important for both men and women (Gregorian 1969).[11]

The first modern secondary school, Habibia College, with new curricula and teaching practices, was established in Kabul at this time, shortly followed by the first national department of education, in 1913 (Samady 2001:26). Habibia College introduced the first real competition between the traditional, mosque-based schools and a more modern system (Gregorian 1964:336).[12] The first ruler of Afghanistan to attend this school, Amanullah, sought a vast expansion of Afghan education as the foundation of his own modernization program, which reflected his belief that an enlightened, educated elite was necessary to administer the country (Gregorian 1969). Amanullah made education compulsory for the children of government functionaries, and primary and higher education were free. Students were also sent abroad for higher education. Administrators who failed to send their children to school risked losing their jobs (Gregorian 1964:480; B. R. Rubin 1995:56).

Amanullah's reforms were met with harsh resistance from the clergy. He shifted control of mosque schools from the mullahs to the government, for the first time removing the mullahs' authority over one of their key functions. He also encouraged these schools to broaden their curricula to include science, math, and geography and "mandated the use of these schools to spread literacy in remote villages" (Nawid 1999:93). The educational system was expanded to include formal education for girls[13] and made compulsory for all children between the ages of six and eleven (Gregorian 1964:481–82; B. R. Rubin 1995).

Resentment of these reforms contributed to the outbreak of civil war in 1929. On their own, however, they were not enough to trigger the conflict. Larger factors included Amanullah's rejection of clergy with whom he had previously aligned himself, corruption within the Afghan government, and, in 1928, a new round of comprehensive social reforms that precipitated a financial crisis (Barfield 2010:184, 190–91). Although schools were attacked at this time, the real objection was not to education but to the threat of government control over people's lives: taxation, conscription, and perceived interference in family life (Barfield 2010:183). While in their larger ambitions Amanullah's education reforms ultimately failed in the face of insufficient funding and popular support, they were enough to sustain a state education system that could serve as an alternative to mosque schools.

Rural-urban tensions—including over education practices—continued to simmer for the next several decades. With the rise of communism in Afghanistan in the late 1970s, long-held fears of secularization were realized as the Afghan communists, and later the Soviet-backed Afghan government, once again launched a massive overhaul of the education system.[14] Although token religion classes were allowed, the majority of the traditional religious curriculum was cut. The Afghan mujahideen made targeting schools and teachers a key feature of their rebellion against the Soviets, and refugees cited changes to the educational system as one of their reasons for fleeing the country. Although today Taliban attacks on schools are unpopular with Afghans, the justifications put forward for them resonate with a section of the population that fears that foreigners—or even modernizing urban Afghans—intend to remove Islam from textbooks. They capitalize not on any innate rural, conservative bias against education, but on traditions of local autonomy and respect for religion. Most Afghans deeply desire greater educational attainment, but on their own terms and not at the expense of local traditions. Thus, the twin forces of religious orthodoxy and xenophobia and the tensions between modernists and religious traditionalists have left a profound legacy, one that extends into the present and complicates humanitarian efforts to reduce conflict through education.

Pathways from Education to Conflict or Peace

Foreign interventions in Afghanistan have run afoul of the tensions and opposing forces described above. Although the history of conflict in Afghanistan shows that simply pursuing more education in the name of "modernization" is not enough to produce peace, this has been the course that many governments have taken when they include education in their aid programs. Since September 11th, it has been an article of faith among law- and policymakers in the US that poverty and a lack of education contribute to increased militancy and violence (e.g., Mass 2001; Zelikow et al. 2004; Sobe 2009) and that aid to education mitigates these ills. Thus interventions have been based on fixed ideas of the role of education in promoting peace, irrespective of the type of education or the environment in which it is undertaken. The dominant argument characterizes the relationship between education and conflict or peace in much the same way Mortenson's books do—one of the root causes of conflict is ignorance, and more education will promote peace. Indeed, for some time, *Three Cups of Tea* was required reading for US military personnel, and David Petraeus, Stanley McChrystal, and colleagues famously sought Mortenson's advice on cultivating peace through building schools and educating Afghans (Bumiller 2010).

This argument is intuitively appealing. It is also supported to some extent by research. A handful of large, cross-national studies that assess the link between education and the likelihood of civil war or militancy finds that lower levels of conflict are associated with higher levels of education (Collier and Hoeffler 2004; Collier et al. 2004; Thyne 2006). They argue that participating in education creates "opportunity costs" for young people who might engage in conflict; in other words, if education must be put aside to fight, this increases the cost of participating in conflict. Some arguments for support to education programs have been based on this logic.

Likewise, if individuals have fewer educational opportunities, the cost of becoming a fighter is lower, thus contributing to the availability of recruits. These findings are supported by Humphreys and Weinstein (2008), who find that among youth in Sierra Leone, those without access to education were nine times more likely to become rebels than those who did go to school (see also Barakat and Urdal 2009). Similarly, in comparing inequalities across subnational regions within twenty-two sub-Saharan countries, Ostby et al. (2009:315) find that regions with low levels of education are more likely to experience conflict. They attribute these outcomes, in part, to relative recruitment costs for fighting, noting that higher levels of education improve the chances of securing a stable livelihood.

Much of the research on "youth bulges"—regional populations that are disproportionally young—and their relation to conflict relies on similar cross-national assessment of educational attainment, showing that countries experiencing a youth bulge have an increased risk of conflict and that this risk is greater the lower the level of educational opportunity (Collier and Hoeffler 2004; Collier et al. 2004; Barakat and Urdal 2009; Brett and Specht 2004, cited in Ostby and Urdal 2010). Using a dataset that encompasses 120 countries over thirty years, Barakat and Urdal (2009) find a significant relationship between large youth populations, low levels of education (particularly secondary education), and the likelihood of conflict.

Yet both the mechanisms of this relationship and the ways its expression may vary across countries remain underspecified. The opportunity-costs argument, for example, has little to say concerning the significance of education for youth who are excluded from it. The argument implies that youth may take up arms simply because they are not engaged constructively in another activity, such as education. But there are other plausible mechanisms—for example, they may take up arms because they are angry for having been excluded from an education system, or because they have missed out on educational opportunities to which others, they believe, have access—and so the opportunity-costs argument may reveal only part of the story.

Thus, education may relate to the likelihood of conflict not only through the absolute levels of attainment in a society but also through how that attainment is distributed across society. If access to education is increased in absolute terms but unequal across groups, then the likelihood of conflict may nonetheless increase. The difference between these mechanisms corresponds to the "greed versus grievance" debate about causes of conflict, famously articulated by Paul Collier and Anke Hoeffler (2004).[15] While the opportunity-costs argument is rooted in an assumption that behavior is based on rational assessment of economic opportunities ("greed" theories), the argument regarding inequality is grounded in an understanding of grievance stemming from Ted Robert Gurr's (1970) classic discussion of relative deprivation. Gurr argues that "while absolute poverty may lead to apathy and inactivity, comparisons with those in the same society who do better may result in violence" (in Ostby 2008:145). So-called *horizontal inequalities,* or inequalities between groups, may result from economic and social inequalities (e.g., in income, land distribution, and access to education) overlapping with social cleavages such as ethnic identities (Stewart 2000, 2002; Stewart et al. 2005). Such disparities are measured by comparing the economic or social outcomes of one group to the average of the society as a whole or to those of a rival group (Stewart 2000). When inequalities coincide with ethnic or other politically relevant cleavages, they may enhance group cohesion, as well as mobilization for conflict (Gurr 2000; Stewart 2000, 2002; Murshed and Gates 2005; Stewart et al. 2005; Ostby 2008:144; Blattman and Miguel 2010).

Qualitative case-study research supports the claims that pronounced social inequalities represented by restricted or denied educational access or a prejudicial educational process can lead to civil conflict. Examples abound (Gurr 2000 on Sri Lanka; Stewart 2002 on South Africa).[16] In Rwanda, the content and structure of the national education system likely contributed to the genocide in the mid-1990s (King 2014). In particular, King (2014) found that teachers often distinguished between ethnic groups in class, teaching practices were often hostile and destructive, and textbooks portrayed the relationship between Hutus and Tutsis as historically and inherently oppositional. Additionally, access to education was, or was at least perceived to be, unequal, with Tutsis reporting feeling discriminated against. This work offers important insights into the way education can be manipulated to aggravate ethnic hatreds, but it focuses on a national system and leaves aside questions of foreign intervention, except for consideration of the missionary role in colonial Rwanda. In sum, higher levels of education are generally associated with steeper opportunity costs for rebellion and thus decreased civil conflict—unless access to education is distributed unevenly, which can contribute to conflict by stirring up grievances. Uneven access to education is particularly likely to enhance the conditions for conflict if it coincides with ethnic cleavages.

Our understanding of the relationship between education and conflict to date primarily relates to countries experiencing civil war, rather than countries where a strong state is fighting a proxy conflict (such as the US, to weaken the Soviet-backed Afghan government in the 1980s), or where a strong state is engaged in direct counterinsurgency operations (such as the US in Afghanistan in the 2000s and 2010s). It is not clear how, in the presence of a strong state, aid to education, as in stabilization programs, may interact with horizontal inequalities. It is essential to understand how education interventions as a component of foreign aid intentionally or inadvertently contribute to conflict or promote peace. Below, I present two ways that education interventions can intensify conditions for conflict: by exacerbating perceptions of relative deprivation and by encouraging militancy directly.

Educational Access and Government Legitimacy

It is an article of faith among some policymakers and aid workers that providing education to a population increases the legitimacy of a government, and that this, in turn, reduces the likelihood of conflict. According to the UNESCO Global Monitoring Report (2011)—a highly respected annual publication that documents the state of education for children around the world—state provision of comprehensive education, support of fair access to education, inclusive and nonviolent curricula, and appropriate teaching practices increase the chances of peace. Populations commonly perceive education availability as a "barometer" of the degree to which a government is committed to them (Thyne 2006; Barakat et al. 2008). Education is considered even more critical than other services in this regard. Although state provision of services in general is a prerequisite for legitimacy, "Education is particularly key given it is the largest, most widespread and visible institution" in most countries (Rose and Greeley 2006:4).

US counterinsurgency strategies are based on a similar understanding of the role of government legitimacy in reducing conflict. Insurgents such as the Taliban in Afghanistan depend on the local population for recruits as well as for resources such as food and housing. They also need local populations to help them blend into their surroundings and operate undetected by counterinsurgent forces. US counterinsurgency ("hearts and minds") doctrine argues that winning trust and support from a local population is necessary to separate the insurgents living among them. When foreign forces support a local government, as the US does the Karzai administration in Afghanistan, successful counterinsurgency requires that the local population hold positive attitudes toward the local government and view it as legitimate. The provision of government services (education, health care, security) are important in this equation, because local populations are unlikely to view their government positively if it does not provide the services they expect from it.

Humanitarians and the international NGOs they work for are deeply concerned about such counterinsurgency strategies because strong states such as the US rely on humanitarian aid to implement them. Many aid workers question the merit of including aid as part of a counterinsurgency strategy. Most are loath to be associated with the military in any way, nor do they wish their programs to be considered in relation to broader strategic interests. Not only are they concerned that any real or perceived affiliation will increase the likelihood of violence befalling their staff, but they also question whether aid driven by strategic interests is effective in meeting the needs of the population. Aid is more effective, they argue, if it follows humanitarian principles that dictate neutrality, independence, and impartiality and heeds the injunction to first "do no harm" (M. B. Anderson 1999; Oxfam 2010). Evidence on this question is mixed, and concerns persist about the extent to which strategic interests of donors may undermine the ability of aid to affect attitudes toward government.

In Afghanistan, two forms of grievance are likely to interact with aid. The first, described above, results from horizontal inequalities and relates to another ethnic group, tribe, or clan. While this type of grievance can contribute to communal conflict, it can also spur resentment toward the government when the government is perceived as creating these inequalities. The second forms in response to a perceived norm or right, in this case, universal access to education, and targets whatever actor is expected to provide that right. A general understanding of education as a universal right has arisen in most societies and has been promoted by media and international human rights instruments around the world. In addition, the "education in emergencies" movement has capitalized on the growth in human rights norms to promote universal access to education in countries affected by conflict. Increased perception in Afghanistan of education as a universal right may contribute to discontent within the population and decreased perception of the government's legitimacy if it is unable to provide access to education. This second type of relative deprivation can exacerbate conditions for conflict by increasing resentment toward foreign forces and toward government, potentially increasing sympathy or support for militancy. It is important to consider this form of grievance when governments are trying to win hearts and minds, build a nation, and establish their legitimacy. In this book I examine how inequitable access to education, even in the name of stabilization programs, can increase the likelihood of conflict by decreasing perceptions of the government's legitimacy.

Education and Militancy

Recent studies have complicated the understanding of education as a force to mitigate militancy and conflict. In fact, emerging research argues the opposite: that those who engage in militancy, particularly suicide bombing, are likely to be *more educated* than the general population. This appears to be particularly the case in Palestine and Pakistan, where increased levels of education are associated with support for and participation in terrorist activities. For example, one study finds that better educated individuals are more likely to participate in Hamas and Palestinian Islamic Jihad (Berrebi 2007). Similarly, an influential piece by Krueger and Maleckova (2003) finds that among Palestinians in the West Bank and Gaza in the 1980s, higher levels of education do not decrease support for violent attacks, and in Lebanon, participation in Hezbollah is associated with higher levels of education.[17] Additionally, Jewish Israeli settlers involved in terrorist activities against Palestinians during the 1980s tended to be well educated as compared to other Jewish settlers (Krueger and Maleckova 2003).

18

It is important to point out that higher levels of educational attainment on their own are unlikely to cause these outcomes. Other factors interact with education to affect attitudes toward militancy or suicide bombing. First, favorable country-specific conditions, such as "sound institutions" and strong economic development, that increase the usefulness of education to an individual and enhance his or her social participation appear to help education reduce domestic terrorism (Brockhoff et al. 2012:3). However, in countries where literacy rates are already low and institutional environments underdeveloped, even low levels of educational attainment can increase support for terrorism (Brockhoff et al. 2012).

Second, a recent study examining how "political dissatisfaction" mediates the effects of educational attainment on attitudes toward suicide bombing across six Muslim countries finds that although educational attainment is generally correlated with reduced support, political dissatisfaction acts as a powerful mediator, reducing the correlation of educational attainment and negative attitudes toward suicide bombing (Shafiq and Sinno 2010). The study finds that "educational attainment and higher income encourage political dissatisfaction and that, in turn, political dissatisfaction increases support for suicide bombing" in some countries (Shafiq and Sinno 2010:167). Findings in Indonesia, Morocco, and Pakistan "suggest that educational attainment, more so than income, increases the likelihood of being politically dissatisfied with domestic policy" (170). Particularly important, Shafiq and Sinno (2010:170) suspect that "the direct effect of educational attainment on suicide bombing attitudes depends critically on the *content of education* and the *values inculcated in educational institutions.* If educational curricula and institutions do not promote peaceful conflict resolution, then educational attainment may not affect attitudes toward suicide bombing" (italics added).

Finally, it is possible that men and women react differently to education. For example, a recent study in Pakistan finds that uneducated women are actually more likely to support the Taliban and militancy as compared to uneducated men, but that men's support for the Taliban increases as they become more educated, while women's decreases (Afzal 2012). This study speculates that while educational content is important, differing teaching practices may also affect outcomes, because in this context women have female teachers.

Notwithstanding suggestions that curricula play a role, none of these studies adequately look inside the "black box" of education to assess to what extent variations in educational content or quality may be related to outcomes. Studies that find a positive correlation between education and participation in terrorism define education so broadly that the implications of the observation are unclear. In other words, they do not assess the direct effects of educational or curricular content on students' participation in violence or support for militancy. Instead, these studies tend to attribute this relationship to political and economic frustration, speculating that more educated people are more likely to participate in politics, which requires effort and leisure time that is less likely to be available to the poor and less educated (Krueger and Maleckova 2003:35). Some suggest that militant organizations may select better educated individuals from the pool of volunteers because of the skills required to carry out a particular mission (Berrebi 2007; Fair 2007) or because more highly educated individuals may be more frustrated by a lack of social opportunity (Berrebi 2007). Additionally, several compelling qualitative case studies examine textbooks for negative portrayals of "the other," (e.g., Bar-Tal 1998; Davies 2005; Lall 2008) but they do not trace the effects of these images.[18] Finally, Shafiq and Sinno (2010) speculate that educational content is an important factor in influencing political dissatisfaction and support for suicide bombing, and Berrebi (2007) goes to some length to assert that hate-filled Palestinian textbooks have played a key role in creating suicide bombers, but neither study tests for the effects of negative curricula in their models.[19] Thus it is critical to assess textbooks and other forms of educational content as a factor that may mediate the effects of education on participation in or support for militancy or violence. To this end, I assess the way US-sponsored jihadist textbooks from the 1980s have likely influenced a generation of Islamist militants.

Overview of the Book

Both qualitative methods (in-depth interviews, archival research, document analysis, observation) and quantitative methods (survey data from a randomized controlled trial to assess a community-based schools program in Afghanistan) provide the data for the findings in this book. To collect the data, I relied on an array of methodological approaches, including historical analysis and qualitative case studies (chapters 2, 3, and 4), and both a qualitative case study and quantitative data from a single large-scale, randomized controlled trial of community-based schools (chapter 5). In addition, my analyses are informed by everyday observations collected from living and working with humanitarians in Afghanistan and Pakistan off and on for the past eight years—part of my two decades of work on "education in emergencies" programs, first as a practitioner and later as a scholar. A brief description of relevant methods is presented in each chapter.

Chapter 2, "Humanitarian Action and the Neglect of Education," shows how education has been neglected by humanitarians and explains the underlying reasons for this neglect. It starts with discussion of the history of humanitarian aid, the debates within it, and an analysis of where education fits into these debates. It provides a framework for understanding some of the problems within the international-aid system that have contributed to ineffective—and possibly dangerous—education interventions in Afghanistan. I rely on secondary sources and qualitative interviews with educators who work in the field of education in emergencies to show how two myths—that of "emergency" and that of a golden age of apolitical humanitarian aid—have constrained the incorporation of education into the humanitarian paradigm. Although new standards have been created, the adherence among humanitarians to a particular definition of emergency and their belief that true humanitarian aid is apolitical continue to undermine efforts to provide the aid that recipients request.

Chapter 3, "Jihad Literacy," presents a case study of the way US aid to education has been used to promote conflict. A low-budget intervention—funding and support for textbook development for Afghan refugees—was a weapon of war and appears to have had an enduring effect on the underlying conditions for conflict in Afghanistan. I show how the US supported education for Afghan refugees living in Pakistan as part of its strategy against Soviet forces occupying Afghanistan in the 1980s and early 1990s. From 1986 to 1992, the United States Agency for International Development provided fifty million dollars to fund the design and development of jihadist curriculum for Afghan youth (Coulson 2004). The curriculum relied on counting bullets and bombs to teach math and on jihadist references to teach literacy (Davis 2002; Spink 2005; Woo and Simmons 2008; A. Jones 2009). Military commanders selected the youth who were included in these education programs, and students were mandated to return to the front in exchange for US support to their education. These textbooks appear to have been powerful particularly because they appealed to the population's religiosity in a deliberate strategy of indoctrination. Although US funding ended in 1992, the books were reprinted multiple times and widely circulated. They were still available in the book market in Peshawar, Pakistan in 2013 and used in schools inside Afghanistan until the mid-2000s (pers. interview, March 5, 2013). Although many Americans are unaware of this far-reaching initiative and of its unintended consequences, most Afghans remember these textbooks. Some Taliban who are currently locked in battle with US and NATO forces have called for a return to this curriculum (Glad 2009).

Chapter 4, "Education for Stability," is a case study of the relationship between education, stabilization, and counterinsurgency, showing how stabilization initiatives can enhance disparities in education. These disparities exacerbate horizontal inequalities and may also undermine the government's legitimacy as an unbiased provider of vital services. This chapter starts by discussing stabilization and counterinsurgency goals in conflict-affected or postconflict countries. Then it explores the tensions between international humanitarian norms and politico-military strategies to stabilize these countries, highlighting the fraught relationship between aid to education and counterinsurgency efforts. International interventions to combat the Afghan insurgency included a new approach that mixed civil, diplomatic, and military efforts. The new US counterinsurgency manual changed the military mission and suddenly gave priority to protecting the population and providing social services (US Army/Marine Corps 2006). As part of this strategy, the US funded rapid educational interventions in targeted districts. These projects were intended to increase the legitimacy of the Afghan government and gain trust from the population. Humanitarians were uncomfortable with this new relationship to a military strategy, arguing that singling out conflict-prone areas for education aid threatened the delicate balance among rival groups, potentially undermining stability rather than promoting it (Fishstein 2010; Oxfam

2010; Burde et al. 2011). Preliminary evidence suggests that their concerns are largely being borne out: local reactions to these projects reflect dissatisfaction with uneven access to education. Furthermore, while this alone can exacerbate conditions for conflict by creating or reinforcing intergroup tensions, it may also reduce the government's perceived legitimacy, although more research must be done to isolate the effect of education access on local attitudes toward government.

In contrast to the previous two, chapter 5, "Education for the World," explains how education may mitigate conflict and promote peace. I argue that a good quality, relatively neutral curriculum that is provided in an equitable, nondiscriminatory way is likely to decrease support for militancy, diffuse underlying conditions for conflict, and enhance government legitimacy. I show first, that community-based schools dramatically increase equitable access to education across the country. Second, I demonstrate that these schools additionally enhance equitable access by protecting education and decreasing the likelihood of violent attacks, and that this has secondary effects that are likely to further reduce conflict. Third, I show that the current curriculum in Afghanistan is neutral and tolerant, albeit religious.

The concluding chapter, "Education as Hope," summarizes the key points from previous chapters and outlines the way outside support for sound education policies can contribute to conflict mitigation, stability, and peace. I provide a short update on the fate of the community-based schools program in Afghanistan described in chapter 5 and offer several policy recommendations for humanitarian aid to education (education in emergencies programs). Finally, I point to further research needed to deepen our understanding of the forces examined in this book.

A Word About Audience

This book is written for two audiences: a scholarly one, which may cut across academic disciplines, and the curious nonspecialist who wishes to understand how education interventions such as those in Afghanistan can contribute to conflict or peace. Among academics, I hope the book will appeal to international-relations scholars, political scientists, international- and comparative-education scholars, education specialists of all kinds, and anyone with a regional interest in Afghanistan. Studies in international relations rarely examine questions that relate to education. The book should appeal to political scientists interested in the role of state-building efforts in promoting peace. In the field of education, there are few books that provide empirical analysis of international interventions in education abroad. And scholars in any discipline with a focus on Afghanistan will be interested. To those who study the politics of humanitarian action, this book offers new insights from the perspective of education intervention. Finally, the idea that education can promote peace maintains a strong hold on popular, civil, and military thinking alike. This book explores that relationship, delineating the pathways to conflict or peace for anyone interested in the power of education.

2

Humanitarian Action and the Neglect of Education

A FEW YEARS AGO I WAS ASKED to give a talk on aid to education in countries affected by conflict, focusing specifically on the relationship between education aid and conflict mitigation. The talk was held at the headquarters of a major international donor, and the audience consisted of representatives from international organizations, nongovernmental organizations, and bilateral donors, all of whom worked on "education in emergencies" programs in one form or another.[1] When I began discussing the role of education programs in conflict mitigation, one of the attendees asked how education programs administered in a country affected by conflict were any different from education programs administered in countries at peace. The question was more rhetorical than anything—the questioner believed, as many educators do, that treating the two contexts differently runs the risk of losing focus on educational outcomes and abandoning the neutrality held so dear by most aid workers.

The question reflected a concern and a belief increasingly common among educators over the past fifteen years or so, as education in emergencies programs have become more standardized, professionalized, and systematically incorporated into humanitarian action. I agreed with the thrust of the question—external support for good quality education programs should follow similar basic principles around the world, with those principles modified according to context and local priorities. But I offered this qualification: the context and priorities in countries affected by conflict are fundamentally different from those in stable, peaceful countries. Moreover, those differences make the apolitical posture of traditional aid programs problematic.

I voiced what many educators who work in conflict-affected countries have long known: the difference between peaceful settings and those affected by conflict lies in the ease with which even well-intentioned aid programs can inflame the underlying conditions for conflict. If well-intentioned educators make a mistake in administering an education aid program in a peaceful country, say by inadvertently favoring one ethnic group over another, that mistake may disgruntle many, but it is unlikely to foment violence. The same mistake in a country with simmering or active conflict and deep rifts between ethnic groups may cause a riot, or worse. And if the education program is meant to enhance the legitimacy of the government, such mistakes may produce the opposite effect.

Our exchange offers a view into a fundamental divide within the worldwide community of humanitarian-aid workers, that between "minimalists" and "maximalists." While nearly all humanitarians believe that aid should be neutral or apolitical, they differ in their approach to this principle. On one side are those who think aid agencies should avoid participating in any activities that may be perceived as political or as possibly favoring one party to a conflict over another. This view often precludes support to education in conflict-affected countries altogether, sanctioning only aid programs that provide for basic needs such as food, water, shelter, and emergency health services. Some educators, as opposed to humanitarians, have similar views, but for them neutrality takes on a slightly different meaning, one allowing for education to be included in humanitarian work: aid to education in countries affected by conflict should be delivered without regard to the conflict's causes, so as to avoid distraction from a focus on education. Minimal attention to conflict is equated with an apolitical, neutral stance.

Those on the other side of this debate hold that humanitarian aid can include ostensibly less urgent support like education while remaining apolitical, and that, further, to be effective, such aid must consider the political context of the crisis. This maximalist approach calls for aid workers to understand the conflict dynamics of the environment in which they are working, so as to avoid exacerbating the conditions that produced the need for humanitarian aid in the first place. Such support, it is maintained, can both satisfy human-rights requirements and promote universal access to education. Thus, while maximalists also recognize the necessity of neutrality, they differ from minimalists in that they believe that ignoring the political context in which aid is delivered risks perpetuating or exacerbating conflict. They are also more likely to consider activities that are often counted as development work, like education aid, as permissible during ongoing conflict. The "conflict-sensitive analysis" that some educators have recently been incorporating into their programs reflects this view.[2]

Even aside from questions of political neutrality and context, however, there persists a mind-set that classifies all crises as "emergencies," during which addressing basic life-saving needs is the only acceptable form of aid. According to this view, education is not urgent or important to people in emergencies, and so should not be included in early responses to a crisis. This reification of "emergency," I maintain, encourages a false understanding of crises that hinders the humanitarian community's ability to respond to an affected population's voiced needs, which almost always include education.

Both the minimalist and maximalist positions are in dialogue with a historical narrative of humanitarian aid from which aid to education has been largely excluded. Education has been part of humanitarian responses for decades, yet its continuing role has seldom been recognized beyond a small group of education-aid practitioners and activists.[3] Thus the importance of education as an element of humanitarian action has rarely been acknowledged, in terms of either its effects on beneficiary populations or the value recipients place on it. This inattention has prevented education aid from reaching its full potential for eliminating suffering during conflicts and accounts, in part, for its underfunding, relative to other forms of humanitarian aid.

Even relatively small interventions, as I describe in subsequent chapters, may produce significant outcomes. Unfortunately, however, the neglect of education in humanitarian aid has contributed to poor implementation of those education programs that *have* been undertaken, resulting in unanticipated outcomes that have undermined efforts to end conflict. If practitioners and policymakers are to design initiatives that are sensitive to the role education plays in conflict or peace, it is critical to understand the historical neglect of education within humanitarian action and the shortcomings in Afghanistan and elsewhere that are its legacy.

In this chapter, I show how both past and current assumptions regarding emergency, basic needs, and recipients' desires that underpin humanitarian aid have created misguided policies that exclude education from a systematic role in humanitarian response and block our understanding of its potential. I argue, first, that debates about the scope of humanitarian action have served to limit both analysis of education programs and support to education for conflict-affected populations. Efforts to maintain an apolitical "humanitarian space" have at times excluded thoughtful consideration of the relationship between education and conflict. The ways that humanitarians have addressed the perceived politicization of aid, coupled with their conception of emergency and the proper role of aid, have had far-reaching consequences for support to education in countries affected by conflict. One such way is the historical absence of recipients' voices in determining the kind of assistance they have received, based on humanitarians' belief that emergencies engendered a set of needs that were rooted in biology, standard across contexts, and therefore addressable with a standard package (Barnett and Weiss 2008). Humanitarian inattention to recipients' requests has often resulted in excluding education, or at best including it as a footnote to a larger effort.

Second, I argue that writing it out of the historical narrative has restricted our understanding of the extent to which education, as an element of humanitarian action, has been freely manipulated as a political tool. Although education has frequently been part of humanitarian assistance, it has never been fully embraced as part of an official aid policy In part as a result, political actors have been able to co-opt humanitarian education programs in pursuit of their own agendas—agendas that often contribute to conflict.

Third, I suggest that these presuppositions and gaps in the historical narrative have also limited the incorporation of emerging standards for aid to education into humanitarian reforms, thus perpetuating its second-class status in the humanitarian worldview.

Together, these three arguments suggest that a revised approach to education that fully includes it within the humanitarian framework would provide a better understanding of how interventions in education may lead to conflict or to peace. As I discussed in chapter 1, existing research points to several possible avenues by which education might contribute to the likelihood of conflict or peace, but the humanitarian community is only just starting to heed this research and consider how it might be reflected in modifications to relief programs. In the meanwhile, the continued neglect of education's humanitarian role may prolong or intensify conflict in ways that have not been anticipated by the aid community.

This chapter proceeds in the following way. First, I discuss definitions of humanitarian aid. Second, I review the expansion of the field and missteps that led to deep introspection among humanitarians. Next, I discuss the place education holds in this process of reflection. Finally, I show how the current debates among humanitarians have influenced the level of support to education within the humanitarian project.

What Is Humanitarian Aid?

High stakes, both real-world (the welfare of recipient populations) and financial, are linked to the struggles over humanitarianism and its definitions. Definitions and classifications matter: they include or exclude particular activities and shape both public and private funding, and international organizations are structured to provide aid based on the ways they categorize their activities.

Today, humanitarian aid is typically defined as relief assistance provided to a population affected by war or disaster.[4] It is managed and funded separately from "development" assistance, which is typically provided to countries at peace, but may also take the form of long-term interventions in infrastructure, institutions, and services in countries affected by conflict.[5] According to humanitarians, war-induced emergencies that trigger a humanitarian response include "massacres, international and civil wars, war crimes, crimes against humanity, and war-induced famines," all of which are considered "acts of violence that place individuals at immediate risk" (Barnett and Weiss 2008:15). Assistance most frequently includes food, water, shelter, and medical treatment. Most humanitarians consider the political neutrality of its implementation to be one of the central characteristics of such aid. Another widely agreed upon feature is urgency—humanitarian aid is defined by its necessity in response to a crisis or an emergency. Although in some contexts the term "emergency" has been supplanted in recent years by phrases such as "complex emergency" and "chronic crisis," the imperative to quickly address immediate, physical needs in a crisis remains central to the humanitarian endeavor, and the term persists among humanitarian organizations.

The origins of modern humanitarian aid can be traced to the founding of the International Committee of the Red Cross (ICRC) in 1863 and the emergence of international instruments—the Geneva and Hague Conventions—designed to protect civilians affected by conflict.[6] Today, humanitarians subscribe most closely to the core principles set forth by ICRC director Jean Pictet in the 1950s: he called on humanitarians to respect humanity and strive for impartiality, neutrality, independence, and universality. Neutrality requires that aid not be used to promote the interests of one side in a conflict over those of another. Impartiality requires that aid be given based on need, without discrimination according to race, religion, ethnicity, or other markers. Independence requires that aid be free of religious, political, or other associations (Terry 2002). Universality requires that aid reach victims of crises regardless of where they are. Organizations that promote these principles are concerned with delivering aid and with gaining and maintaining access to victims, regardless of what party to a conflict they support. Violation of any one of the principles might be perceived by a warring party as an attempt to benefit another and thus result in denied access to affected populations. These principles have remained central to the humanitarian movement since their original promulgation (Barnett and Weiss 2008; Barnett 2011).

Beyond these core principles, however, agreement ends. As aid has expanded in the last two decades, debates have erupted over what constitutes relief, how it should be distributed, and who should be involved in its distribution (see for example, De Waal 1997; Terry 2002; Barnett and Weiss 2008; Oxfam 2010). Today, many humanitarian organizations include activities such as education, peace-building, and institution-building that have at other times been categorized as "development," a classification very different from relief assistance. To understand the nature and scope of contemporary debates surrounding humanitarian programs, it is best to examine the circumstances in which Pictet first formulated his principles of aid and how the aid community has since evolved.

Humanitarian Expansion

President Harry S. Truman's 1949 inaugural address formally launched state commitment to international development. In the aftermath of World War II, international law was expanded and governments came together to establish international institutions such as the United Nations and the World Bank to protect human dignity, promote economic well-being, and guard against such devastation as had come with the war.

Perhaps as early as the 1960s, international organizations such as CARE, Save the Children, and Catholic Relief Services had begun to distinguish between two types of assistance, development and relief (Duffield 1994; Barnett and Weiss 2008:24). Development was provided to countries at peace and included training, institution-building, and construction, while relief, or humanitarian assistance, included immediate support for populations affected by conflict or disaster. Although these were not entirely fixed categories, most organizations that provided international assistance began to identify themselves with one or the other or created divisions within their offices that corresponded to these distinctions. Donors, likewise, maintained distinct funding mechanisms for one category or the other.[7] For aid to education, the segregation between relief and development served conceptually to preclude any official role in relief, since education was categorized firmly in the development camp, because of the perception that it was both inherently politicizing and not necessary in an emergency (Burde 2005).[8]

The end of the Cold War rearranged the global political map and saw an expansion of humanitarian action, sometimes in ways that challenged the relief/development dichotomy. First, aid workers identified a greater need for their services as geopolitical events appeared to cause an increase in the numbers of civilians requiring aid. In the early 1990s, the two superpowers retreated from states that they had propped up as well as from states where they had been engaged in proxy wars (Terry 2002).

Conflicts shifted from interstate to intrastate as stable governments collapsed as the external assistance on which they had relied was withdrawn. In the 1990s, 94 percent of all armed conflicts were civil wars (Paris, 2004). Their more frequent occurrence resulted in increased numbers of internally displaced people and civilians killed or living in the midst of conflict (Macrae and Leader 2001; Terry 2002:13; Le Billon 2003; Paris 2004). These circumstances brought aid workers into more direct contact with conflict, as well as with aid recipients who lived with long-term unrest and wanted to continue to educate their children despite such conditions.

Second, new ideas of state sovereignty and human rights created new space and standards for humanitarian aid. After the collapse of the Soviet Union, the principle of sovereignty was weakened, because it was no longer so firmly linked to balance-of-power geopolitics. As a result, aid organizations were able to work in areas previously off limits and reach populations affected by conflict more directly. Deference to sovereignty was also undercut by the increased standardization, internationalization, and institutionalization of human rights instruments. A new norm began to emerge: states had obligations to their citizens, the fulfillment of which could take precedence over their sovereignty—if they did not fulfill these obligations, other states might intervene on behalf of their citizens (Barnett and Weiss 2008:20). At its most extreme, this led to the doctrine of "humanitarian intervention"—military intervention to protect citizens whose rights were perceived to have been violated by their state, as, for example, the NATO bombing of Serbia to protect the rights of Kosovar Albanians (Woodward 2001). Similarly, providing access to education was one of the rights-based aims President George W. Bush used to justify the US invasion of Afghanistan in 2001.

In contrast, however, the advent of the twenty-four-hour news cycle and the dramatic worldwide expansion of media coverage, particularly on television, fed the growth of humanitarian action, but in ways that did not blur the lines between development and relief. Instead, journalistic coverage, with its inevitable emphasis on acute suffering and the immediate effects of conflict and disaster, served to solidify the distinctions. It contributed to the expansion of humanitarian action by strengthening the link between the "distant suffering of strangers" (Boltanski 1999) and the desire among some in wealthy countries to help. Among humanitarians, increased visual coverage, especially, of wars and disasters in "real time" appeared to increase demands among populations in wealthy nations to end suffering, to increase donations to aid agencies, and to contribute to a surge in numbers of people interested in and willing to move to conflict-affected areas to offer their assistance. Although visual images can contribute to "donor fatigue," on balance they appear to have added "impetus to humanitarian response" (Calhoun 2010:6). At the same time, they reinforced the link between crisis and urgency of humanitarian response, thereby undercutting consideration of education as an element of such response.

Growth in Aid, While Funding for Education Lags

In response to these global shifts, there has been a huge increase in the numbers of humanitarian organizations worldwide, with a parallel expansion in staff and activities. Official assistance—that is, funding from states—grew from $2.1 billion in 1990 to $5.9 billion in 2000 and rose again to over $10 billion in 2005–6 (Barnett and Weiss 2008:33). By 2011, funds (including both official and private giving) devoted to humanitarian aid worldwide had reached approximately $18 billion (Barnett 2011) (see figs. 2.1 and 2.2).[9] In terms of personnel, in 2010, 274,000 humanitarian workers were estimated to be employed worldwide, of whom approximately 141,400 worked for international NGOs (ALNAP 2012).

As a percentage of official development assistance (ODA),[10] humanitarian aid increased from an average of 5.83 percent in the early 1990s to 10.5 percent in 2000. The US government is responsible for a large share of this increase, with its commitments rising from 20 percent of the total of humanitarian assistance in 1995–97 to 30 percent in 2000. Although a large number of humanitarian organizations remain active, the bulk of the work has become concentrated among a few. In 2001, six organizations controlled $2.5–$3 billion worth of aid, or 45–55 percent of the total (Barnett and Weiss 2008:31–33).

Despite this overall growth, education ranks at the bottom, or next to the bottom, of nearly every inventory of humanitarian aid commitments, as is apparent from figures 2.1 and 2.2. According to USAID, the

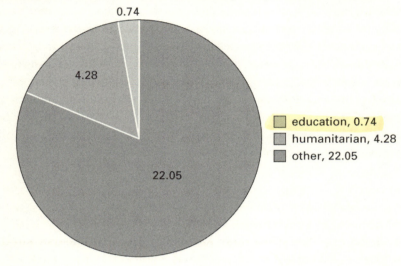

US Bilateral Aid as a Portion of ODA (2011) = USD 27 Billion

0.74

4.28

22.05

education, 0.74
humanitarian, 4.28
other, 22.05

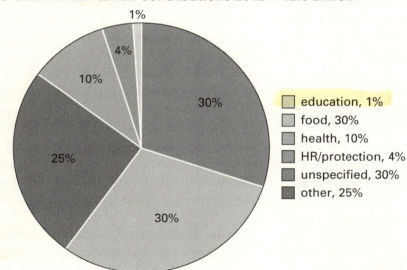

Global Humanitarian Contributions 2012 = 12.8 Billion

1%

4%

10%

30%

25%

30%

education, 1%
food, 30%
health, 10%
HR/protection, 4%
unspecified, 30%
other, 25%

US government's total net ODA for 2011 was $30.8 billion (USAID 2011e), including both humanitarian and development funds. Of $27 billion given in US bilateral aid, only $742 million was for education development assistance, while $4.28 billion was given to the humanitarian sector.[11] These funds are not disaggregated, so it is not clear what percentage of humanitarian funding may have gone to education (USAID 2011d). The United Nations Office for the Coordination of Humanitarian Affairs' (UNOCHA) Financial Tracking Services traced global humanitarian contributions made in 2012, including UN Consolidated Appeals, natural disaster response, bilateral aid, and all other reported humanitarian funding. According to its report, a total of $12.8 billion was provided for humanitarian assistance in 2012, of which *1 percent* went to education. Education was the least funded of all sectors, save monies designated for the safety and security of humanitarian staff. By comparison, food aid received roughly 30 percent of the total, health 10 percent, protection/human rights/rule of law 3.8 percent, and approximately 30 percent unspecified (see also Save the Children 2013, 19–22). One observer suggests that underfunding of education has conditioned humanitarians to request small sums for their education portfolios, knowing that this sector remains a low priority for donors (Karpinska 2012).

Thus, despite the changing nature of conflicts and their effects on civilians and local populations' increased demand for education, the role of education in this expanded system of aid has hardly changed. And yet international agencies that found themselves ever closer to the effects of conflict started to realize that linear notions of response to emergency crises, with clear transitions from relief to development phases, were inadequate (Buchanan-Smith and Maxwell 1994; Duffield 1994). By conventional understanding, "emergency" calls for urgency, immediate relief,

FIGURE 2.1 *(top, opposite page)*
US Bilateral Aid as a Portion of ODA (2011) (United States Agency for International Development, 2011) *Source:* USAID (2011) U.S. Official Development Assistance (ODA) FAST FACTS: CY2011

FIGURE 2.2 *(bottom, opposite page)*
Global Humanitarian Contributions 2012 (United Nations Office for Coordination of Humanitarian Affairs, 2012)

and resolution, but this definition was proving a poor fit with crises in which huge groups of people were forcibly displaced or caught in the midst of civil conflict for extended periods of time. As debates concerning the accepted forms for addressing crises intensified, many international agencies revised their concept of emergency aid to include what previously had been referred to as development assistance.

Humanitarian Missteps

Aid programs were hardly well-adapted for their expanded role. Along with their greater access to war-affected populations and their increased overall budgets, together with the expansion of television news, came greater scrutiny of aid programs. The image of humanitarianism changed dramatically after a series of tragic and highly publicized debacles in the mid-1990s left many questioning whether humanitarianism mitigated or contributed to conflict. Afghan and Rwandan refugee camps were accused of harboring "refugee-warriors"—combatants who blended in with civilians, using camps to regroup and remilitarize (Terry 2002). Bosnian "safe-areas" established by the United Nations to protect civilians and facilitate the provision of humanitarian aid failed to do so; in one of the most notorious acts of the war in the Balkans, approximately eight thousand men and boys were killed in Srebrenica. In Somalia, a sizeable amount of aid funding was used for security for aid workers or otherwise diverted (Terry 2002). These cases raised questions regarding the role of relief in conflict. Many aid workers questioned deeply the doctrine of neutrality and its apparent consequences. These crises also created a general outcry in the West, spurring demands for investigation of humanitarian efforts that apparently had gone very wrong.

These high profile examples of aid failures triggered a cycle of critiques, much soul-searching among humanitarians, and, ultimately, reforms to international humanitarian assistance. They raised questions about the power and benefit of humanitarian aid and its possible role in (re)igniting conflict. Fiona Terry (2002), a former employee of Médecins Sans Frontières (MSF; Doctors Without Borders), one of the most respected aid organizations in the world, compiled a damning portrait of aid abuses in refugee camps from Central America to Asia. The use of Afghan refugee camps in Pakistan by the mujahideen (an aspect of which I discuss in the next chapter) was among the high-profile examples Terry cited to argue that aid could exacerbate or prolong conflict. Many policy-makers and aid workers portrayed the humanitarian impulse as naïve and questioned whether aid could really be neutral. Yet despite, for example, the key role that education had played in the Rwandan genocide (King 2014), it was virtually excluded from these critiques.

Militarization of Aid

In the post-Cold War period states started to realize both that with in-creased globalization protracted foreign intrastate conflicts could threaten their own security and that they could harness humanitarian aid to their own strategic goals (Barnett and Weiss 2008:25). The attacks of September 11, 2001, reinforced these realizations. Strong states that had previously considered humanitarian aid a minor element in their foreign policy be-gan to see a larger role for such programs. Development aid, too, took on a more important role, as weak states were identified as the biggest secu-rity threats. Many within the foreign-policy community argued that in the post–September 11th world failed states appeared to pose a danger not only to those living within their borders, but also to many living comfort-ably beyond those limits (Barnett 2009; Burde 2011; Colenso 2012). In the US, a policy shift was marked by the publication of the 2002 National Se-curity Strategy, which, for the first time, included development along with defense and diplomacy, the three together forming the pillars of US for-eign policy. USAID was subsequently more closely affiliated with the US State Department, and in 2010 the two issued their first joint review: *Leading with Civilian Power: The First Quadrennial Diplomacy and Devel-opment Review.* Some aid programs in weak or failed states were explic-itly intended to promote stability via livelihood development, health care, civic engagement, economic empowerment, and education for marginal-ized, uneducated, and undereducated populations (USAID 2006a).

As official aid has been bound more closely to states' political objec-tives, bilateral organizations have sharpened their focus on both conflict mitigation and stabilization initiatives. USAID defines conflict mitigation as "activities that seek to reduce the threat of violent conflict by promoting peaceful resolution of differences, reducing violence if it has already broken out, or establishing a framework for peace and reconciliation in an ongoing conflict" (USAID 2005a:5). Guiding principles for pursuing these activities call for using a "conflict lens" to approach all traditional aid sectors, such as agriculture, democracy and governance, and economic growth.[12] Those involved in such stabilization efforts may work closely with the military to provide social and economic aid explicitly "to build confidence and trust" between a government and its people (USAID 2011c). Thus, while USAID is the principal actor in providing aid, it may also deploy mixed civil-military teams to deliver aid in the interest of promoting stability—for example, using Provincial Reconstruction Teams (PRTs) in Afghanistan and Iraq, units consisting of an aid worker, a diplomat, and a military officer intended to meld aid, diplomacy, and military strategy.

The increased use of humanitarian aid, including on occasion education interventions, to promote security is also reflected in budgets. While funding for international assistance nearly tripled in the 1990s, most of these funds came from strong states that often placed conditions on the aid to ensure that it be used in ways that would satisfy their interests (Barnett and Weiss 2008:18). From 2002 to 2005, the US Department of Defense (DOD) increased its share of US ODA from 6 to 22 percent, while USAID's global share decreased from 50 to 39 percent (Fishstein and Wilder 2012:13). US aid in Afghanistan from both the State Department (including USAID) and DOD is intended to "stabilize and strengthen the Afghan economic, social, political, and security environment so as to blunt popular support for extremist forces in the region" (Tarnoff 2010, cited in Fishstein and Wilder 2012:13). Stabilization programs typically enlist NGOs to perform statelike functions, and post–Cold War trends toward smaller government created more space for NGOs to play a bigger role (Terry 2002; Barnett and Weiss 2008:17).

As among humanitarians generally, educators' concerns over the politicization of aid have intensified alongside the post–September 11th efforts to align humanitarian aid with states' security interests (see, e.g., Novelli 2011). In policy, education is often linked directly to conflict mitigation, which, in turn, is linked to stabilization and security goals. This is especially true in "critical priority countries" such as Afghanistan, which receive the majority of USAID funds. Adhering to humanitarian principles such as neutrality, impartiality, and independence sits uneasily with both conflict mitigation and stabilization efforts. Yet many aid agencies that have already expanded their mandates beyond minimalist humanitarian approaches manage to incorporate humanitarian principles into conflict-mitigation approaches. They see their role as that of impartial outsider who may mitigate the effects of war by addressing the root causes of conflict—a process that is by necessity political but that has the relatively impartial goal of creating a sustainable peace for all local parties. In contrast, they see stabilization as narrowly focused and defined by the security interests of outsiders, and thus necessarily partial. Educators and humanitarians working in conflict-affected countries express deep concern about the extent to which education may be affected by strategic priorities and subordinated to political goals (UNHCR 2007; SCHR 2010).

Humanitarians Respond to Missteps and Militarization

The aid calamities of the 1990s and the militarization of aid in the twenty-first century required humanitarians to adjust their approach. Before the 1990s, humanitarian aid had received little criticism or oversight from outsiders. Media reports usually focused on the selflessness of aid workers and the altruism of the movement. Workers were viewed as motivated by a higher calling—as having sacrificed a comfortable (Western) lifestyle to pursue efforts to alleviate the suffering of others in challenging and often dangerous environments. Scant scholarly work examined humanitarian efforts, and in cases where aid was the focus of an academic study, it was usually to assess the process or impact of an aid program, rather than to examine the industry as a whole or the role that it might play in preventing or promoting conflict. Data on funding for emergencies, still difficult to find, is only "reasonably complete back to 1995," in part because donor reporting was flawed and also because the information did not come online until the mid-1990s (Fearon 2008:54). The bulk of reports on aid that existed beyond the media were authored by the aid organizations themselves and often written in the service of advocacy campaigns to garner funds. Humanitarians did not question the outcomes of their efforts. They assumed that humanitarian action "did more good than harm" (Barnett and Weiss 2008:13).

The Debate Between Minimalists and Maximalists

This has begun to change over the last two decades. Humanitarians launched their criticisms of aid and embarked on an extensive review of their work in response to the aid crises of the mid-1990s and the perceived politicization and militarization of humanitarian aid. The internal critiques followed two main lines, each arguing for a particular response to the perceived danger of politicization—"minimalist" (also referred to as traditionalist) and "maximalist" (also referred to as new humanitarian). The first holds that humanitarianism ran amok because of its departure from fundamental principles and its extension into messy statebuilding activities; the second suggests that the problems aid encountered arose from its inability to address root causes of conflict, and that therefore an even greater expansion of its activities is essential. Neither approach takes adequate account of education.

Minimalists defined themselves in opposition to politics and adhered to the core principles outlined by the ICRC. These represented traditional humanitarianism at its purest, they argued, providing for "relief and nothing but relief" from the effects of conflict (Barnett 2011). Yet the criteria for the appropriateness of aid programs were restricted by minimalists' adherence to a narrow—and problematic—concept of emergency. By defining a situation as an emergency, humanitarians cue in the popular imagination certain images and ideas—a sudden, life-threatening crisis that requires an immediate response. These, in turn, influence and often determine decisions about the kinds of interventions needed. The centrality of "emergency" thus fosters a needs-based approach to aid focused on specific "biological requirements that do not vary" across contexts: food, water, shelter, and urgent medical care (Barnett and Weiss 2008:47). Characterizing such environments as emergencies does little to suggest the need for education among affected populations and does much to inhibit its support. Some educators nonetheless adhere closely to the minimalist outlook, even while subscribing to a generous understanding of emergency, one that allows for the provision of education aid. They eschew activities that contribute to state-building—since this process necessarily involves political decisions about what the state will look like—but consider it possible to deliver education aid without implicating themselves politically or violating principles of neutrality, impartiality, universality, and independence.

Yet at the same time minimalists have recognized that sometimes even aid that adheres to ICRC principles can have negative consequences. Many policymakers and aid workers questioned whether "neutral" humanitarian aid has not in certain instances prolonged conflict. The minimalists began to revise their position to include Mary Anderson's (1999) suggestion that aid be approached in the way that doctors approach their patients, that is, in the spirit of the Hippocratic oath to "do no harm." Fiona Terry (2002) modified this stance, arguing that "all aid does some harm and will have unforeseen consequences, and that the best that aid agencies can do is try to minimize the harmful effects of aid" (cited in Barnett and Snyder 2008:149). She recommended that aid agencies guard against the influence of politics while at the same time increasing their efforts to monitor and track the use of aid (Terry 2002). Aid actors discussed calculating risks so as to avoid potential harm. Minimalists believed they could preserve their apolitical, neutral positions while structuring aid with checks to insure against abuses and unintended consequences.

Maximalists, too, saw the importance of maintaining neutrality and apolitical positions, but they split with the minimalists over the narrow scope of aid programs permissible in emergencies and articulated several counterarguments. First, they embraced an expanded humanitarian mandate, one they considered consistent with core principles. They questioned the traditional goal of saving lives, if saving lives meant condemning people to live in dire conditions and remain at risk for many years afterward (Barnett 2011). They sought programs that could provide more comprehensive support to people living amid protracted crises. Eager to ensure that populations would cease to be at risk after receiving aid, they sought also the transformation of social structures. Organizations that embraced this expanded mandate—for example, Save the Children, International Rescue Committee (IRC), and the United Nations Children's Fund (UNICEF)—believed in the power of aid to transform underlying social inequalities. An expanded humanitarian mandate gave these organizations license to address inequalities by reforming economic and social systems—including education systems. The fact that bilateral government aid agencies often supported this expanded mandate was not generally deemed problematic by these NGOs; many encouraged such aid by calling for increased coherence and coordination between their own relief and state-funded development efforts (Barnett 2005). However, the enduring influence of "emergency" as a framework for aid programs meant that even when some humanitarians began to accept education as a necessary component of aid, the design and implementation of such aid did not receive adequate attention. Most maximalists remained loyal to a hierarchy-of-needs approach inherent to the concept of emergency. Though their hierarchy of needs was more inclusive than that of the minimalists, it nonetheless continued to consider support for education less important than other forms of relief.

Second, some maximalists held that aid should be expanded further, arguing that it should be closely coordinated with peace-building, that it should be determined by rights as well as needs, and that it should not always be neutral, especially in circumstances when it could potentially do harm. In many crises these humanitarians experienced a coincidence of interest with government funders (Barnett 2005). As humanitarianism expanded to include conflict resolution, capacity building, and occasionally education projects, it played a part in what minimalists saw as the more insidious role of aid, that of promoting "global governance" (Duffield 2005; Sobe 2009). Maximalists, however, perceive their positions as apolitical to the extent that they "act according to universal values and avoid partisan politics" (Barnett 2005:728). Today most major international aid organizations have shifted to focus on transforming societies—only MSF and ICRC eschew the expanded humanitarian mandate (and both focus on functions other than education). Thus, while the maximalist position is better suited to providing aid that could promote peace, it remains insufficiently committed to education to do so effectively.

Standardization and Professionalization
of Humanitarian Activities

Part of the shift among the maximalists has been a call for greater stan-dardization and professionalization, to increase accountability among aid organizations. The Active Learning Network for Accountability and Per-formance (ALNAP) and the Sphere Project were established in 1997, fol-lowed by the Humanitarian Accountability Project (HAP International) in 2003. By setting standards and framing them in human-rights language, the Sphere project took a step away from a needs-based approach to humanitarian action and toward a more codified, professionalized, rights-based one.[13] The Sphere Handbook marked another significant expansion of the humanitarian mandate (see Weiss 1999; Minear 2002; Barnett 2005; Alexander et al. 2010). The handbook initially excluded education. In 2008, however, the Inter-Agency Network for Education in Emergencies (INEE) and Sphere signed an agreement that led Sphere to include guidelines pertaining to education in the core chapters of the Sphere Project hand-book. In addition, information on the INEE Minimum Standards was inte-grated into all Sphere training. Despite such improvements in attitudes and policies, however, in practice education continues to play a limited role in humanitarian action.

The expansion and professionalization of humanitarian aid, then, with few exceptions has only further limited incorporation of education into humanitarian action. This despite the efforts of educators who have ad-opted a number of strategies and initiatives to advocate for including edu-cation in the humanitarian response paradigm. First, in 2000 they formed INEE to support education in countries affected by conflict and crises. In doing so, they distinguished education in emergencies from education for development in order to incorporate education into traditional hu-manitarian assistance (Burde 2005). Education in emergencies refers to a set of program interventions that are supported by international, bilat-eral, and multinational organizations worldwide to help children living in disaster- and conflict-affected countries gain access to education. They comprise a subset of programs that overlap with and attempt to unite two global efforts: humanitarian responses to alleviate suffering and develop-ment efforts to promote Education for All (EFA). EFA initiatives, launched in the early 2000s, are intended to expand access to quality education. For different reasons, neither of these global initiatives has wholeheartedly embraced education in emergencies programs. On the one hand, although humanitarians possess the financial and management mechanisms required to deliver aid quickly in hard-to-reach places, they have been reluctant to consider education a crucial element of emergency aid. Humanitarians continue to vacillate between "needs-based" and "rights-based" approaches, still prioritizing interventions deemed to be "life saving" over those considered nonessential, such as education. On the other hand, although education is, of course, central to EFA goals, EFA initiatives lack the financial and management mechanisms to support education in countries and regions affected by conflict and crisis. In addition, many educators and humanitarians are still reluctant and perhaps ill-prepared to consider the relationship of education to conflict or conflict mitigation in their programs (Burde et al. 2011); these educators may not have much experience working in crises and prefer not to dilute their education interventions with a focus on conflict, so as not to undermine educational outcomes.

That said, in the new rights-based paradigm that competes with the old needs-based one, education has been more frequently included as part of a humanitarian response. The Convention on the Rights of the Child (CRC), introduced in 1989 and signed and ratified by 192 countries, is the most widely ratified rights treaty in history. The CRC outlines basic human rights for children everywhere, including "the right to survival; to develop to the fullest; to protection from harmful influences, abuse and exploitation; and to participate fully in family, cultural and social life" (UNICEF n.d.). These rights are further elaborated by the standards the CRC sets forth to protect them—articulating standards in education was a first and critical step toward extending access to education for children all over the world, including children living in countries affected by conflict.

Educators and networks such as INEE seized on this instrument for protecting children's rights and used it to advocate for greater attention to education from bi- and multilateral agencies and NGOs. Placing emphasis on delivering education as a "service" that could be packaged (i.e., UNICEF's "school in a box") highlighted its compatibility with other forms of packaged emergency aid. Stressing "service delivery" had additional implications. Educators hoped it would help distance education from politics, further deepening its compatibility with core humanitarian principles. If it also resulted in a rhetorical emphasis on access, at the expense of discussion of quality, the focus on simply delivering a service and maintaining distance from politics (and, by extension, from the specifics of content) likely helped aid workers incorporate education into the humanitarian paradigm, insofar as this has happened (Burde et al. 2011).[14]

Despite such successes, however, interviews and program literature show that educators still struggle to insert education programs into typical humanitarian responses. According to those in the field, many international organizations continue to view education as a dimension of development assistance, not a "life-saving priority" (Winthrop et al. 2010). Some of the largest aid donors have yet to add education to their humanitarian response protocols (e.g., the USAID Office of Foreign Disaster Assistance [OFDA], the Humanitarian Aid department of the European Commission [ECHO]). In addition, donors typically separate humanitarian from development funding and view the investment in education as too risky for humanitarian crises (UNESCO 2011).[15] The USAID education strategy included education in conflict and crisis-affected environments for the first time in 2011, although not without significant internal debate. The explicit focus on education in emergencies remains controversial. Education still often remains on the sidelines, either not systematically included in a humanitarian response, underfunded when it is included, or excluded altogether.

Fact-Checking the Aid Narrative: Making Room for Education

The aid narrative described above, largely determined by a needs-based approach and conceptions of emergency, has dominated and guided the work of humanitarians over the past two decades. It has shaped the kind of aid that has been delivered, the way aid has been implemented, and the way future aid is conceived. Although the rights-based approach has begun to emerge as an alternative, it enjoys only limited acceptance. The most prominent debate within the community remains that between minimalists and maximalists, and the two are united in positions that hinder their ability to provide education aid that reduces conflict. First is the assumption that aid at its purest is politically neutral, as embodied by ICRC principles and past practice—even if, as some aid maximalists believe, neutrality does not equal the absence of interventionist programs. Second is the assumption that aid had an apolitical golden age. Third, and most important to my argument here, is the definition of humanitarian aid as a response to an emergency, such that aid must prioritize life-saving interventions that respond to basic needs—even if, again, maximalists accept a broader range of interventions as necessary in the long run. Finally, both accept that basic needs are the same the world over.

Even though most aid organizations today are committed to expanding humanitarian aid beyond the basic-needs paradigm, a hierarchy of needs continues to frame humanitarian action within both bilateral organizations such as USAID and NGOs. These key elements—belief in aid as apolitical and a conception of emergency that warrants primarily interventions that respond to basic needs—sideline education and prevent it from assuming a fuller role in humanitarian efforts. However, both beliefs are predicated on a selective history that does not accurately account for how aid programs work—and have always worked—in reality.

Was Aid Ever Apolitical?

Although humanitarianism has taken many forms, emergency humanitarianism, as we know it, began in the 1800s with efforts to relieve the civilian suffering caused by the wars in Europe. This form quickly assumed representative dominance and became the "official face of international humanitarianism" (Barnett 2011:76). Today's humanitarianism retains this emergency focus. If, however, a conventional understanding of the proper response to emergency—impartial aid on a strict needs basis—has developed alongside this history, that does not mean that historically emergencies have been insulated from political decision making or that political challenges to humanitarianism began only with the end of the Cold War.

Early emergency humanitarians depended on the state and took political positions in the service of governments. For example, the ICRC "started as a quasi-public, quasi-private body, an arm of states even as it was independent of them" (Barnett 2011:81). National Red Cross societies were patriotic and nationalistic, and relief organizations tended to focus their efforts on the allies of their countries. The ICRC was slow to respond to atrocities committed by Italy during its 1935 invasion of Ethiopia, in part because of the ICRC's "civilizational mentality," which viewed Westerners as superior, and in part because many at the ICRC sympathized with Italy (Barnett 2011). In other clear violations of humanitarian principles, during the Cold War many workers used aid in biased and questionable ways in, for example, El Salvador, Lebanon, Cambodia, Pakistan, Vietnam, Nicaragua, and Nigeria (De Waal 1997; Barnett and Weiss 2008). Analysts have since argued that in many cases aid served to prolong the fighting, yet during the Cold War there was no discussion among humanitarians about negative consequences of aid or the root causes of conflict.

Humanitarians who pursue the minimalist paradigm believe that politics can be avoided either by limiting the types of activities included in aid (thereby justifying the exclusion of education) or by ignoring the causes of a conflict. Yet adherence to humanitarian principles of neutrality, impartiality, universality, and independence is itself inherently political. Promulgating norms as ICRC does makes it a key player in humanitarian politics: organizations that abide by them still need to decide when a situation requires aid and who is worthy of receiving it (Barnett and Weiss 2008). Similarly, MSF "gives witness" to report on abuses, but also to take action. Although both of these organizations consider themselves apolitical, they clearly assume political positions (Barnett and Weiss 2008:35–37; Barnett 2011). Likewise, maximalists who are committed to addressing the roots of conflict, and restructuring the global order in the process, have assumed fundamentally political positions. The claim that their organizations are merely "operating on behalf of humanity and furthering universal values" should not mask the fact that they are deciding which behaviors represent these universal values (Barnett and Weiss 2008:38).

Although education has been included in humanitarian aid, it has yet to be acknowledged as a necessary element of the humanitarian paradigm, and the histories of humanitarian action generally exclude it all together (Burde et al. 2011). In practice, although it was not typically included as part of a standard aid package for the first several years of a crisis, and it was rarely supported for civilians living in the midst of conflict, it was sometimes supported for refugees living in camps. Aid to education for Palestinian refugees started in the 1950s and continues as one of the most successful aid initiatives provided to these displaced people. The teacher training afforded refugees is considered one of the top achievements of the United Nations Relief and Works Agency (UNRWA).[16] The UNRWA school system provided nine years of free primary and preparatory education (Pillsbury and Nashef 1964) in the West Bank, Gaza, and regional refugee camps, and many countries in the region hired teachers trained by UNRWA. Education throughout the Middle East benefitted from this investment. Even so, the United Nations High Commission for Refugees (UNHCR) did not create an agency-wide policy for education until 1994, and did not review this policy until 2011 (Dryden-Peterson 2011).

Conversely, aid provided to Afghan refugees in Pakistan in the 1980s initially included only "emergency essentials: tents, blankets, quilts, clothes, water, and health facilities as well as basic food items such as skim milk and edible oils" (Girardet 1985:204). This is typical of the types of aid permitted under the minimalist paradigm. Girardet (1985:204) suggests that there may have been an operative distinction between humanitarian and development aid, noting, for example, that "the Pakistani government discouraged anything that tended toward the development of a Palestinian-style situation. Only reluctantly did it permit refugees to construct walls around their tents against the heat, wind, rain, or snow." By 1985, aid to refugees in Pakistan and to civilian populations living in "free Afghanistan" included education, but the humanitarian framework lacked structure and the aid community did little to guard against strategic interests.[17] indeed, aid workers permitted excessive political interference by the US government. As I discuss in the next chapter, this had far-reaching effects that ultimately contributed to conflict.

The perpetuation of the view that humanitarian aid has once been truly apolitical serves today to define and restrict humanitarianism in a way that is counterproductive and that inhibits aid workers from engaging constructively with the political dilemmas they face.[18] Denying that aid is inherently political leaves aid workers poorly prepared to deal with politics when they encounter it and may unnecessarily restrict the type of aid supported for affected populations. The result is that aid may fail to ameliorate—and may even exacerbate—conflict. An apolitical approach to aid is necessarily blind to its effects within a volatile political context and to the causes of violence in conflict-affected areas.

The Emergency Imaginary

While some of the responsibility for education's continued absence from humanitarian programs lies with efforts to adhere to an unrealistic ideal of political neutrality, the neglect also reflects a restricted concept of emergency aid, one that, even when making room for education, has kept its priority low and thus has prevented it from receiving adequate attention or effort. The whole humanitarian enterprise is based, in part, on an imagined construct of "emergency," or the "emergency imaginary" (Calhoun 2004). The notion of emergency in humanitarian action becomes what sociologist Emile Durkheim would call a "social fact"—a concept like "sovereignty" or "nation" that exists because we agree collectively that it does. It is produced and reproduced, shaping the way we both understand and react to specific events, as well as our understanding of the limits of possible action. The word "represents as sudden, unpredictable and short-term" events that are usually "gradually developing, predictable, and enduring." It assigns "particular [that is, uniquely local] settings" to crises that are "in fact produced, at least partially, by global forces," thus absolving the wealthy global North of responsibility for their production, while at the same time encouraging a particular form of outside intervention for their control (Calhoun 2004:376).

Although the idea of a humanitarian emergency has existed for a long time, it is only relatively recently, since the growth of media with a global reach and the acceleration of the news cycle, that the effects of war have been portrayed on television and online almost in real time—with images from the moment of an explosion, the aftermath of a suicide attack, or the myriad of other common scenes that have come to signify war (see Calhoun 2008, 2010 for an exploration of how the media frame emergencies). In reality, injured people in that place at that moment in time need urgent care, but there are many around them who do not. The images convey an emergency, and they serve to represent a larger crisis, but they do not capture life beyond the bounds of the incident that defines the emergency, nor the days that preceded or followed the incident. In many cases the life that continues beyond a particularly disruptive event is marked by a search for normalcy and a drive to return to a daily routine as quickly as possible after immediate caring and mourning is over.

This constructed, almost mythical idea of emergency and all that it entails frames every aspect of aid work, from fundraising, to organizational structure, to program implementation. In the world of humanitarian aid, the "emergency" has become a term of art. In other words, while its meaning is rooted in the layperson's definition—the sudden occurrence of an atypical event or condition that requires immediate action (for example, a bombing), among humanitarians it is used to describe many varieties of difficult and complicated situations. The word takes a range of qualifiers to convey this diversity of conditions: "disaster" (e.g., caused by hurricane, flood earthquake), "acute," "chronic," and "complex" are some of the terms used to differentiate the types of emergencies that aid workers encounter. Humanitarians are aware of the multiple uses of the word, but they generally accept its elasticity since using it encourages the desired response—immediate action.

The problem with discourses of emergency is not that they constitute reality, but that they constrain it. Neither aid recipients' voices nor education fit into this model, which permits only certain types of aid, those dictated by the logic of immediate relief. This needs-based approach belies both the quotidian reality of life in a conflict zone and the diversity of contexts and beneficiaries. It is true that there are needs common across emergencies, but the emergency imaginary serves to restrict humanitarian action in at least three ways.

First, it bases the humanitarian response on a notion of emergency determined by the popular definition of the word—an urgent, life-or-death situation. Emergencies of the humanitarian variety are not like this. Or they may be for some but not for all. Or there may be moments, even days, when an urgent response is required to mitigate suffering, but this moment passes quickly, after which needs change. Emergencies are uneven. And conflict—even in high intensity areas—is uneven, too.

Second, this mythical idea of emergency assumes that people living in these conditions are in such dire straits that they think only of survival and have no other concerns. Most people who have lived in an area affected by conflict—even in a situation designated as an emergency by aid organizations or in a country defined as at war according to the numbers of battle-related deaths per year—know that this is not true. It is not an accurate representation of how people living in such contexts feel or think. In fact, in most war zones, there are very few moments when survival is the only thing the affected population thinks about. This is likely to be different, of course, if the population is affected by a war-induced famine, or if the food supply is abruptly cut off for other reasons. Under such conditions, affected populations may be more likely to think exclusively in terms of basic needs. And reactions will vary according to personal circumstance: when one is oneself caught in a cross fire, or when oneself or one's family member is injured—these are of course emergency moments. However, as long as people stay in their homes, they try to continue their normal routines as much as possible. And when they continue their normal routines, they are interested in more than simple survival. During the siege of Sarajevo in the 1990s, for example, people organized their own primary and secondary school classes when the government shut down. Famously, a cellist played in ruined buildings in Sarajevo during the first year of the siege—a poignant example of the general desire to return to normalcy, despite a situation that was commonly portrayed as dominated by an overwhelming concern for survival and immediate life-sustaining support. This is not to suggest that individuals affected by conflict are not *also* concerned with survival—only that, in many cases, their need for relief for immediate, biological needs is not so overpowering as to rule out their interest in other types of aid *at the same time*.

Third, a logical extension of the emergency imaginary is that aid agencies are precluded from reaching their intended beneficiaries because the same conditions that produce urgent needs also keep a population isolated from humanitarians. Even in high risk environments, however, delivering aid is often possible. There are only a few circumstances in which it is not: when civilians are fleeing, it is difficult in the midst of their flight to provide them with aid, and when civilians are held hostage by governments that prohibit aid, it is not possible to provide it. Heavy bombardment complicates aid delivery, but many civilians flee under these conditions. In addition, some environments are more hostile to those delivering the aid than those receiving it. Yet a needs-based response is predicated on a physical presence—that humanitarian agencies can be present during the moment when a crisis requires the most urgent response. Thus, if aid organizations can deliver any aid at all, they can also provide support to education.

If a needs-based approach to relief is only warranted during extreme conditions, then this approach is necessarily invalidated, since these same conditions would also prohibit aid organizations from operating. Because in practice, then, aid organizations can only operate outside of the emergency imaginary, the hierarchy of needs model is flawed and adhering to it does not make sense beyond the moment of immediate aftermath—that is, beyond the short time in which individuals needing assistance have been identified and located, hunger and thirst are quenched, and urgent health conditions that affect individuals are addressed. So aid provided to civilians during conflict—during what we call an emergency—should not be limited to basic needs. Unless civilians are in the process of fleeing, or unless they have been directly bombarded, the basic-needs approach does not apply.

Outside of the frame of the emergency imaginary, aid recipients repeatedly demand access to education for their children. These demands have likely become more common as globalization has intensified and as calls for universal access to education have increased. It is also likely that more educated populations caught in conflict would be more likely to demand support for children's education, in addition to other forms of relief (e.g., Bosnians in the 1990s, Syrians today). But even societies with low literacy rates, such as those in Afghanistan, demand access to education. As principles have shifted at some organizations from needs-based approaches to a rights-based approach, there are fewer express justifications for providing "relief and nothing but relief." Then why do aid organizations continue to follow the basic needs paradigms? Why is education rarely included as part of a standard relief package?

One reason is that agencies have often assumed that they knew better than the aid recipients. Consent from beneficiaries was not required. Many aid agencies acknowledge today that recipients have often been left out of the equation, and it remains unclear to what extent beneficiaries bestow authority on aid agencies or to what extent agencies operate with their consent (Barnett and Weiss 2008:47). Discourses of development and security empower aid agencies, shape them, and convey legitimacy to them (Duffield 2002). In this context, the voice of affected populations is limited; aid agencies can claim to speak on behalf of beneficiaries in part because aid recipients cannot speak—they have no voice (Duffield 2002; Barnett and Weiss 2008; Calhoun 2010).

In addition, there is a clash between what humanitarians want to give and what recipients of aid want to receive. People who fund and deliver aid feel better when it includes only basic relief—the more obvious the impact, the better people who give feel about their donations. Similarly, the closer the outcome is to an idealized model of humanitarianism, the more genuine or important it appears to be. To couch this point in a reversed version of the old aid cliché, it is easier—more direct, with more visible results—to give a man a fish than to teach him how to fish.

Conclusion

Because of the emergency imaginary and the dominant interpretation of aid, many humanitarians, as well as bilateral agencies, overlook three critical issues. First, they are unable to assess the important role that education has played in promoting conflict, because they are preoccupied with short-term relief that fits preconceived notions of what is appropriate and necessary. Second, these same preconceived notions make them unable to consider the role of education in mitigating conflict. Third, they are unwilling to listen to what recipients really want as part of relief, because emergency relief can only include food, water, shelter, and medical treatment, prioritized in that order. The result is that education has been largely absent as a positive force toward peace. When education has been present, inadequate humanitarian attention may have led to its contributing to the causes of conflict.

The following chapters present three examples from Afghanistan of US-supported education interventions. Their histories show how poorly conceived education interventions—in part made possible by poor integration of education into humanitarianism—can deliberately or inadvertently undermine peace efforts. They also demonstrate how such aid could be designed to effectively reduce conflict. The first two examples seem to reinforce humanitarians' concerns about the politics of aid, showing that strong states use humanitarian aid to education to serve political goals. Humanitarians colluded with USAID in the 1980s to promote jihad against the Soviet Union. They have pushed back against the political goals of counterinsurgency in the 2000s, but with weak arguments and questionable results. These examples illustrate the need for humanitarians to assume greater control over education interventions to prevent their perversion in support of nonhumanitarian goals. Instead of arguing that aid is apolitical and must remain so, they need to assert that all aid is political and acknowledge a "politics of solidarity" (Barmett and Weiss 2008) with aid recipients. In this way they can be prepared to respond to the abuses of education aid as well as better advocate for providing it when populations demand it. Finally, chapter 5 shows how aid to education, provided in solidarity with aid recipients and distributed equitably, can have positive implications for peace.

3

Jihad Literacy

IN 2010, I GAVE A TALK at a prestigious English university on protecting education from attack in Afghanistan. There was a young woman in the audience who appeared to be listening particularly intently. After the talk she approached me to ask if I knew anything about "the mujahideen textbooks." When I replied that I did, she said, "I'm from Afghanistan, and you know, the Americans created these jihadi textbooks, and we all used them?"

I nodded. I knew these books had been used to educate Afghan refugees, and at first I assumed she had grown up in a refugee camp in Pakistan. She explained that she had not grown up in a camp but that she had used the same books in her school in Afghanistan. They were also used in the refugee camp schools that her sister had attended. The woman was indignant.

When I learned of these books on my first trip to Pakistan, in 2005, I was shocked at the irony: the US today is one of the biggest promoters of counterterrorism and democratic state-building in the region, yet so few Americans (including me) were aware that our taxpayer dollars had once been used to fund violent jihad and build a militantly Islamist society. The movie *Charlie Wilson's War*[1] offers some understanding of the Cold War rationale for providing military support, but none of the popular coverage of that time describes US efforts to indoctrinate children and young men. In fact, the US created children's textbooks (for grades 1–12) designed to inspire militancy, as well as the *Alphabet of Jihad Literacy*, a series of adult literacy lessons for mujahideen. All were funded and supported by a US government aid project, administered through the University of Nebraska at Omaha, designed in large part to support the Cold War struggle against the Soviets.

I told the young woman that most Americans do not know about these books. She looked at me incredulously, thought for a minute, and then said: "Most Americans don't know about them? Really? But every Afghan does." Indeed, reference to these books has arisen persistently in my numerous conversations with Afghans and Pakistanis. US activities in the region feature prominently in the local press, and the US effort to create jihadist textbooks is no exception, even if the project is long discontinued. In a 2011 blog post, one Pakistani journalist summarizes the story in just three sentences:

> Imagine that you learnt the alphabet and numbers with images of Kalashnikovs and tanks instead of apples and oranges. During the mid to late 1980s, a USAID funded project printed millions of textbooks in Peshawar. The funds came from Saudi Arabia and the books were distributed amongst school children in Afghanistan and in new *madrassas* across Pakistan. (El Edroos 2011)[2]

Schools throughout Afghanistan used these textbooks, or slightly modified versions of them, from the mid-1980s until the mid-2000s. Many madrassas—schools dedicated to the study of Islam—on the Afghan-Pakistan border also used these materials (El Edroos 2011), and despite the fact that the Afghan government has a new (and improved) set of books, many schools and madrassas on both sides of the border continue to use the US-sponsored jihadist books today because of the way they teach violence as an obligation of religion. Indeed, in insurgent-controlled regions of Afghanistan, reports indicate that the Taliban demand that schools use these texts if they want to remain open (pers. interviews March 4, 2013; Glad 2009).

It is difficult to understand the extent to which these activities undermined US credibility in the region and contributed to underlying conditions for conflict without first returning to the history of education in Afghanistan. This chapter begins with a short discussion of the theory and empirical evidence suggesting a relation between negative, biased curricular content and the likelihood of conflict. I then briefly describe the role that education played in the struggles between urban-modernizing and rural-traditionalist forces from the 1930s to the 1970s (up to the time of the Soviet invasion), as a basis for understanding the extent to which US-sponsored jihadist curriculum was able to permeate Afghan society. Then I discuss the Soviet invasion and the responses from the US, Saudi Arabian, and Pakistani governments that supported the Afghan mujahideen. The discussion of the Soviet invasion provides an understanding of the geopolitical context that encouraged humanitarian interventions in education and allowed it to have such drastic effects. Finally, I show how the US became involved in the business of promoting violent jihad and provide an analysis of the jihadist textbooks sponsored by US-AID and the University of Nebraska at Omaha. I argue that a minor program, an afterthought to a larger strategy, conceived as something of a low-risk long shot, had a major influence on the normative acceptance of jihad and violence in Afghan society, contributing to the indoctrination of several generations of Afghan children and young people into violent militancy, first against the Soviets and later against the US and its NATO allies. These textbooks endorsed a form of violent jihad that had not previously been part of Afghan religious education (Linschoten and Kuehn 2012; Brown and Rassler 2013) and that later helped form the basis of Taliban ideology, thereby contributing to conflict.

The Power of Negative Curricula

Currently, there is no data isolating the effects of negative curricula on children's behavioral outcomes—none that show, for example, what percentage of children who are exposed to such curricula go on to participate in violence. Thus, it is not clear to what extent teaching hate and violence is a direct causal mechanism for producing violent civil conflict. Even if a direct link has not been tested for, however, there is strong evidence that using textbooks to create a culture of intolerance and hate is likely to increase public support for militancy, particularly when these messages are framed in religious lessons exhorting young people to engage in violence and defend their faith. Under these conditions, militancy may not be considered extreme, but rather a logical and rational response to a perceived threat. Indeed, the influence of negative curricula can explain some of the correlation between higher educational attainment and increased support for militancy or suicide bombing noted in chapter 1.

The power of negative curricula appears to manifest in at least two ways. First, there is evidence that educational content that teaches bias or hatred toward a particular group fosters discriminatory and exclusionary attitudes and behaviors, which contribute to underlying conditions for conflict. In countries with a history of troubled ethnic cleavages, it is likely to exacerbate ethnic tensions. In Rwanda, for example, essentialized images of the "other" were a key element in fomenting conflict (King 2014; see also Lall 2008 on India and Pakistan). As discussed above, these textbook lessons and images were accompanied by particular schooling practices that interviewees believe fueled the Rwandan genocide, including aggressive and negative teaching methods directed toward an ethnic group, in the absence of any concern with fostering critical thinking skills. Similarly, students who lived in eastern Europe and Germany during World War II and in Afghanistan during the post-1979 armed conflict attribute polarized identities to their school curricula (Dicum 2008).

Second, curricular content that glorifies war, militancy, and the use of force is likely to increase normative support for violence and militancy more generally. In Pakistan, for example, the curriculum was overhauled by Zia ul-Haq, the military dictator who took power in 1977. An independent review conducted in 2004 by Pakistani scholars found that the resulting textbooks contain inaccuracies and lack emphasis on critical thinking. In addition to discriminating against minorities, they contain "incitement to militancy and violence, including encouragement of *Jehad* and *Shahadat* [violent struggle and martyrdom]" and "glorification of war and the use of force" (Sustainable Development Policy Institute 2004). Both Palestinian and Israeli textbooks have been blamed for contributing to the intractability of conflict. A team of highly respected American, Israeli, and Palestinian academics recently conducted an extensive empirical analysis of Israeli and Palestinian textbooks to assess levels of bias. Preliminary results indicate that although "extreme examples of dehumanization" are rare on both sides, each side presents a strongly nationalist narrative that lacks a positive representation of the other, or indeed any representation apart from that of enemy (Kershner 2013). Generally, neither side marks the existence of the other on its maps, and both sets of textbooks contain glorifications of martyrdom and self-sacrifice for the cause of the nation. Both societies are mobilizing young people to defend their nation, and textbooks are likely one factor contributing to this process (Kershner 2013). Because this chapter examines jihadist textbooks sponsored by the US in the 1980s to support the Afghan mujahideen against a foreign invader, I focus here on content designed to mobilize a population for war and glorify violence, rather than content that aims to stoke discrimination and internal divisions. However, the jihadist textbooks' emphasis on defending the faith also served, during the Taliban's rule, as the basis for an ideology of that encouraged violence against Afghan Muslims labeled insufficiently observant. Given the prevalence and endurance of such negative curricula in Afghanistan, it is important to consider exposure to it as one pathway toward increased participation in and increased public support for militancy and violence.

Finally, because Islam is often characterized in the West as a religion that incites adherents to violence, it is important to review the much-discussed link between madrassas and militancy. There is no evidentiary basis for asserting such a relationship, considering madrassas as a whole. This is not to say that discriminatory or bellicose education does not exist in madrassas; it does, but such "extremist" madrassas as there are in Pakistan, for example, represent a minority, nationally (Andrabi et al. 2006; Bergen and Pandey 2006; Graff and Winthrop 2010; Khan 2012). Negative curricula are problematic whether they are used in religious or secular schools. An important difference may be, as I suggest here, that the potential for negative outcomes is higher in religious schools.

Since education is formative by definition, negative, biased textbooks likely have an enduring effect on those who come in contact with them. Thus, biased education aid in Afghanistan may have contributed to violence and destruction not only in the late 1980s and during the civil war of the early 1990s, but also today, as students from decades ago fight the US.

Modernization and the Continuing Struggle
Over Education

The US education intervention in Afghanistan was particularly effective because it was able to capitalize on long-held fears in rural areas of foreign intervention and loss of local autonomy, as described in chapter 1. Urban-rural tensions were still sharp in the decades after Amanullah's failed reforms. Indeed, concessions to rural leaders following the civil war of the 1920s made by the new king, Nadir Shah, reinforced the power of the clergy and local tribal leaders at the expense of the center. Although the 1931 constitution included free compulsory education for all, it allowed mullahs to resume control over mosque schools. This protected schools from attack, but at the same time institutionalized the division between parallel education systems. Suspicion of state schools persisted in rural areas across Afghanistan, with some villagers even suggesting that they were "a ploy of the infidels" (Ward 1978:123). To calm such fears, textbooks were revised in 1933. Education for girls was abandoned. By 1937, four years after King Zahir Shah had assumed the throne, enrollment and literacy rates were lower than they had been ten years earlier (Ward 1978:124).

Religious Education in Afghanistan:
Mosque Schools and Madrassas

Rural Islamic clergy played a major role in weakening the state's authority over education. The religious and state schooling systems persisted as rivals, with no coordination between them until the 1950s. As discussed in chapter 1, mosques and madrassas were often the most readily—or only— available sources of education for Afghans. Given the threat the clergy[3] have posed to state elites based in Kabul, gaining control over this system of religious learning was (and remains) an important priority for the central government. In 1953 the state, backed by the urban elite, attempted once again to assert control over traditional religious education. Mohammad Daoud Khan, prime minister and a cousin of the king, established new state-run madrassas; mosque schools were "converted to public village schools with mullahs paid by the state in return for teaching Persian, Pashto, and mathematics as well as religion to grades one, two, and three" (Ward 1978:123). A faculty of theology had been established at the University of Kabul in 1951 with support from Al-Azhar University of Cairo, and soon afterward the state-run madrassas in district and provincial centers began to offer higher-order religious studies. By the end of the 1950s, the Afghan monarchy no longer needed the support of the clergy (Roy 1990; B. R. Rubin 1995).

It should be underscored that the difference between the two schooling systems—state-controlled and traditional—was not a simple secular-religious division. In fact, the Afghan state was "concerned to monopolise religious instruction, not to destroy it" (Roy 1990:45). By controlling religious higher education, the state intended to "shape the education the 'ulema receive, and play a key role in their selection" (Roy 1990:45). The difference between clergy educated in the government system and those who come through traditional (private) mosque schools and madrassas is that the latter are more traditionalist, while the former are more modernist and more closely linked to the intelligentsia. The majority of Afghan clergy have been traditionalists educated in the private system, through the 1980s and into the present. In keeping with its aims of monopolizing religious instruction, the current Afghan government has issued many requests for support from donors to sponsor religious education across the country (pers. interviews November 9, 2006). For USAID, these requests clash with the establishment clause of the First Amendment to the US Constitution, which mandates the separation of religion and state.[4] Thus while the Afghan government's requests stem logically from the country's internal tensions, USAID, equally logically, has been unable to comply.

Expansion of Aid for Modern Education

Beginning with Daoud Khan's reforms in the mid-1950s, then, initiatives to modernize education began to reemerge. As the Afghan government sought to wrest control over education from the clergy, it requested significant amounts of aid from the US and Soviet governments. Although it accepted Soviet aid for its armed forces and for building roads and other

public works, the Afghan state kept Soviet influence away from education, because of the communist state's commitment to atheism. And so
Americans were allowed to take charge of developing elementary and
teacher education (Ward 1978:144).

From the US perspective, the type of aid was not important—Washington
was using aid mainly to maintain a role in Afghanistan, which both superpowers perceived as an important buffer state. Education did matter,
however, to Teachers College, Columbia University (TC), the implementing partner that won the American education-development contract. In
1956, TC won nearly $7 million from USAID to train English teachers for
secondary schools. Ten years later TC started its USAID-funded curriculum and textbook project, which lasted approximately another ten years.
The curriculum project was heavily studied and reported on; Afghans
and foreigners considered it a significant success, at the time and for
many years following its closure.[5] Studies attribute the project's success
to its careful management and intense collaboration with Afghans in the
Ministry of Education (Easterly 1974:40). The project introduced a number of reforms, including emphasis on child-centered classrooms and
community participation. It seems clear in hindsight that a firm focus on
education and the long-term commitment from staff contributed to the
project's success.

Schooling expanded dramatically at this point, perhaps assisted by the
TC project, and the 1964 constitution again made education compulsory
for both boys and girls. Mosque schools, now called village schools and
folded into the state, were critical to realizing this goal. Children who
performed well in their first few years in these schools were eligible to
continue their studies in a middle school in the nearest town. Approximately 20 percent of eligible children were enrolled in state schools by
1970, and by the middle of the decade, middle and high schools were
available in all provincial capitals and major towns (Ward 1978:126–27).
At this time, the total enrollment is reported to have reached approximately 622,000 students in grades 1–6, of whom approximately 140,000
attended village schools and 90,000 were girls (Ward 1978:132).[6]

But tensions surrounding education persisted, through the late fifties
and into the sixties. Many rural families did not understand what government schools were, exactly, or what they were intended to do. Their igno-

rance stemmed in part from government's heavy-handed tactics in launching schools across the country. The Ministry of Education would determine where schools were to be built and the minimum number of children to be enrolled. Next, the provincial education director, "often accompanied by police, would inform the people of these plans and then commence with the project" (Sullivan 1973:69). Reports from the time indicate that many rural families were convinced that sending their sons to school, especially outside of their village, was tantamount to giving them over as slaves to the government. As one young Afghan reported, "Children were enrolled through the use of police force. Those who entered the school were thought to belong to the government. Most of the children who entered the school were the sons of poor people who could not avoid doing so" (an unidentified student in Kabul, quoted in Sullivan 1973:70–71). Suspicions among parents and village elders were so strong that some families who could afford to do so would pay for poorer boys to attend school as substitutes for their sons (Sullivan 1973:69–70).

Children themselves often resisted attending school because of the harsh corporal punishment employed by teachers and student monitors. In a short, vivid, fictionalized account, Ashraf Ghani[7] (1993) describes life in Afghanistan from the mid-1950s to the late 1970s: Education is characterized by harsh discipline, including frequent beatings with a switch. Children who are sent to boarding schools are subject to additional indignities, including forced labor for the school principal. The state enforces compulsory schooling by holding "the headmaster accountable for the number of enrollments per year. . . . Those students unwilling to attend the classes [are] dragged there by the school's orderlies" (Sullivan 1973; Ghani 1993:338).

The government's tactics gradually changed. By the early 1970s, King Zahir Shah's administration was employing new rural development models that were endorsed by Western organizations. The government sent representatives on awareness campaigns to introduce the idea of school and to garner support among communities. Villagers who agreed to sponsor a school would be responsible for providing the labor to build it. In exchange, the government would pay the teachers' salaries (Roy 1990:94). In this way, the King hoped to overcome traditional rural fears of an encroaching central government.

Thus, in the late sixties and early seventies many rural Afghans moved from shunning education to demanding it. During parliamentary debates in 1969, for example, "perhaps the most often expressed demand of the representatives was for more schools, more teachers, and upgraded schools in their districts" (Sullivan 1973:76). It appears that the rewards of education became obvious as village boys with an education moved into the government bureaucracy. Gaining a government position meant a guaranteed income and job security, advantages that were not available to most villagers.

Yet the struggles between modernists and traditionalists persisted. Some reports indicate that mullahs and *maulawis* (more educated mullahs) had lost control of their network of mosque schools by the 1980s because of competition from government primary schools, where classes were taught by students of state secondary schools. Many students preferred government schools because the state recognized their diplomas but not the certification from the "private" madrassas. With government-recognized diplomas, students were guaranteed employment on graduation (Roy 1990:46). Still, the prestige of the clergy remained high in rural areas, and the conservative religious establishment continued to express suspicion toward "innovations from infidel lands" (Ward 1978:137; Roy 1990). The introduction of foreign-aid workers to support the education system aggravated rural Afghans' fears of outside influence. Reports from 1973—several years before the Soviet invasion—indicate that many Afghans harbored intense hostility toward outsiders, some even calling for the expulsion of all foreigners from the country (Ward 1978). On the eve of the Soviet invasion, rural leaders and their conservative, religious base remained as devoted as ever to their long-held independence from foreign and central control.

Soviet Invasion

The Soviet invasion only intensified these deeply held rural attitudes. Current historical assessments of the war are dramatically different from interpretations dominant at the time. In contrast to the previous assumption that the Soviets long intended to appropriate the country as a satellite state, it now seems clear that the Soviet Union in fact showed little interest in Afghanistan until a number of changes within the country and in its relations with its neighbors prompted the Soviets to intercede (Gibbs 1987; Coll 2004). Likewise, prior to the invasion, the US was content to maintain its presence through the provision of aid and saw no need for increased competition with the Soviets for Afghan hearts and minds (NSC 1952; Galster 2001). Internal correspondence from the early 1960s confirms this: US intelligence reports note that the Soviets were not involved in ongoing subversive activities (USG 1962, cited in Gibbs 1987) and even praise Soviet aid to Afghanistan. For example, one report remarks, "Soviet aid to Afghanistan has been immensely successful. . . . Even American officials are hard pressed to find major flaws" (Goldman 1967:122–23, cited in Gibbs 1987:369). The US appeared comfortable with the type and extent of Soviet involvement it observed in Afghanistan.

The turn in the US attitude toward the Soviet presence originated in events outside Afghanistan. Until the late 1970s, the US believed that it had secured its influence in the Middle East and the Persian Gulf. The alliance between the US and the Shah of Iran was at the foundation of American power in the region. After the Shah was overthrown in the Iranian revolution of 1979, the US suddenly viewed Soviet involvement in Afghanistan very differently. The American foothold in the region had been weakened, and the language in US intelligence and media reports to describe the Soviet presence in Afghanistan shifted from tolerance to outrage (e.g., USG 1962; Getler 1980). On this evidence, if the Iranian revolution had not happened, the US would not have responded to the invasion of Afghanistan as it did.

The Soviets, for their part, were clearly reluctant to invade Afghanistan— as their declassified intelligence from the time shows (Gibbs 1987). Furthermore, they feared that an intervention would antagonize and radicalize the rural population and prompt an Islamist backlash—precisely the outcome that they wanted to avoid. They were aware of the conservative values of the rural population and were concerned that Afghanistan was not ready for a modernizing socialist influence (Gibbs 1987). When the Afghan socialists took power, they immediately began arresting mullahs and prominent landowners (Girardet 1985). They were extremely oppressive in their rule, implementing land-reform policies, intervening in marriage customs, and suppressing rural rebellions through disappearances,

torture, summary executions, and mass killings of civilians (Feifer 2010).
When the Soviets did finally invade Afghanistan, they did so in part to
temper what they perceived as the heavy-handed and misguided communist regime led by Hafizullah Amin (Gibbs 1987; B. R. Rubin 1995).

Yet Soviet-directed efforts proved similarly oppressive. They singled
out particular groups for persecution: Maoists, Islamic fundamentalists,
and nationalists, as well as those accused of being CIA or other foreign
intelligence agents. An omnipresent KhAD (Afghanistan's state security)
also suppressed resistance. The agency had "a broader structure, access to
more money, and more numerous personnel than any other ministry, it
had the power not only to look into matters of public significance but also
to intrude into the private domains of persons and families and to make
arrests. Except for Babrak Karmal [the Soviet-installed Afghan communist leader], no one under the regime was beyond its reach. It had the
power and the means to torture men and women to the point of death
with impunity" (Kakar 1995:156; see also Girardet 1985).

The US was well aware of the conservatism the Soviets faced in the
Afghan countryside after the invasion. A US government report from 1980
characterizes rural attitudes in the following way:

> Any change in the traditional way of life is considered wrong, and
> modern ideas—whether Communist or Western—are seen as a
> threat. . . . Some of the reforms that have incensed the tribes—
> education of women for example—are neither Communist nor anti-
> Islamic, but they conflict with the tribesmen's perception of what is
> right. . . . In the tribal villages it is in the interests of the most influen-
> tial men—local landowners, religious leaders, or both—to reject re-
> forms, especially Communist ones, that threaten both their property
> and their political power (USG 1980, cited in Gibbs 1987:371).

This report describes women's education as being particularly potent in
causing anger and resistance among Afghan tribes.

According to multiple reports, Soviet efforts to pacify Afghanistan after occupation included heavy-handed efforts to reform its agricultural
and education systems, including a forced literacy campaign that required
mixed gender classes (e.g., Roy 1990:94; Giustozzi 2000; Coll 2004:39;

Barfield 2010:231; DOD 1983). The initiatives took shape in several ways. First, Soviet advisors assumed control over the central administration, moving into the Ministry of Education and taking control of decision-making and human resources. The "Party office" screened MoE employees to ensure that they maintained sufficient loyalty to the Communist Party. Second, the structure of the state education system—village schools, primary schools, secondary schools, and lycées—was changed to reflect the Soviet system. Finally, the Soviets revised the Afghan school curriculum to nearly match that used in the Soviet Union, with the exception of religious studies. They preserved one hour per week for theology in grades 1–4, and two hours per week in grade 10 (AED 1985). This was of course a significant reduction from the numbers of lessons devoted to theology, Qur'anic studies, and Arabic in the pre-Soviet curriculum.

Thus the Soviets, and soon after, the Americans, entered into the now generations-old battle over efforts to reform education in rural Afghanistan. The Soviets assumed the role of the modernists, albeit with a communist twist, while the Americans would defend the religious leaders (both the rural traditional ulama and the urban Islamists). The US showed what in hindsight looks like remarkable lack of concern for the fervor of the religious leaders they supported. In an interview in 1998, President Jimmy Carter's national security advisor, Zbigniew Brzezinski, was asked if he regretted having armed "Islamic fundamentalists" to fight the Soviets. Brzezinski replied, "What is most important to the history of the world? The Taliban or the collapse of the Soviet empire? Some stirred-up Moslems or the liberation of Central Europe and the end of the cold war?" (Gibbs 2000:242). Across Afghanistan, South Asia, and the Middle East, the US supported Islamist movements, believing that the "three monotheistic religions" share a repugnance toward the atheist ideology of communism, "and this factor could become an important asset in promoting Western objectives in the area" (NSC 1952).

The Geopolitical Context

As is now well known—and as Brzezinski's reflections above highlight—US concerns regarding Soviet and communist expansion blinded it to many other foreign policy issues and underlined its policy choices in nearly every way. This focus combined with a confluence of events and circumstances in the late 1970s to unite an unlikely group of collaborators. It is important to understand these conditions, which predate the US efforts to provide aid to Afghan refugees and shaped the US decision to fund education interventions to promote conflict. There were at least five factors that combined to underpin these interventions.

The US was deeply disturbed by the Soviet invasion of Afghanistan and looked to the mujahideen as the best available force to counter it. Just ten months earlier the US had experienced its dramatic and humiliating ouster from Iran, which deprived it of a key hub of regional influence. Also, in February 1979, the US ambassador to Afghanistan, Adolph Dubs, was kidnapped and then killed during a botched rescue attempt by Afghan police and their Soviet military advisors (Kakar 1995; B. R. Rubin 1995; Galster 2001) further turning US opinion against the Soviets and raising alarm about the stability of the region. Meanwhile, President Carter was engaged in a bruising reelection campaign in which his opponent, Ronald Reagan, and other hard-line conservatives accused him of appeasing the Soviets. Desperately wanting to present a more hawkish posture, in January 1980 Carter declared that "aggression unopposed becomes a contagious disease," committed US military might to protecting national interests in the Persian Gulf (Galster 2001), and authorized additional covert aid to support the Afghan resistance (Gibbs 2000).

At the same time, the brutal campaigns of the Soviets and the Afghan communists who preceded them were drawing wide condemnation from humanitarians and political moderates, which provided the US an opening to pursue its Cold War agenda. Headlines declared the devastation of the Afghan countryside by Soviet aerial bombardment. US officials accused the Soviets of pursuing a scorched-earth policy—"draining the sea" in order to kill the fish. Reports of death tolls and destruction in the Afghan countryside promoted sympathy for the Afghan cause among conservatives, moderates, and humanitarians alike (Roy 1990; Terry 2002).

The exodus of millions of Afghans to neighboring countries during the occupation presented clearly visible notice of unfolding events. Most reports put the total number of refugees at approximately 6.2 million, with roughly 3.2 million seeking refuge in Pakistan alone, slightly fewer in

Iran, and the remaining dispersed among other nearby countries and the West (UNHCR 1999).[8] At the height of the crisis in 1980, 80,000–90,000 refugees were arriving in Pakistan each month (Maley and Saikal 1986:9, cited in Grare and Maley 2011). The US took the opportunity to step up its covert aid to mujahideen based in neighboring countries, where such support was logistically easier.

At the same time that the US and the Soviets were escalating the Cold War, Sunni-Shia tensions also increased, prompting the Saudis to also take a greater interest in the Afghan mujahideen. Saudi Arabia had been funding madrassas in Pakistan's North West Frontier Province (NWFP) since the 1950s, seeking to counter other Islamic movements and increase its influence (Roy 1990).[9] Its focus on and funds for the region began to increase in 1973, with skyrocketing oil prices, and it began supporting the mujahideen in Pakistan soon after (Coll 2004).[10] With the transition in Iran from the secular rule of the Shah to the Shia Islamic rule of Ayatollah Khomeini, the Sunni Saudis also became increasingly concerned about the role of Iran in the region. The Wahhabi sect of Islam, which has been dominant in Saudi Arabia since the early twentieth century, views the Shia as polytheistic heretics. There has been significant violence and discrimination against the Shia since the Wahhabi movement first began to spread across the Arabian peninsula at the beginning of the nineteenth century, and systematic marginalization of Shia by the Saudi Arabian government has continued to feed tensions between the sects.[11]

The Afghan mujahideen were crucial to furthering Saudi efforts to promote Wahhabism and protect what Saudis perceived as their own interests in the Muslim world and beyond. Aid from Saudi Arabia took off in 1984, when the government began pursuing a two-pronged strategy to support the Afghan resistance. The first step was to send a significant number of Saudi men to fight alongside Afghans, and the second involved expanding traditional Saudi support to madrassas. The Saudis built and funded hundreds of madrassas to train Afghan mullahs living in refugee camps in Pakistan (Roy 1990). The more traditional and more tolerant Hanafi madrassas were poorly funded and could not compete with the extremist, Wahhabi-supported schools, which provided meals and monthly allowances to students. In addition, Saudi Arabia offered scholarships to the students who wanted to continue their training in Saudi

Arabia. Their efforts and their funds, along with those from the US, helped tip the balance away from moderate nationalist Afghan parties and toward the Islamists, whose views were more in line with their own.

The deepening relationship between Arab jihadists and Afghan mujahideen was not without difficulties. Saudi Wahhabis believed that Afghans were poorly educated, having received their religious training in the Hanafi branch of Islam rather than the Hanbal branch that is dominant in Saudi Arabia (Van Linschoten and Kuehn 2012:70–71; see also Brown and Rassler 2013). For their part, although the Deobandi-educated Taliban had a profound respect for Arabs, in interviews conducted by Van Linschoten and Kuehn (2012:30), Taliban express preference for Deobandism over Wahhabism and describe this sentiment as universal among them.[12] Significant tensions have been reported between Wahhabis and the Taliban.

For its own geopolitical reasons, Pakistan shared Saudi Arabia's commitment to supporting the most Islamist among the mujahideen. The Pakistani government was deeply concerned about Pashtun nationalism, which it viewed as a threat to its own foundations. In 1893 the British had clumsily separated India from Afghanistan along the Durand Line, which split the Pashtuns into two groups. Afghanistan had for many years been eager to unite the Pashtun regions that spanned the border. Such designs unnerved the young government of Pakistan, already fearful of encroachment by India. Under Zulfiqar Ali Bhutto, concern about Pashtun loyalty began to guide Pakistan policy toward Afghanistan (Roy 1990:230). Pakistan was wary of Pashtun nationalism and of former king Zahir Shah's power to unite Afghans under a nationalist banner (Roy 1990). In addition, the border between Pakistan and Afghanistan was notoriously porous, which created many opportunities for cross-border interference; accusations of such interference had already caused problems on several occasions since Pakistan's independence. Thus the Pakistanis supported the Islamists—Burhanuddin Rabbani and Gulbuddin Hekmatyar—whose ideology most closely resembled their own and who were not interested in promoting Pashtun nationalism. These two started to build relations with the Saudis and the Pakistanis in the mid-seventies, before the flood of refugees began.

The mujahideen, already welcome in Pakistan, received a dramatic boost after General Zia ul-Haq deposed President Zulfiqar Ali Bhutto in a coup in 1977. General Zia was intent on Islamicizing Pakistan and embarked on a series of reforms of the country's military, legal, and educational institutions meant to ensure that a particular interpretation of Islam permeated every aspect of life in Pakistan. The reforms also focused on schools and included textbook revisions featuring references to violence and glorification of war. The reforms were profound and far-reaching, and their effects are still prevalent in Pakistani society today. Under Zia, Pakistani support to the Islamist mujahideen was all of a piece with domestic policy initiatives.

Pakistan responded to the Soviet invasion of Afghanistan by organizing "camps" for the refugees in such a way that they could maintain some control over the displaced population. However, the camps grew into large villages or small cities, and refugees could move freely in and out. Although Pakistan never signed the 1951 Convention Relating to the Status of Refugees or the 1967 Protocol Relating to the Status of Refugees, it did absorb large numbers of refugees. Yet because Pakistan was not a signatory, it was able to administer the camps as it chose. It became the gatekeeper for all aid—military and otherwise—that flowed to the Afghan refugees. Pakistan explicitly organized aid to the refugee camps to support the mujahideen, prepare them for battle, and provide for them when they returned (Terry 2002).

Pakistan's plan for controlling the flow of aid required that refugees declare an affiliation with a particular political party in order to receive rations and other forms of assistance. The political parties subsequently gained strength when they were enlisted to channel relief aid throughout the camps (Baitenmann 1990:12). In response to its concerns over Pashtun nationalism, the Pakistani government selected the most religious leaders among the Afghan parties to receive aid, hoping a strong Islamist ideology would weaken support for ethnonational irredentism. However, according to a 1987 poll by the Afghan Information Centre, these parties were not representative of the refugees. At the time, leaders like Rabbani and Hekmatyar had very little support at home. They were part of an urban Islamist movement that had had limited opportunity to establish itself in the countryside. As a result, they were reliant on foreigners—via Pakistan—for support (Roy 1990).

Aid workers present in Pakistan and Afghanistan at the time of the struggle against the Soviets noted the lack of interest in and support for education outside of the pursuit of political goals. It was only when the mujahideen requested educational support (around 1984) that the US offered it, and only as a small component of the larger war effort. Humanitarians largely allowed US interests to dominate education interventions, in part because the prevalent humanitarian framework saw education as outside its purview and in part because Afghanistan now was considered so important to US goals. Despite UNHCR concerns over Pakistan's insistence that refugees "join a fundamentalist Muslim political party in order to draw refugee rations," reports at the time indicate that there was "[pressure] by the USA, the largest single funder of the programme in Pakistan, not to interfere with Pakistani policy" (Baitenmann 1990:68). UNHCR acquiesced.

Education as Part of the War Effort

As US and Saudi funding to the refugees increased and as the US stepped up its military support, both countries pressured the government of Pakistan to create a more united opposition to the Soviets among the Afghan refugees and political parties. While the US was concerned with defeating the Soviets, the Saudis were concerned with spreading Wahhabism. The Seven Party Alliance was formed in 1985 under the official name the Islamic Unity of Afghan Mujahideen. Figures vary, but according to most accounts, the US provided close to $500 million per year to support the mujahideen during the 1980s, and Saudi Arabia matched these contributions dollar-for-dollar (B. R. Rubin 1995; Terry 2002; Wright 2006).

This support for the military struggle is in stark contrast to typical international education aid during the period. In the early 1980s, several funders, including the US, German, Dutch, and Canadian governments and UNHCR, sponsored rudimentary schools that were managed by the Pakistani Commissionerate for Afghan Refugees (CAR).[13] Attendance was poor. Figures are unreliable, but UNHCR estimated that 5–6 million school-age refugee children lived in the camps, but only approximately 100,000 were receiving an education by the end of 1986 (Centlivres and Centlivres-Dumont 1988:88).[14] Of 555 schools, most provided only primary education; only approximately 50 were for girls. Only 68 of the total went as far as eighth grade, and only two offered classes up to twelfth grade. When refugees arrived in the camps, they reportedly felt antipathy to secular schools because they associated them with the rise of Marxism that led to the coup in Afghanistan (Centlivres and Centlivres-Dumont 1988).

The Afghan political parties reinforced this view, disapproving of the UNHCR/CAR schools as ideological and inadequate. However, Western academics at the time described them as "politically neutral . . . centered on a Pakistani context" (Centlivres and Centlivres-Dumont 1988:88). As an alternative to these schools, political leaders argued for Islamic education, and religious schools (madrassas) affiliated with each party were founded for primary and secondary students. The schools reportedly offered their own curricula, including "geography, languages, Pashtu and Dari literature . . . arithmetic, science, drawing, and paramilitary training" in addition to religious instruction. The madrassas generally used the same classroom materials regardless of party affiliation and enrolled a total number of students "at least equal to that of the UNHCR schools" (Centlivres and Centlivres-Dumont 1988:89).

While funds for these schools were made possible by the mujahideen parties' support from external sponsors, they were not specifically the result of international education interventions. By the mid-1980s, though, the US started to see such interventions as potentially beneficial. The confluence of interests between the US government and Afghan resistance parties produced strange bedfellows: in deference to its political aims in the region, USAID underwrote the printing of pro-mujahideen textbooks for Afghan primary school children by the Education Center for Afghanistan, a group jointly appointed by the seven mujahideen political parties[15] and supported by Pakistan's Inter-Services Intelligence and the United States' Central Intelligence Agency (Coulson 2004).[16] Designated education representatives from at least some of the seven political parties designed and wrote the books autonomously, although the US project managers reported their approval of the contents (see Education Sector Support Project reports referenced below). One set of textbooks was entitled *Alphabet of Jihad Literacy*.[17] All volumes in the set included explicit references to jihad, the Russian enemy, illustrations of guns and mines, and other forms of indoctrination into the ideology of conflict and religious resistance; all were intended to complement the covert

US support for the Afghan Islamic "freedom fighters" (Davis 2002). In addition, the project hired teachers based on refugee group leaders' recommendations rather than on qualifications (Iqbal May 19, 2005, cited in Burde 2005). Refugee group leaders, in turn, were determined by their affiliation with one of the seven mujahideen parties (Terry 2002).

A needs assessment commissioned by USAID in 1985, before the creation of the curriculum and textbooks, describes multiple meetings with "Afghan freedom fighters." The mujahideen recommended and prioritized key activities for the USAID-funded education program for Afghan refugees in Pakistan. The recommendations were comprehensive and included the following: (1) administrative support for the Free Afghanistan Department of Education, (2) support for primary and secondary education, (3) establishment of an Afghanistan Academy, (4) scholarship options in Pakistan and abroad, and (5) miscellaneous "other assistance options" (AED 1985:2–5). The Afghanistan Academy is cited as a priority, to provide for those freedom fighters whose education had been interrupted. Admission to the Academy was to be contingent on a letter of introduction from a "freedom fighter commander and party leadership to verify Jihad involvement" (AED 1985:61). Education for girls and women was mentioned briefly under "other options"; human rights and peace education were not mentioned at all.

USAID contracted and funded the University of Nebraska at Omaha (UNO) to provide education for Afghan refugees in Pakistan, as well as for Afghans remaining inside Afghanistan, through the Education Sector Support Project (ESSP) from 1986 to 1994.[18] The project was closed abruptly and ahead of schedule when USAID decided to withdraw the Afghanistan mission after Najibullah's government (that is, that of the last Soviet-supported leader) collapsed.[19] Although the project was funded solely by the US with no contributions from the government of Afghanistan, ESSP created the Education Center for Afghanistan, managed by the Seven Party Alliance, to implement the project within Afghanistan. ESSP became "the cornerstone of educational services in the resistance-controlled areas of Afghanistan" as well as for Afghans in refugee camps in Pakistan. UNO was a key player in all ESSP plans and programs and remained so after the US invasion of Afghanistan in 2001. The project included literacy training for mujahideen in refugee camps and for women through home schools, training and payment for teachers, school management training, vocational training, and the provision of scholarships for study in the US.

The most damaging effects of the project were likely produced by the development and distribution of the textbooks and by the curricular guides for grades 1–8 for social studies, language arts, math, and science. These are discussed in detail below.

Textbook Analysis

The educational rationale for indoctrinating students into jihad and militancy appears to rest on an assumption of the importance of starting early. The bulk of the violent material appears in grades 1–6. Until recently, the only academic discussion of these books appeared in a short but compelling article by Craig Davis (2002). Davis' excerpt from the introduction to the Dari alphabet[20] in a first-grade language-arts book warrants repeating here:

Alif [is for] Allah.
Allah is one.

Bi [is for] Father (*baba*).
Father goes to the mosque . . .

Pi [is for] Five (*panj*).
Islam has five pillars . . .

Ti [is for] Rifle (*tufang*).
Javad obtains rifles for the Mujahidin . . .

Jim [is for] Jihad.
Jihad is an obligation. My [uncle] went to the jihad. Our brother gave water to the Mujahidin . . .

Dal [is for] Religion (*din*).
Our religion is Islam. The Russians are the enemies of the religion of Islam . . .

Zhi [is for] Good news (*muzhdih*).
The Mujahidin missiles rain down like dew on the Russians. My brother gave me good news that the Russians in our country taste defeat . . .

Shin [is for] Shakir.
Shakir conducts jihad with the sword. God becomes happy with the defeat of the Russians . . .

Zal [is for] Oppression (*zulm*).
Oppression is forbidden. The Russians are oppressors. We perform jihad against the oppressors . . .

Vav [is for] Nation (*vatn*).
Our nation is Afghanistan. . . . The Mujahidin made our country famous. . . . Our Muslim people are defeating the communists. The Mujahidin are making our dear country free.

"Violence for the sake of Islam" is the dominant theme throughout the language-arts and mathematics series for grades 1–6 (Davis 2002:90). One can imagine how easily boys and young men using the books today could reappropriate their original messages for the current conflict against the US and NATO allies.

Given the limited analysis presented by Davis, I wanted to reexamine the full texts to determine the extent of their violent content. My analysis yields similar findings. For this study, I acquired several old copies from local sources (fifth grade and tenth through twelfth grades) and a colleague purchased recent (2011) Pashto editions of the old books (first and second grades) from a bookstore in Pakistan in February 2013. Although these books contain some modifications to the originals created in 1986–87, the sentiments are the same. For example, the 2011 edition of the first-grade Pashto textbook contains individual lessons for the 41 letters in the Pashto alphabet. Of these 41 lessons, 17 are neutral, 16 contain religious messages, and 8 glorify violence in the name of Islam. A passage analogous to the one above appears as follows in the 2011 Pashto edition:

Letter A: (Allah) Allah is great, Allah is great. Mohamed, Peace Be Upon Him (PBUH) is the leader; Mohamed (PBUH) is the leader. We are going the right way. Allah is one. Mohamed (PBUH) is Allah's messenger.

Letter B (capital B and small b): Father (*Baba*): Father is reading the holy Qur'an. The Holy Qur'an is Allah's book.

Letter T (capital T and small t): Sword (*Turra*): Ahmed has a sword. He does Jihad with sword.
Gun (*Topak*): My (maternal) uncle has a gun. He does Jihad with the gun.

Letter G (capital G and small g): (*Jihad*): Jihad is a duty. Seraj (boy's name) has gone to Jihad. He is a good Mujahid.

Letter D: Religion (*Din*): Our religion is Islam. Muhammad (PBUH) is our leader. All the Russians and infidels are our religion's enemies.

Letter Ghain: Honor (*Ghairat*): Every Muslim honors and protects Islam. Muslims of Afghanistan do not accept to be slaves of anyone. They keep the flag of freedom.

Letter K (capital K and small k): (*Kabul*): Kabul is the capital of our dear country. No one can invade our country. Only Muslim Afghans can rule over this country.

Letter M (capital M and small m): (*Mujahid*): My brother is a Mujahid. Afghan Muslims are Mujahideen. I do Jihad together with them. Doing Jihad against infidels is our duty.

Letter Y (capital Y and small y): One (*Yo*): All Muslims are followers of the same and one Allah/God and they are followers of one prophet. All Muslims take order from one Islamic law. Our Allah/God is one, our holy Qur'an is one, our prophet is one, our religion is one and our *qiblah* (direction towards Mecca) is one. Nobody can compete with Muslims.

The covers of the 2011 textbooks have been changed to show allegiance to the Taliban, and images of faces have been removed. Otherwise, these editions appear to be very similar to the originals, leaving intact the references to Russians, communists, Parcham and Khalq (the Afghan communist parties) and replete with Kalashnikovs and bullets, used to teach math.

A systematic review of the fifth grade Persian/Dari language book for Pashto speakers published with USAID funds in 1986 shows that 18 of the 78 lessons contain religious instruction. This is not a problem in itself—it would be expected if the book were about religion—but it is worrisome given that it is ostensibly intended for language learning. The more significant issue, however, is the association between religion and violence. Of the 18 lessons on religion, seven are explicitly devoted to inciting students to violence, martyrdom, hatred, and militancy. Here are two representative examples:

Jihad
It is obligatory for Muslims to fight in the way of God. The Prophet said wage jihad against kafirs [infidels] with your wealth, with your life, and with your speech. The Muslims of Afghanistan by the order of God and His Prophet, started jihad against the Russian Communists and their slaves. In this cause, they lost their wealth and their lives, and achieved manifold success. We read about that in the newspapers and magazines of Islamic revolution every day (66).

Mujahideen
We Muslims wage jihad in the way of God. With the power of belief and faith in God, we began jihad against the Russian unbelievers, empty handed. The brave mujahideen attack the communist Russian unbelievers from every side and capture/seize their weapons with the help of God, the great and the exalted. Also, they inflict defeat/destruction

on the enemies of our faith and our homeland. Hence, we can say that whatever successes that are the destiny of mujahideen are a result of believing in God and are in accordance with the law of God and a result of acting upon the sharia of the Holy Prophet (Peace Be Upon Him) (15).

Titles of the other violent lessons include, "Manners of a Mujahid," "Homeland" (about driving out foreigners), "Love of Country/Homeland" (about fighting the enemies of Islam who have destroyed the country), "Success of Mujahideen," and "Where the Mujahideen Fight the Enemy." These textbooks continually reinforce the lesson of violence in the name of Islam and the expulsion of foreigners that are introduced in the initial lessons on the alphabet.

Scope and Reach of Jihad Literacy

The reach and prevalence of the UNO textbooks is unparalleled in the history of Afghan education and yet difficult to measure, since records are poor and the books proliferated widely. To complement the textual analysis above, I assessed the availability of this violent curriculum through reports from the time and interviews with aid workers who participated in education programs around the time of publication. Although at the height of ESSP the textbooks were officially used by only approximately 100,000 children in UNHCR schools, in fact they were also used by roughly the same number of students in private schools or madrassas supported by the mujahideen parties in the refugee camps. They were also widely used in General Zia's Pakistani madrassas along the border, where Afghans also enrolled. Reports indicate that they were the only textbooks available in Afghanistan—that is, in "Free Afghanistan"—and that they were used in some schools in Pakistan supported by Arab states (pers. interviews October 2, 2012). Indeed, among young educated Afghans today, it is unusual to meet someone who was not at some point exposed to some version of these textbooks (pers. interviews October 2, 2012; November 10, 2012; March 4, 2013). Thus, nearly wherever

Afghan children attended school, they were taught from these incendiary textbooks.

Official reports from UNO to USAID at the time reveal that ESSP activities from 1987 to 1992 included support for primary schools, literacy training, and teacher training, with the latter two designed for mujahideen residing in refugee camps in Pakistan outside Peshawar (USAID 1988).[21] A report submitted from UNO to USAID notes, "From FY87 to FY92 Mujahideen were offered literacy courses in the winter camps along the border, using the 'Alphabet of Jihad Literacy' books prepared by ESSP" (USAID 1994a:4). An earlier activity report notes, "Five hundred and ninety-eight literacy courses in six winter camps for Mujahideen have given over 12,000 adults the opportunity to learn to read and write and become effective fighters" (USAID 1988:15). Subjects included reading and writing, math, and religious studies. According to a final report, "Over 1,600 primary schools and 446,000 students received ESSP textbooks in Afghanistan, and 1,031 primary schools and 167,022 students received ESSP textbooks in the refugee camps in Pakistan" (USAID 1994b).

In keeping with fervent efforts among humanitarians to support the Afghan resistance against the Soviets, UNO educators took a holistic approach to fostering militancy. Local staff used achievement tests to select mujahideen for teacher training, after which "members of the Education Council and their respected military representatives or camp commanders" (USAID 1988:9) decided which would become teachers. After training as primary-school and adult-literacy teachers, they would return to Afghanistan to "upgrade" the quality of schools and education. Political parties selected the schools that were to receive educational kits (these appear to have contained textbooks and training materials), which party representatives distributed in "summer vacationing areas" and in nine southwestern provinces of Afghanistan.[22] In 1991 ESSP shifted its focus from "relief-oriented educational assistance" to reconstructing the Afghan education system (USAID 1994). Toward the end of the project, teachers were trained in refugee camps in Peshawar and in Afghanistan, with priority placed on female teachers. By the close of ESSP, over six hundred women had been trained as teachers (USAID 1994).

The Cold-War Education Strategy and its Influence on the US Invasion of 2001

During the eighties and early nineties, throughout the refugee camps and in mujahideen-controlled territory inside Afghanistan, life was organized to support the fight first against the Soviets and later against Najibullah's government. Schooling, too, supported this end. The violence-infused textbooks transmitted the goal of pursuing jihad from political leaders to the teachers they had selected to students in the classroom. Promoting violent jihad in the classroom from the earliest age served to inculcate the jihadist message through children's formative years, and within the most upwardly mobile segment of the Afghan refugee population. Although the conflict with the Soviets was already underway when these textbooks were created, the US intervention supported and reinforced it by instilling norms of violence and solidifying the links between violence and religious obligation or jihad. In addition, these textbooks contributed to the radicalization of young Afghans in a way that fueled later violence during the civil war of the 1990s and the insurgency of the early 2000s.

In today's geopolitical environment, it is difficult to grasp how such a program could have been funded and supported by the US government. As discussed above, the US's nearly single-minded focus on defeating the Soviets provides some explanation. Indeed, there seems to have been no effort to mask the motivations. At a Brookings Forum on Universal Education (December 17, 2001), Thomas Gouttierre, director of the Afghan education project (the Center for Afghanistan Studies) at UNO and dean of International Studies and Programs, explained that decisions on educational content were made by local Afghan educators on behalf of the Afghan refugees and in the interest of providing a culturally appropriate, locally determined curriculum. His deputy notes, "We helped all of these seven parties with school supplies, developing curriculum, paying teachers, teacher training and manpower training. . . . They were taught about love for the country, love for freedom, hating the Soviet occupier" (quoted in Williams 2003).

Moreover, some independent education experts argue that the books had little educational value *except* as political propaganda. According to reports from educators working in Afghanistan and Pakistan, the books were poorly conceived and of limited pedagogical value (pers. interview August 3, 2012; August 14, 2012). They were poorly written, did not allow for teachers' creativity, and did not engage children. Some parents reportedly disliked them (pers. interview August 3, 2012).

In recognition of the inappropriate pro-war content in the UNO textbooks, the books were reportedly revised in 1992–93. However, according to educators in Afghanistan and Pakistan, while the revisions excised some passages and images related to violence, they left much of the overall sentiment of the books intact. For example, they continued to exhort students to jihad and to link Islam to militancy. In addition, the *original* violent books, albeit with some of the Taliban regime's modifications (e.g., removing images of faces), were reprinted multiple times over the years, and in 2002 the *Washington Post* noted that the original books, "filled with talk of *jihad*" and featuring "drawings of guns, bullets, soldiers and mines," have served since the end of the Cold War "as the Afghan school system's core curriculum." The original books could still be found (with a little searching) in bookstores in Peshawar as recently as 2013.

By the late 1990s, as the UNO books became discredited among members of the aid community, UNICEF and Save the Children launched a project to support a diverse group of Afghan educators to create new education materials.[23] To avoid criticism from the government in Afghanistan, which was sensitive to international interference, the project referred to these materials as the Basic Competencies and presented them as supplemental to whatever was being used already in Afghan classrooms. The materials, however, were devised to stand alone and to provide good-quality support to teachers who had limited training and limited access to resources outside of the classroom. From all reports, accomplished Afghan educators, with support from experienced international colleagues, created materials that were widely viewed as a significant step forward for the Afghan educational system (Stephens and Ottaway 2002; Rugh 2012; pers. interviews August 3, 2012; August 14, 2012).

When the US launched its attack against Afghanistan in 2001, UNICEF and its partner organizations stood ready to provide support to the education system as soon as conditions permitted. By the end of 2001, UNICEF had negotiated with the interim Afghan government to allow it to provide the Basic Competencies textbooks to schools across the country in its "Back to School Campaign." As UNICEF was in the process of printing the books, Chris Brown, described as the "head of book revision for AID's Central Asia Task Force," met with the Ministry of Education (MoE) (Stephens and Ottaway 2002). Shortly after these meetings, news arrived in the UNICEF offices that the MoE had changed its mind and decided to distribute the UNO textbooks (Rugh 2012). The UNICEF educators later learned that rather than pressing for use of the Basic Competency materials, Brown appeared to have instead urged the MoE to distribute the UNO books. The *Washington Post* notes that in February 2002, "Brown arrived in Peshawar . . . to oversee hasty revisions" to the textbooks' printing plates. Afghan educators scrambled "to replace rough drawings of weapons with sketches of pomegranates and oranges." According to Brown, "We turned it from a wartime curriculum to a peacetime curriculum" (quoted in Stephens and Ottaway 2002). However, these new books were of poor quality, given the way they had been hurriedly redacted, and much of the problematic text remained (Spink 2005).

Despite the widely acknowledged problems with the original UNO textbooks and the deficiencies in the revised books, and despite access to a better-quality alternatives available from UNICEF, UNO was awarded another education contract for $6.5 million in 2002, this time to print and distribute the revised textbooks to all schools across Afghanistan. In 2001, according to the Center for Public Integrity (CPI), UNO hired the Washington-based firm Van Scoyoc Associates Inc. to lobby "Congress, the White House and other agencies on budget and appropriations, science and technology, and education" and spent a total of $60,000 to do so. The following year, "UNO spent . . . $120,000 lobbying Congress, the White House and other agencies on the same issues" (Williams 2003). Although the lobbying may have been effective, UNO likely benefitted further from the fact that the US simply lacks substantive policy on providing aid to education abroad, since policies deemed to be of secondary importance are more readily subject to manipulation.

In this case, the manipulation was probably facilitated by Thomas Gouttierre's long-standing ties to the US government. Gouttierre's career in Afghanistan began with the Peace Corps in 1965 and continued for the better part of ten years. He was a Fulbright fellow and later the executive director of the Fulbright Foundation. He also worked as the coach of the national basketball team in Afghanistan (UNO n.d.) and formed some lasting ties in this role. One of the members of the team was Zalmay Khalilzad, who would later become part of the G. W. Bush administration and serve as US ambassador to Afghanistan from November 2003 to June 2005 (Williams 2003). Upon his return to the US in the mid-1970s, Gouttierre established the Center for Afghanistan Studies at UNO. He was deeply dedicated to supporting Afghanistan, maintaining his relationship to Kabul University, and hosting many Afghan scholars at UNO. The close personal relationship between Gouttierre and members of the US government continued over the years and may have helped Gouttierre garner grants (Williams 2003).

Thus, when the Soviet Union invaded Afghanistan, Gouttierre was well-positioned to assist in the US response. He became a member of the Afghanistan Relief Committee—a US-based NGO that advocated for increased aid to Afghan refugees—and was a passionate supporter of the Afghan resistance. According the Boston Globe, as cited in a report from the Center for Public Integrity, "The Center for Afghanistan Studies at the University of Nebraska at Omaha has longstanding ties with Washington policymakers and collaborates regularly with intelligence" (Williams 2003).

The Relationship Between Textbooks and Violence

The US supported the design and printing of the jihadist textbooks before the collapse of the Soviet Union, during what many have identified as the golden age of humanitarianism, when aid was supposedly apolitical. Clearly this period was not apolitical, as I have shown and as many had already established (Terry 2002; Barnett 2011). In fact, the progress reports written by UNO to USAID clearly reflect awareness of the political nature of the intervention they were implementing. But examination of the education intervention in Afghanistan is also important for a better understanding of the effectiveness of negative curricula in cultivating violence. This history demonstrates that simply including education in international aid interventions is insufficient to create peace—the content of the intervention must also support this goal.

As discussed in chapter 1, a number of recent studies of militancy show a correlation between increased levels of education and increased likelihood of supporting suicide bombing or becoming a militant or suicide bomber (Krueger and Maleckova 2003; Berrebi 2007; Fair 2007; Shafiq and Sinno 2010). Yet these studies do not explore the possible role of negative curricular content as a mechanism behind the correlation. In addition, although many studies focus on the textbooks used in politicized contexts, they usually examine how differing historical narratives socialize students into political identities (e.g., Freedman et al. 2008; Muller 2011) or how new textbooks may reform systems (e.g., Wray 1991). Those that focus on the impact of textbooks on students usually examine their effect on learning (e.g., Fuller 1987; Glewwe et al. 2009). Virtually no studies examine the causal effect that textbooks may have on producing militants or support for militancy. From the data presented in this chapter, it appears likely that negative content coupled with religious instruction influenced a generation of young men to support militancy and violent jihad—not only during but also beyond the struggle in which they were then engaged.

Conclusion: Jihad Literacy Textbooks, US Credibility, and the Rise of the Taliban

The link between the US-government-funded jihadist textbooks and the conflicts in Afghanistan appears to have formed in several ways. First, the prevalence of these textbooks likely strengthened the normative support for violence and conflict by endorsing a form of jihad that had not previously been sanctioned by Afghan religious education. The moderate Hanafi school of Islam was the most common throughout Afghanistan. Deobandism, an offshoot of the Hanafi school and the dominant form among the Taliban, had generally maintained a separation between religion and politics since its founding in the 1800s and remained generally apolitical until the Soviet invasion of Afghanistan (Van Linschoten and Kuehn 2012). Although historically *jihad* had been used to refer to personal, internal struggle and introspection, in the 1980s the word assumed the meaning with which it is most commonly associated today, of a call to war specifically to defend Islam (Van Linschoten and Kuehn 2012; Brown and Rassler 2013). Imbued with this new meaning, it was invoked throughout the Afghan refugee camps and in the madrassas in Pakistan along the Afghan border to incite young people to participate in armed struggle for the purpose of dislodging the Soviet occupier from Afghanistan, thereby protecting Islam from the infidels. What likely has made these jihadist books so powerful—far more powerful than, for example, communist textbooks that also attempted to indoctrinate children—is the link they foster between violence and religion. In a society where nearly every aspect of life revolves around religion, teaching violence through religion is likely to be more authoritative than other forms of indoctrination. The books' manipulation of rural fears of external domination—especially at the expense of religion—also contributed to their appeal.

Such were the historical and cultural conditions that left Afghanistan's citizens particularly vulnerable to US-supported education that served as one of the key mechanisms for transmitting the message of violent jihad. As chaos deepened in Afghanistan after the departure of the Soviets in 1989 and the country fell into full-scale civil war, the Afghan madrassas in refugee villages and in the borderlands in Pakistan changed from training centers for the mujahideen into training centers for Taliban fighters. This change occurred as the Hizb-e Islami Party run by Gulbuddin Hekmatyar fell from favor and Jamiat Ulema-e-Islam (JUI)[24] assumed control of the broad networks of extremist religious schools and military training camps on both sides of the border. In an effort to stabilize Afghanistan, JUI and the government of Pakistan shifted their support to Mullah Mohammad Omar and the Taliban, mobilizing "thousands of Afghan and non-Afghan students . . . into the training centers run by the Pakistani interior minister in support of the Taliban military adventure" (Nojumi, 2002; Nojumi et al. 2009:105).

Although the US abruptly dropped its support to education after the collapse of the Soviet Union, it left behind poorly revised or unrevised jihadist textbooks and scant support for secondary education for the Afghan refugees still languishing in Pakistan. Educators working in the region at the time speculate that the post–Cold War neglect of refugee education drove students to continue their studies in the schools that were available, which were often extremist madrassas (pers. interviews September 7, 2012). The jihadist textbooks continued to be available in book markets in Peshawar, Pakistan, and reprints were discovered in wide use as recently as 2000 (Davis 2002). Reports indicate that nearly all of the Taliban leaders received religious education from madrassas in Pakistan (DOS 1996, 2002; Elias 2013; Van Linschoten and Kuehn 2012:21; Brown and Rassler 2013). Most histories of the Taliban's formative years note that a significant proportion of the Taliban leadership attended the Dar ul Uloom Haqqania madrassa in northwest Pakistan (Van Linschoten and Kuehn 2012:23; Elias 2013). Given its location and its collaboration with mujahideen leaders during the struggle against the Soviets, it is likely that the Haqqania used the UNO books at some point. The Taliban themselves referenced these books in a threat letter in 2009, justifying their attacks on schools by the absence of appropriate education and demanding that the mujahideen textbooks be reinstated (Glad 2009), and respondents report that Taliban require these books to be used in the schools under their control today (pers. interviews March 4, 2013). Set along the path begun by the US-supported pro-mujahideen curricula, these madrassa graduates rejected "scientific" education in favor of Qur'anic studies and supported strict seclusion of women. In this way, the US likely supported the growth of an extreme and unconventional strand of Deobandism that formed the basis of Taliban ideology.

Thus, the concerted US, Pakistani, and Saudi efforts to promote violent jihad through education created a normative support for war among some Afghans. The formative influence of schooling permeated every aspect of society, and the new form of jihad became so foundational that it persisted after the US abandoned the region. In fact, jihad as war found a new target—other Muslims in the Afghan civil war—and then gave justification to the next generation of Taliban fighters, those fighting the Americans.

Finally, perhaps as important as the influence these textbooks may have had in creating support for militancy, the wide awareness among Afghans of their sponsorship by the US undermines US credibility and legitimacy among many in the region. Credibility is particularly important in a culture in which so much depends on personal relations. The irony of the

US teaching violent jihad is not lost on well-educated Afghans. Among poorly educated Afghans, however, irony can easily morph into suspicion of conspiracy. Given the role the US played in providing foundational support to jihad, it should not be surprising that many in the region believe that the US currently funds the Taliban (see, e.g., Shafi and Sharifi 2013). An idea that seems so preposterous in the West appears entirely plausible in much of Afghanistan and Pakistan.

4

Education for Stability

IN THE LEAD-UP TO THE MILITARY SWEEP through Marja[1] in spring 2010, General Stanley McChrystal declared that the US had a "government in a box" ready to assume its role once the area was cleared of the Taliban. Although the US cleared many Taliban from Marja, this achievement came at a significant cost and had mixed long-term results. Allied forces suffered high casualties, and flaws in the planned civilian surge emerged immediately. The UN refused to participate in reconstruction efforts, trained staff were scarce, and the public learned quickly that the US-selected Afghan governor-in-waiting had spent four years in a German prison for killing his son-in-law (A. J. Rubin 2010). Several months later, the Taliban reasserted themselves. After the offensive in Marja failed to bring much civil progress, one pundit declared that once McChrystal's box had been opened, "there wasn't much inside" (McManus 2010). Although the operation has recently received better press, problems with its implementation continue to create resentment among the local population. (A. J. Rubin 2013).

Despite its mixed legacy, the operation in Marja remains representative of the US military's approach to the war in Afghanistan, which embraces social, political, and economic development as a key element of counterinsurgency (US Army/Marine Corps 2006). In addition to tracking down militants, current counterinsurgency doctrine calls for "hearts and minds" strategies that are intended to increase the perceived legitimacy of the state and provide the economic opportunities that make insurgency less attractive, thus persuading the civilian population—upon which insurgents depend—to support the government and reject insurgency. Without the resources, recruits, and information garnered from the population, insurgents are unable to sustain an insurrection against a government. For the US in Afghanistan, the "hearts and minds" approach entails winning the support of the population—through stabilization programs that decrease insecurity and provide services to the local population—the sine qua non of successful counterinsurgency.

Yet the implementation of the strategy in Afghanistan has largely failed to take into consideration its interaction with regional and ethnic tensions or local expectations for government services. Preliminary research indicates that as a result education aid has been distributed unequally, undermining the goals of counterinsurgency and creating conditions that could exacerbate conflict. In fact, stabilization programs are administered unevenly by design, with priority given to the most unstable regions. This may be particularly problematic in Afghanistan, where Pashtun regions exhibit far more instability than areas dominated by other ethnic groups. In addition, stabilization models assume near-perfect design and administration of projects, and such is rarely if ever the case. Not only are projects unlikely to be perfectly designed; they are also unlikely to be perfectly executed. There are inevitably instances, for example, where aid is prevented from reaching its intended destination, whether by unforeseen events, such as a setback with distribution, or foreseeable problems like corruption. These problems may have greater consequences in an already unstable region than in more stable areas. For example, if ethnic divisions are a possible source of conflict (Lieven 2012; Rashid 2012), the mere appearance of favoring one group over another may exacerbate tensions. Thus, stabilization initiatives may contribute to underlying conditions for conflict by augmenting perceptions of horizontal inequalities (inequalities between groups) and undermining government legitimacy.

By their nature, stabilization programs require services that ordinarily fall within the purview of humanitarian and development agencies, and aid workers generally have better expertise and experience in providing relief services than the military. However, humanitarians, recovering from the missteps of the 1990s and equipped with new professional standards, have been uncomfortable with a relationship with military intervention. Many foresee dangers in the distribution of aid as an element of counterinsurgency. They argue that singling out conflict-prone areas for aid can threaten the delicate balance among rival groups, potentially increasing tension rather than defusing it (Fishstein 2010; Oxfam 2010; Burde et al. 2011). Although some aid workers have assumed such a role, most nonprofit organizations are loath to be associated with the military in any way, and they do not wish their programs to be considered as part of broader strategic goals.[2] Not only are they concerned that any perceived affiliation will increase the likelihood of violence befalling their staff, but they also question whether aid driven by strategic interests is effective in meeting the needs of the population. Aid is more effective, they argue, if it follows humanitarian principles of neutrality, independence, and impartiality, and adheres to the "do no harm" principle (Oxfam 2010; M. B. Anderson 1999; Barnett and Weiss 2008). There is some empirical evidence to support the humanitarians' concerns, in the fledging exploration of the impact of stabilization initiatives and from data on the role of horizontal inequalities in civil war (Ostby 2008; Fishstein and Wilder 2012; Bohnke and Zurcher 2013).

This chapter explores the tensions between international humanitarian norms and strategic goals of stabilizing conflict-affected countries, highlighting the fraught relationship between aid to education and counterinsurgency efforts in Afghanistan and arguing that uneven support to education can exacerbate underlying conditions for conflict—despite positive, well-intentioned curricula.[3] The chapter proceeds in the following way. First, I discuss the relationship between stabilization programs, uneven access to education, and the likelihood of conflict. Second, I describe the emergence of the Taliban after the fall of Afghanistan's communist regime and the dire conditions for education that resulted from Taliban rule. Third, I discuss the evolution of the US military strategy as it came to incorporate humanitarian aid as part of stabilization operations. Fourth, relying specifically on civil war and counterinsurgency literature, I reiterate and expand on what we know to date about the relationship between unequal access to education and conditions for conflict. Fifth, I present preliminary evidence to show how some US education-aid practices may decrease the perceived legitimacy of the Afghan government through unequal and inconsistent implementation. Finally, I suggest that although this evidence reveals important tensions in stabilization models, additional mixed-methods research must be conducted to test more definitively a number of questions that the qualitative and historical data presented here cannot alone settle.

Unequal Access to Education

My argument in this chapter is twofold. First, I contend that because stabilization programs support uneven access to education—both by design and by default—they appear to contribute to perceptions of horizontal inequalities. Thus, uneven access to education, or perceptions of being denied access, is likely to fuel resentment between groups (clans or ethnicities) that have disparate educational opportunities. Second, I argue that uneven access also results in resentment that focuses group grievances against the government, and thus may decrease government legitimacy. As a result, faulty stabilization practices that create unequal access appear to have fomented resentment toward the foreigners who implement aid programs, the Afghan government, and other ethnicities seen to benefit at the expense of peaceful groups. A belief that access to education plays a unique role in affecting grievances, and that these grievances can provide a particularly potent motivation for conflict, underpins these positions. Yet at the same time, current research is unable to isolate and better understand the roles that key public goods such as education play in undermining or promoting conditions conducive to peace or conflict.

"Unequal access" refers to differences in the ease with which groups in a society benefit from certain services. Access to education can be described as unequal or uneven when one community's educational aspirations are blocked in a way that other communities' are not, exacerbating or creating horizontal inequalities. There are many ways stabilization programs can create the perception that some populations are being deprived of certain services or rights. Such perceptions may emerge from allegations of corruption perpetuated by internationals or co-ethnics (Berdal and Malone 2000; Keen 2000), or from comparisons of relative prosperity across time (e.g., life was better before the US forces arrived), or space (e.g., conditions are better in neighboring countries, where family members may reside), or simply from comparisons to an idealized, imagined community (B. Anderson 1983). Because what little research there is on these associations has emerged from civil-war literature, it focuses on horizontal inequalities between ethnic groups. What is missing from this discussion is attention to horizontal inequalities in the context of internationalized civil war or counterinsurgency. I argue for the importance of relative-deprivation perceptions as they manifest not only in relation to another ethnic group, but also in relation to expectations of services from government and foreign forces—a key feature of counterinsurgency.

The first type of grievance arises from horizontal inequalities across ethnic groups, created by unequal assignment of aid, either by accident or by design, mapping onto and thereby exacerbating existing group tensions. However, grievances against the government can also be dangerous. For example, in Sierra Leone, former combatants repeatedly identified anger and frustration regarding their inability to realize their educational aspirations as the primary motivation for joining armed groups (Peters and Richards 1998:187; Richards 2003). Thus, the failure of the Sierra Leone government to provide access to an adequate education for its citizens was in itself the catalyst for rebellion—combatants considered lack of education to be their grievance and the government to be responsible for it (Richards 2003; Richards, cited in Thyne 2006:735–36).

It would be mistaken, however, to focus exclusively on how individual educational aspirations contribute to individual motivations for conflict. Education cannot be considered in this light alone, because access to it has a multiplier effect across society. It does not simply affect the individuals who are enrolled in classes. It also affects the parents, siblings, and extended family members who may depend on the student who is enrolled. In addition, inequitable access to education affects parents and older family members who are committed (and in some cases, desperate) to send their children to school—whether because they need the economic opportunities education brings or because they desire the higher social status associated with it. Today, stabilization programs in Afghanistan support unequal access to education, thus creating grievances that may increase the likelihood of conflict. After September 11, 2001, the US mandated humanitarian aid as part of its counterinsurgency and stabilization strategy, requiring that aid be allocated to populations considered at greatest risk of conflict. Due to the nature of the conflict, this rule inevitably favors Pashtun regions—since ethnically the Taliban are primarily Pashtun—over regions dominated by other ethnic groups. In a recent intervention in Afghanistan intended to boost education access, USAID directed particular schools to receive support from an education program used to enhance stabilization, while others in more stable regions were passed over. In some instances, aid failed to reach intended villages in conflict-affected areas due to endemic corruption. Villagers whose schools did not receive the support became resentful and complained of inequity. They did not understand why they had been excluded from receiving these benefits (Burde et al. 2011). Some in these villages appear to have become increasingly resentful toward foreigners and the Afghan government, which they perceived as unjustly and without reason denying them access to a highly valued service. In some cases, where villagers recognized that the education support went to villages of another clan, this resentment also extended to the other group, which was seen to benefit at their expense. In either case, this increased resentment likely exacerbated the conditions for conflict.

Education Policy During Taliban Rule

Resentment toward those perceived as denying Afghans access to education evolved over time. Much of Afghanistan had been without stable, competent educational opportunities throughout the Soviet occupation, and the situation only deteriorated after that war. When the Soviet military completed its withdrawal in 1989, the Soviet-supported Afghan administration and its president, Najibullah, faced numerous mujahideen assaults around the country. Once the administration finally collapsed, in 1992, the mujahideen were no longer able to sustain the facade of unity that they had maintained in exile. They turned on each other, launching the period of civil war that has the distinction of being the first conflict to reduce much of Kabul to rubble (Barfield 2010).

It was during this period that the Taliban emerged as a prominent actor in the region. Yet how they did so has been the subject of significant debate. The word *taliban* is rooted in *talib*, which has come to refer to a student in a madrassa—*taliban* is the plural form. This is an evolution in meaning, however. In Pashto and Urdu *talib* actually means "to seek," and the full expression for student is *talib-e-ilm*, "one who seeks knowledge."[4] *Taliban* was used to describe the many students who left their madrassas to join the civil conflict in the mid-1990s. It may seem ironic to many in the West that the Taliban, so often associated with crushing knowledge, are associated linguistically and historically with seeking it.

Recent research indicates that a variety of loosely organized groups of mujahideen called Taliban formed in the mid-1980s during the struggle against the Soviets (Zaeef 2010; Van Linschoten and Kuehn 2012). Education in Pakistan's madrassas throughout the period served to strengthen their solidarity and cultivate transnational networks (Dorronsoro 2005:278). The modern Taliban, which surfaced as a more organized force in 1994, appears to have been constituted from these groups. Today's Taliban and its predecessors drew their leadership from the same regions—centered around Panjwai district near Kandahar—and were nearly exclusively comprised of ethnic Pashtuns born and raised in the south and east (Van Linschoten and Kuehn 2012). The Taliban's rise to power in the mid-1990s was a direct result of the infighting and subsequent weakness among the other, better established, mujahideen groups. The disunity and ineffectiveness among the disparate mujahideen groups convinced Pakistan that it needed to support a strong Pashtun force that would provide "strategic depth"—as Pakistan refers to its access to Afghanistan[5]—and at the same time would not promote Pashtun nationalism, which would threaten its border. The Taliban commitment to Islam tempers their ethnonational identity, which is, in part, why Pakistan chose to back them. With Pakistani support, by 1996 the Taliban had gained control of most of the country, except for the city of Mazar-i-Sharif and Badakhshan Province in the northeast (Rashid 2001).

A common misunderstanding of the Afghan civil war pits the religious, fundamentalist Taliban against the open-minded, secular-leaning Northern Alliance, led by Ahmad Shah Massoud.[6] In fact, nationalist and royalist parties had been progressively eliminated from the struggle against the Soviets, leaving only deeply religious actors to assume opposing sides in the subsequent conflict (Dorronsoro 2005). The differences among these players were rooted primarily in their urban or rural origins, though they also adopted different strategies. Massoud was a key commander in the struggle against the Soviets. He, like many of his colleagues—for example, Gulbuddin Hekmatyar and Abdul Rasul Sayyaf—was an urban intellectual Islamist educated in Kabul. Another party leader, Burhanuddin Rabbani had received his education at Al Azhar University in Cairo, taught at Kabul University, and was president of Afghanistan during the civil war of the 1990s.[7] Their understanding of Islam included an Afghan perspective, but was much broader, shaped by reading and studying Islamic scholars outside of the country. The Taliban, in contrast, were educated in local Afghan village mosques, studying with local mullahs. If they had any exposure to religious thinking outside of Afghanistan, this came from madrassas across the border in Pakistan.

The rural mosque schools and madrassas the Taliban attended in Afghanistan and Pakistan conveyed a narrow understanding of Deobandi Islam that at times violated the Pashtun social code known as Pashtunwali[8] and at other times melded together with it. For example, public flogging or stoning of women generally offended Pashtun and Afghan sensibilities. Pashtunwali considers public violence against women shameful and "unmanly."[9] Likewise, the Loya Jirga (grand council) is a venerable institution for determining justice within the Pashtun tribal code, yet for the Taliban (and other Islamists) "the Loya Jirga represented political forces they opposed, not a primordial tradition" (B. R. Rubin 2002:193). Although Islam is an essential component of Pashtunwali, with mullahs playing a central role during tribal *jirgas* and in other important aspects of village life, Taliban may perceive Pashtunwali as a secular legal codification in competition with the sharia (Dorronsoro 2005).

The Taliban's perversion of Islam into a religion that denies access to education for girls and women seems to have stemmed, at least in part, from how they reconciled their particular religious education with their interpretation of the requirements of Pashtunwali and their rejection of modernity. First, Pashtunwali, like other pre-Islamic social codes in Central and South Asia,[10] considers women the embodiment of men's honor and, in keeping with this belief, often mandates severe restrictions on the mobility of women, teenage girls, and girls nearing puberty. This honor must be protected from intrusion of any sort. If it should be violated in any way, Pashtunwali requires that men respond.[11] Violations are broadly interpreted; for example, they might include a boy taunting a girl as she walks to school. Even a misplaced glance from a man toward a woman may stir trouble. The "protection" of women (i.e., honor) has been extended so widely as to effectively bar the appearance of women in all public spaces in any urban or semiurban area that is frequented by men who are not relatives of the woman. However, since many villages in Afghanistan are small and inhabited by large extended families, women are often free to move about within their villages.

Second, the Taliban of the 1990s and early 2000s rejected modernity, as a Western phenomenon. Much has been written about their destruction of televisions, cassette tapes, and videos. Their rejection of girls' education and any education that was nonreligious was also a reaction to modernity, as promoting a Western lifestyle. These policies were a new iteration of the old xenophobic fears of the corrupting influences of education that were promulgated among some sectors of the population in the nineteenth and twentieth centuries. The Afghan communist and Soviet efforts to secularize education had reengaged these old concerns, such that the Taliban efforts to ban education resonated with the general fears of modernization that were common in some sections of rural society. It is important to note, however, that this reaction to modernity was in some ways incompatible with Pashtunwali. Although Pashtunwali restricts the mobility of women and adolescent girls and typically mandates gender-segregated classrooms, it does not prohibit their education or mandate that education be exclusively religious. Many among the Pashtun population on both sides of the border chafed under these interpretations of their religion and culture, which undermined support for the Taliban among their base.

Furthermore, under the Taliban, the tensions between rural and urban social structures persisted. As in the past, these tensions were most pronounced in relation to education and women's rights. New laws were enacted to enforce a mixture of a narrow interpretation of sharia and Pashtunwali: women were removed from their jobs and barred from appearing in public places without a male escort. By the time the Taliban were pushed from power, enrollment in education had declined from a high of roughly 1.4 million in 1980, just after the Soviet invasion, to approximately 900,000, of whom the vast majority was boys (Samady 2001).[12] Education infrastructure also fell into greater disrepair. Although the Taliban today claim to have held more tolerant views of education during their rule, interviews and numerous reports from the time say otherwise (Rashid 2000). Interestingly, however, there is some evidence to suggest that Taliban commanders did not uniformly accept the policy of barring girls from school or educating sons in exclusively religious classes. Some commanders sent their girls and boys to school in the refugee villages where their families had remained, as reported by one of their former teachers (pers. interview October 1, 2012). In addition, when questioned, some Taliban leaders offered security as an explanation for "temporarily" denying girls access to school, promising that when security improved, girls would be allowed to attend (pers. interview October 1, 2012; B. R. Rubin 2002).[13]

US Aid, Stabilization, and Counterinsurgency

Thus, when the US and its NATO allies invaded Afghanistan in 2001, they found a country badly broken, by the years of Soviet occupation, the subsequent civil war, and the Taliban rule. Although there was a clear demand for many basic services from the population, including education, the US did not initially see the role for these services in counterinsurgency. Shortly after the US launched its offensive in October 2001, many believed the worst of the crisis was over and the Taliban had disappeared. As the *New York Times* reported in November 2001, "As the negotiations went on . . . the hard-core Taliban fighters and an unknown number of foreign Islamic zealots had simply melted away. They crossed the brown hills and ridge lines, and slipped away" (Kifner 2001). Allied forces faced no resistance among civilians, and many among the Taliban army left their regiments and returned to their villages. The majority of Afghans disliked Taliban rule; they were exhausted from decades of conflict and craved calm and prosperity. In contrast to the later reactions to US forces in Iraq, when the US and NATO invaded Afghanistan, many Afghans were relieved and welcomed their presence. The promise of peace was tantalizing.

The subsequent events are now well-known—funding and personnel arrived only very slowly in Afghanistan, military efforts focused on routing Al Qaeda, and US and allied forces relied on former warlords to track militants. After the US invaded Iraq, the war in Afghanistan was all but forgotten. Although the majority of Afghans initially welcomed the foreign presence, they were profoundly disappointed with the US decision to support former warlords as proxies against the Taliban. As the warlords-turned-governors gained strength, corruption reemerged and security deteriorated once again. Despite their notoriously poor treatment of women and their draconian justice system, the Taliban had had two remarkable achievements: first, they largely eliminated opium production;[14] second, they virtually ended the civil war and improved security throughout the country. These accomplishments contrasted sharply with the subsequent US and NATO failures and allowed the Taliban to regain strength and support. By the time the US began to refocus its efforts on Afghanistan, the Taliban had reorganized, and a full-fledged insurgency was underway.

Failing to understand the rural-urban dynamics at the outset, NATO and US military forces pressed for control from the center. The deposed Taliban took the opposite approach. A village leader's description of his tribal relationships characterizes local dynamics: "My allegiance is to my family first, then to my village, sub-tribe, and tribe" (quoted in S. Jones 2009). Understanding this structure, the Taliban sought to extend their influence from the bottom up. They relied on networks of local commanders who conducted operations within their home provinces, where they maintained tribal affiliations (Christia and Semple 2009). They started at the village level and typically sent an envoy from the same tribe or subtribe to coerce or persuade a local leader to join them (S. Jones 2009). To rally support, they would cite grievances against foreign forces and point to the Karzai administration as a corrupt puppet government—both common complaints among the civilian population.

When it became apparent that Afghanistan was becoming increasingly unstable and that the war in Iraq was going badly, the US overhauled its military strategy. This was part of a larger reorientation of US defense strategy around a supposition that failing, unstable states posed the greatest security threats toward the country (USG 2002). To stem the losses, the US adopted a new counterinsurgency field manual that changed the military mission and gave priority to winning by gaining the support of the population (US Army/Marine Corps 2006). The new US Army Field Manual (FM 3–24), prompted by experiences in Iraq and largely credited to David Petraeus, placed a premium on protecting the civilian population and rebuilding government services. Stabilization programs play a key role in this strategy: "Stability operations is an overarching term encompassing various military missions . . . to maintain or reestablish a safe and secure environment, provide essential governmental services, emergency infrastructure reconstruction, and humanitarian relief" (US Army/Marine Corps 2006:2–5). With this new policy, the military not only united "development, diplomatic, and defense" initiatives under programs like the provincial reconstruction teams (PRTs, discussed below) but also envisioned closer collaboration with international NGOs and other humanitarian actors who had a history of keeping their distance from the military.[15] The Department of Defense stressed the importance of stability operations over and above "traditional combat operations" and eventually "elevated stability operations to a status equal to that of the offense and defense" (US Army 2008:3–7).

In accordance with this elevated status, stabilization strategies receive significant funding from USAID and other government sources. From 2002 to 2006, these programs in Afghanistan received approximately $3.5 billion—a large amount in its own right—but in the two years after FM 3–24, from 2007 to 2009, another $3.8 billion was obligated (Colucci 2007; SCFR 2011). In 2009–10, approximately 77 percent, or $1.65 billion, of USAID's total budget for Afghanistan was spent in the south and east, and by 2011, 80 percent of US government nonmilitary aid to Afghanistan went to programs in these turbulent regions (SCFR 2011). In contrast to US policy language endorsing development, the large majority of stabilization interventions were quick-impact projects with visible results expected often within several months, rather than programs that demonstrated a longer-term commitment to peacetime development. Most of these funds were managed by private, for-profit contractors, with the Louis Berger Group Inc. and Development Alternatives Inc. winning "more than half the total of USAID's contracts" (SCFR 2011:15).[16]

How Stabilization Is Intended to Work

In service of counterinsurgency, stabilization programs are meant to work by protecting the population from conflict and providing it with social services. Populations at the greatest risk for joining insurgency are targeted the most, in keeping with the idea that better services decrease grievances while increasing the opportunity cost of rebellion. Since the population becomes the prize, reconstruction and other forms of development and humanitarian aid assume a central strategic role. Thus, as it had done in fighting the Soviets in the 1980s, in Afghanistan the US incorporated aid to education as a political tool in its military strategy, rather than only as a form of humanitarian relief. In contrast to the use of education in the 1980s to foster an insurgency, the focus of education in the 2000s was the opposite—counterinsurgency. According to strategy documents, initiatives by the US government and its NATO partners are intended to promote stabilization in several spheres: "rule of law," a "secure environment," "social well-being," a "sustainable economy," and "stable governance" (USIP and US Army 2009:15). Access to and delivery of education is included in the sphere of social well-being. Aid is intended to improve civilian well-being by delivering services (e.g., education, health care); the delivery, in turn, is intended to improve awareness of and attitudes toward government, leading to increased government legitimacy and therefore reduced conflict.

To respond to these new policies in Afghanistan, USAID began to explicitly endorse—at least on paper—its role in counterinsurgency efforts, describing its projects as intended to "contribute to political and social stabilization, social cohesion, and better governance." USAID defines these aims as key to the ability to "hold areas 'cleared' by military or police action and hamper the insurgents' ability to draw support from the local populace" (USAID 2011c). Thus it required that most aid be allocated to populations considered at greatest risk of conflict, since insecurity both undermines "confidence in the legitimacy of the central government" and threatens to roll back any progress. Because of the inextricable links among "security, governance, and development in establishing stability in Afghanistan," USAID claims to support the Afghan government in its efforts to improve these key areas at both the provincial and district levels, especially by encouraging "popular participation in governance" (USAID 2011c).

In this model, USAID is meant to design its program activities to be fully and strategically integrated into counterinsurgency operations at each phase of the stabilization initiative. Activities during the earliest phase, "shape," focus on "assessing community grievances and assisting coalition

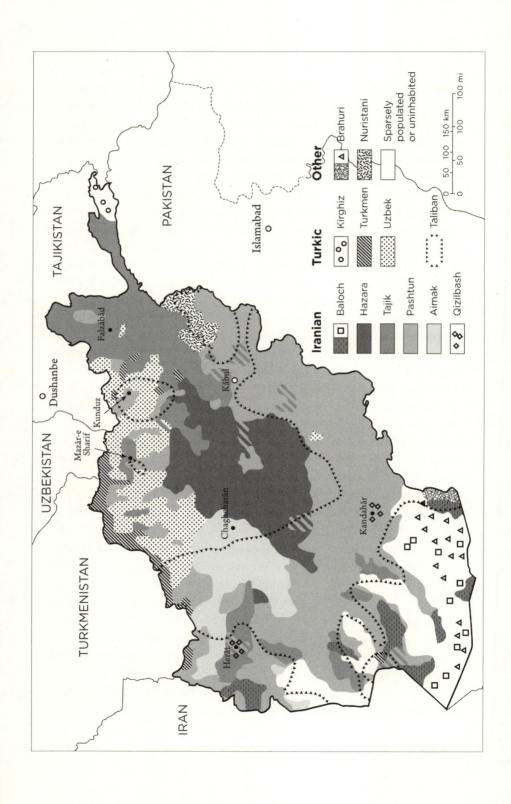

TAJIKISTAN

PAKISTAN

Islamabad

UZBEKISTAN

Dushanbe

Faïzābād

Kunduz

Mazār-e
Sharif

Kābul

Chaghcharān

Kandahār

Herāt

TURKMENISTAN

IRAN

Iranian

☐ Baloch
Hazara
Tajik
Pashtun
Aimak
◇◇ Qizilbash

Turkic

°°° Kirghiz
Turkmen
Uzbek
Taliban

Other

△ Brahuri
Nuristani
Sparsely
populated
or uninhabited

0   50 100 150 km
0   50   100 mi

forces" with determining important projects. Next, during the "clear" phase, USAID implements "quick-impact activities" that are intended to meet "recovery needs" in communities designated as priorities for regional stabilization. Activities during the "hold" phase are supposed to address the "grievances of at-risk populations." Finally, the "build" phase is intended to include "activities that support the transition from stabilization efforts to longer-term development" (USAID 2011c:1). In reality, though, USAID is heavily influenced by the military shift toward stabilization and so, in keeping with this mandate, the agency focuses more on implementing quick-impact and other stabilization projects in the most restive areas than on longer-term development initiatives across the country. However, a number of USAID officers object to close coordination with the military (per. interviews July 2013).

In addition to USAID work, US interventions to combat the insurgency include PRTs—units launched in late 2002 in Afghanistan that mixed civil, diplomatic, and military efforts (US Army Combined Arms Center 2011). By integrating civilian initiatives into the military strategy, these projects were intended to address local grievances, increase the legitimacy of the Afghan government, and gain trust from the population. Some early reports praised the PRTs. An assessment published by USAID, for example, found that PRTs "have been an effective tool for stabilization in Afghanistan, strengthening provincial and district-level institutions and empowering local leaders who support the central government." The evaluation argued that these teams "helped create conditions that make increased political, social, and economic development possible" (USAID 2006b:5).

Both speed and visibility are considered central to the success of stabilization programs, because according to the theories that guide them, it is important to provide clear evidence of progress, so as to decrease willingness to join insurgency. As a result, interventions stress improvements to physical infrastructure over intangible outcomes. Or, in the case of education, "hardware," such as school buildings, boundary walls, desks, and latrines, is typically emphasized over "software," such as teacher training

FIGURE 4.1 Ethnolinguist Groups and Taliban Presence in Afghanistan
Source: (c) 2009, Carnegie Endowment for International Peace.

or other forms of support for human resources. As a small but highly visible part of its stabilization strategy, the US funded rapid educational interventions in targeted districts either through PRTs, as a subcomponent of an omnibus stabilization program, or (less frequently) as a subcomponent of a larger education program. PRT education projects consist almost exclusively of building schools.[17]

One of the most defining characteristics of stabilization programs is the way they are targeted exclusively toward restive districts that are considered unstable and hostile toward the government. Stabilization efforts in service of counterinsurgency have not been concerned with how implementation may affect existing horizontal inequalities in society. But even a stabilization program that is successful in gaining the confidence of its targeted population may simultaneously exacerbate grievances in other sections of society. Thus, in focusing on providing education to communities that have been seen as contributing to violence and instability, stabilization programs risk producing conflict in communities that previously had been peaceful. See figure 4.1 for the rough distribution of ethnolinguistic groups and Taliban presence in Afghanistan in 2009.

Revisions to Stabilization Programs

Given the fluid political environment in Afghanistan, the persistence of the Taliban, increasing evidence of widespread corruption and waste, and US and NATO concerns about the impending Western military withdrawal, stabilization efforts have come under significant scrutiny from Congress and elsewhere, as described below (SIGAR 2011; SCFR 2011). In response, practitioners indicate that stabilization programs have evolved rapidly away from a strict emphasis on strategic military goals and toward a broader concern with building up long-term governance and local participatory processes (pers. interviews February 2013). Earlier programs (2006–11) created by the US military's Counterinsurgency Training Center-Afghanistan in collaboration with USAID were designed to prioritize coordination among foreign actors (military, aid, diplomatic) and were expected to be short-term, stop-gap measures to smooth the impending transition from conflict to peace (USAID 2011a). According to many reports, how-

ever, these programs were implemented quickly and haphazardly in response to what were later deemed superficial community requests, with
little consideration for program contradictions and inconsistencies (SIGAR
2012a, 2012b). One practitioner notes that these projects were executed
with little initial consultation with local government or communities, resulting in the kinds of mistakes frequently criticized by humanitarians—
for example, schools built in the wrong places and later serving to house
livestock, or built in communities that had no teachers. These projects
likely undermined government legitimacy by failing to demonstrate a commitment to providing the services requested by the local population.

In an effort to remedy some of these flaws and strengthen government
legitimacy, USAID and its implementing partners designed new initiatives with increased emphasis on governance and worked more closely
with communities and local government from the outset. They simplified
previously elaborate plans to determine "sources of instability" and re-
structured the guidelines to facilitate working with local governments
and villages. Yet activities considered part of long-term "development"
were still not included in stabilization initiatives, in part due to the typically short time frames allotted to projects—thus limiting the types of
education aid that could be provided.

In contrast to many of those who worked on earlier programs,[18] and in
keeping with conceptually distinct categories created by aid agencies and
aid workers, stabilization program implementers working on USAID-
funded projects today go to some lengths to distinguish themselves from
both development and humanitarian workers, pointing out that they do
not "focus on needs" but instead on "drivers of conflict" (pers. interview
February 15, 2013). They argue that, for example, while development and
humanitarian projects may include a range of programs that respond to
community needs in areas related to water, health, and education, stabilization programs are based on a detailed analysis that implementing partners conduct with community members to determine "causes of instability." After working with community members to identify root causes,
practitioners plan activities to address exclusively the issues that have
been identified as drivers of instability (pers. interview February 15, 2013).
USAID (2011b:12) guidelines recommend identifying activities that will:
(1) increase support for the national government, (2) "decrease support

for Anti-Government Elements," and (3) "increase institutional and societal capacity and capability." Thus, only activities that will address these goals are meant to be funded, and practitioners go to great lengths to attempt to determine which activities will best serve this purpose (pers. interview February 15, 2013).

According to these guidelines, practitioners work with communities to prioritize only those problems that can be identified as contributing to conflict or reducing social cohesion. In sorting through community priorities that qualify for funding under these criteria, practitioners note that many requests for services or infrastructure are dismissed "by colleagues, donors, evaluators, and others" as "wish lists," unrelated to drivers of conflict (pers. interviews February 2013; pers. comm. November 8, 2013). One stabilization practitioner speculates that these requests are likely to be dismissed if a community asks for aid for services or infrastructure that it has never had. For example, if the community complains about a lack of access to education and requests a school to remedy this problem, but they have never had access to school, according to this respondent the stabilization logic assumes that lack of access to education cannot be a driver of conflict, because the community has never before had access to education. Another practitioner notes that the requests for support to services such as education "are often simplistically viewed as pre-engineered to benefit special interests" (pers. comm. November 8, 2013). Whatever the reason, practitioners agree that community demands are often dismissed as illegitimate, and stabilization programs may not consider funding for education a priority.

Yet within the stability assessment framework, according to practitioners currently engaged in stabilization initiatives in Afghanistan, the top grievances identified by communities involve irrigation for agriculture, inequitable distribution of resources, unresponsive government, and lack of access to education. And in reviewing data collected from nine districts, one practitioner notes that every community has requested support for education. This reveals that, despite efforts to improve project implementation, the stabilization logic misses a major cause of perceived government illegitimacy and thus of conflict: the denial of services that the population considers vital. However, it is important to remember that it is not enough to provide a targeted community with the services they want; it is equally necessary to offer support to more than just the most violent communities that stabilization programs target.

The Limits of Stabilization Programs: Unequal Access

According to recent research, development aid, and in particular, provision of social services—usually loosely defined as improved provision of and access to education, health care, and security—is integral to undermining civilian support to insurgents and reducing violence.[19] Local populations will favor the source of social services, increasing civilian willingness to support and share information with the provider and, in turn, reducing willingness to do the same for the nonprovider. Berman et al. (2011) cite information sharing as the key mechanism in hearts-and-minds strategies and argue that in this regard improving "quality of government services" is preferable to supporting "short term employment/job creation programs" (519). They find that a higher level of unemployment is correlated with fewer attacks against counterinsurgents and that "there is no significant relationship between unemployment and the rate of insurgent attacks that kill civilians" (496). Thus, although the research in this field is nascent, successful government provision of social services appears to be more closely linked to successful counterinsurgency operations than short-term employment programs.

In addition, if the local government is too weak to provide these services, there is a danger that insurgents will "fill the vacuum." If NATO forces do not help the Afghan government provide services, insurgents may provide them instead, gaining influence over the population in the process. In this way, some rebel groups have garnered significant support and goodwill from local populations, as Hezbollah has in southern Lebanon. Indeed, the more effective insurgencies are at providing social services to their base, the greater their ability to conduct high-stakes attacks against the government or occupying forces (Berman and Laitin 2008:1944). This underscores the importance of counterinsurgents providing services successfully.

Development projects undertaken for development's sake—as opposed to for strategic ends—appear to have a positive effect on attitudes toward the government in Afghanistan because their implementation is understood to be more equitable and because they address the population's desires. The National Solidarity Program (NSP) is a nationwide development program that makes grants of up to $60,000 to community *shuras* (local councils) after they have decided what they need to promote development in their villages. Community boards decide collectively how to spend the money, typically prioritizing water pumps, roads, and other infrastructure. As noted above, construction projects are often favored by US military, since they are a visible and semipermanent representation of the assistance and goodwill offered by the government and outsiders to the local population. In relatively stable districts, male and female respondents in villages with NSP presence had more positive attitudes toward both local and central government officials (Beath et al. 2012). According to records of security incidents from the International Security Assistance Force (ISAF),* NSP villages were less likely to experience violent incidents, although the effect was more pronounced in the long term. In these districts, "the provision of development programs appears to make noncombatants more inclined to view government actors as working in their best interest, which in turn makes them less likely to support the insurgency" (Beath et al. 2012:23). Strikingly, however, these positive findings do not hold in the two most volatile eastern districts in Nangarhar Province included in the study. In these, the NSP had no positive impact on perceptions of government bodies, NGOs, or ISAF, and, in fact, these respondents held negative attitudes toward the president and the national police. Thus, according to this study, in the most restive areas, even well-designed and equitably implemented development programs may have little impact on community perceptions. In fact, development aid may be more effective in preventing the spread of violence than in reducing its existing levels (Beath et al. 2012).

Similarly, humanitarian initiatives undertaken for the sake of humanitarian rather than strategic ends may effect positive changes in attitudes toward foreigners. Research in northern Pakistan shows that direct aid to populations immediately after the devastating earthquake of 2005, substantially improved recipients' trust in foreigners. Census and survey data

* ISAF is the NATO-led security force in Afghanistan.

from four earthquake-affected districts used a natural experiment (distance from the fault line) to measure trust toward a range of people including family, people of the same village, people of the same clan/kinship group, foreigners and Americans. Pakistanis living in the regions closest to the fault line that received aid trust Americans and Europeans (48.7 percent) significantly more than they trust their neighbors (16.9 percent) or clan (29.7 percent) (Andrabi and Das 2010:12) and more than those living in regions that received less aid.

Despite their apparently lending evidence to the argument that aid decreases grievances and increases government legitimacy, neither of these programs was designed as part of a counterinsurgency strategy. In fact, both interventions clearly distanced themselves from any motive beyond providing relief and development. The NSP is widely known across Afghanistan as a government program intended to reach all villages, not only those that may harbor hostility toward the US or the Afghan government. Similarly, in relation to the earthquake relief in Pakistan, it is possible that because the assistance was visible, immediate, badly needed, and not obviously strategic—that is, there was no public discussion of strategic interests or connection made to such interests—the aid was effective in increasing trust precisely because it was not perceived as trying to do so (Andrabi and Das 2010). Thus, it is unlikely that in these instances assistance produced grievances and perceptions of horizontal inequality in communities that did not receive it. Applied to stabilization programs, which are more explicit in their strategic targeting, these findings may suggest that communities that receive effective aid perceive the government as more legitimate, but they say nothing about the effect in places that were not targeted.

Several other studies of the relationship between development aid and levels of trust or incidence of insurgent activity examine projects that provide support in a range of sectors, including education, electrification, health, transportation, reconstruction, economic opportunity, and water and sanitation (Berman et al. 2011; Crost and Johnston 2010; Andrabi and Das 2010). The omnibus nature of these initiatives does not allow for specification of a causal variable, one that distinguishes the effect of social services from that of promoting economic opportunity or a number of other interventions. To date, most academic literature remains agnostic as to the likely different effects of particular types of social services.[20]

Stabilizing Afghanistan

In Afghanistan, the jury is still out on how well stabilization programs work—either in increasing government legitimacy or decreasing violence. And despite the integral role of social services in the counterinsurgency strategy, research has focused little on these services, isolated from other types of interventions, or on the effect of one particular type of social service, such as education.

Nonetheless, the qualitative data presented below, as well as several other studies, call the effectiveness of stabilization programs in Afghanistan into question. Although recent USAID stabilization interventions appear to have improved on previous efforts by the military, these programs are still likely to produce mixed results. In fact, stabilization operations may have the opposite of their intended effect because, by both accident and design, they create unequal access to aid, and in particular, to education. Unequal access creates perceptions of relative deprivation, which is counterproductive in two ways.

First, perceived relative deprivation creates or intensifies the perception of horizontal inequalities, exacerbating tensions between ethnicities and communities. This creates conditions that make conflict more likely, as resentment between groups increases. As the gap widens between expectations and reality, the risk of conflict is also likely to increase. This may be particularly true when it comes to education, where evidence suggests that intergroup inequality in access fuels conflict (Ostby and Urdal 2010).

Second, as noted in the previous section, stabilization programs are designed to focus narrowly on sources of instability and so avoid supporting community needs unless these have been convincingly demonstrated to relate to conflict. Thus, by design, stabilization programs may fail to respond to community grievances, including those concerned with access to education. Access to education, as has been established, constitutes a perceived right for the vast majority of Afghans across the country, and they expect their government, and sometimes the international community, to guarantee this right. When this expectation remains unmet, it not only adds to community grievances but also drives community members to seek fulfillment elsewhere. While failure to address the issues that are most important to targeted communities can increase grievances against the government, choosing which communities to respond to based on their prior levels of conflict can also undermine perceptions of government legitimacy in communities that do not receive aid.

Stabilization Projects and Unequal Access in Afghanistan

To understand better the role education plays in stabilization programs, I gathered qualitative interview data on current and recent stabilization programs in Afghanistan and compared my findings to existing qualitative and quantitative research, culling information on the effects of education from previous studies of stabilization and counterinsurgency efforts.[21] I conducted interviews with key staff members of two projects and reviewed program documents and reports. Education figures in stabilization programs either as a stand-alone project (in other words, as a specialized program that is devoted to stabilization), or, more typically, as a component of a larger program that includes funds to support education when it is deemed necessary. To preserve the anonymity of my respondents, I do not name these projects. For convenience, I refer to them simply as the education program and the stabilization program (although, as noted, both are intended to work as stabilization programs). I group my findings into three sections: unintended weaknesses, program-design flaws, and community responses. Both unintended weaknesses and program-design flaws result in inequitable distribution of aid, which, in turn, results in inequitable access to education. Communities respond to poor educational options as they do all over the world (including the US), by moving if they can or by seeking education access elsewhere. More research is needed both to identify the effects of particular aid programs—that is, how interventions in education differ from economic interventions or other social programs—and to understand better the prevalence and impact of the outcomes reported here. However, evidence from my data lends support to the notion that stabilization programs produce unequal access in ways that are likely to—and in some cases clearly do—exacerbate grievances against other groups and the government.

Unintended Weaknesses

Some of the causes of unequal access to education in stabilization programs are unintentional. Often, unforeseen problems result from challenges to delivering aid in a hostile environment. Plans may be unrealizable because they are difficult to implement. For example, one of the essential goals of USAID's stabilization programs is increasing "popular participation in governance" (USAID 2011c). Yet broad community participation in extremely volatile communities is very difficult to guarantee. Often, it may appear expedient to hire community mobilizers from nearby villages, but if such people are not already sufficiently known, they may remain outsiders in the eyes of the community and, in reaction, maintain a low profile. Keeping a low profile is not conducive to effective community mobilization.[22]

Stabilization programs also face the problem of corruption. Corruption has plagued all kinds of programs in Afghanistan—stabilization, development, humanitarian, and other. Instability and poor oversight create a permissive environment that invites corruption and encourages questionable decisions regarding implementation of programs, decisions which have resulted in aid not reaching its intended locations.

In relation to education programs, corruption aggravates unequal access, exacerbating differences between groups (Heyneman 2004). Corruption in education is cited in relation to both delivering materials and employing contractors. Regarding materials, stabilization programs have historically emphasized infrastructure and rehabilitation or delivery of other kinds of visible, durable goods. In the context of education, such "hardware" investments usually include building and rehabilitating schools and boundary walls,[23] as well as providing classroom furniture. For education in stabilization programs, infrastructure investments outweigh "soft" investments, such as teacher training or other forms of support.[24] Building schools is especially favored because it provides excellent photo opportunities: highly visible, public shows of support for one of the most widely recognized manifestations of progress and modernization. Sometimes, programs also promise equipment. However, delivering equipment in environments with minimal supervision comes with the risk of encountering corruption. One staff member notes:

But you know a lot of things went missing. In a few of the schools, USAID were insistent that we give them IT equipment—photocopiers, computers, printers and stuff like that. . . . [We] sent an external monitor, unrelated to the program, to check on some of the schools, to make sure what we had paid for was actually there. . . . Well there was a 'goods received note' signed by the principal saying that he had received equipment, but there was nothing there. This happened in a number of schools, not just one school, but probably 8 or 9 schools. And so the equipment wasn't there. So then we had to try and ascertain where equipment was, because we paid for it, we've got the 'goods received note', and the driver who'd shipped it over there said that he had done that, but there's no equipment there. . . . Well, the shop, the shop sold the stuff, we had receipts and they were insistent. The driver, we contacted the driver, 'Yes, yes, I did deliver all those things . . .' He rang back two days later, and said, 'Actually, look, it's Ramadan, we have to be telling the truth . . . and this is the time for us to be honest and actually, well, I didn't deliver that stuff at all. They paid me to tell you that I delivered that stuff, but I didn't deliver that stuff.' Ok, ok, so then we said to the principal, 'So why did you sign the 'goods received note' on these items if you didn't receive them?' 'Oh they paid me to sign off on this stuff. They gave me a bit of money so I would sign the form.' Now where that equipment is, I have no idea. Whether the principal received it and then sold it? Whether he took it home to his family? Whether the shop sold it to somebody else? No one knows where that equipment is, but it's not in the schools and we paid for it. It's just so ridiculous . . . to give people in the middle of [Province] a brand new photocopier with color cartridges. Like who's going to use that? Do they even have sufficient electricity? You know, they get one paper jam or finish the cartridge and that's the end of it.

Quickly delivering highly visible projects—like new school buildings—is a hallmark of stabilization initiatives. But it is inherently risky, since it requires providing easily lootable goods, including construction equipment, materials, and school supplies. These are especially difficult to track in volatile environments.

With regard to contractors, although another key aim of stabilization programs is to provide additional employment for community members (read: local, and presumably idle, young men), many programs have instead relied on contractors from the provincial capital or even from Kabul to carry out the work on schools. Respondents report that when contractors are involved prices inevitably rise. On one of the projects discussed here, a staff member noted that although he had a very positive assessment of the program overall, corruption between contractors and school principals was routine. Another staff member expressed concern about relying on distant urban centers for infrastructure support. In this example, a number of communities requested furniture for their schools that skilled local laborers could have been hired to build. Hiring local labor would increase employment opportunities, and, from an educator's perspective, it could also engage the community in school management, potentially increasing interest in what happens inside the school. Instead of relying on local labor, however, the organization had a contract with a furniture company in Kabul, from which it needed to procure all of its furniture. Furniture was ordered from Kabul and, according to the staff member, "loaded onto a truck at enormous expense, and then delivered to the school." Like other interviewees, this staff member noted that it was challenging generally to achieve project goals in such a volatile environment.

It has been widely acknowledged that aid for stabilization in Afghanistan has had insufficient oversight (SIGAR 2011, 2012a, 2012b; SCFR 2011; Fishstein and Wilder 2012). A Senate Foreign Relations Committee report is damning. Among other examples, it cites a case of fraud involving the Louis Berger Group Inc. (LBG):

A New Jersey-based engineering consulting firm that accounted for over a third of USAID's total contract obligations in Afghanistan between FY 2007 and FY 2009, LBG recently admitted to submitting "false, fictitious, and fraudulent overhead rates for indirect costs . . . [resulting] in overpayments by the [US] government in excess of $10 million" from 1999 to 2007. Such instances of fraud undermine our reconstruction efforts in Afghanistan and highlight the need for vigorous oversight of our war-zone contracts (SCFR 2011:15, citing Voreacos 2011).

The report also describes poor oversight with respect to education:

> In another case involving an education project for teachers, USAID's contracting officer was unaware and did not consent to the award of subcontracts and did not approve of significant subcontract modifications totaling $23.4 million out of a $94 million contract. These modifications included changes in the duration of subcontracts and terms of subcontractor performance, as well as significant funding increases. (17)

These examples do not suggest any inherent problem with well-thought-out stabilization projects that are implemented in the absence of corruption— as difficult as this would be to achieve. Even if stabilization projects were implemented perfectly, however, they would still create unequal access to education because they provide aid predominately to unstable districts and regions. And in doing so, they map on to existing tensions between groups.

Program-Design Flaws

Stabilization programs distribute aid inequitably by design, which may create or exacerbate tensions both regionally (which is also to say ethnically) and locally. Non-Pashtun-dominated regions in the north and west of Afghanistan perceive that unstable Pashtun areas are receiving the bulk of the available aid. These perceptions are accurate. According to official records of funding levels for aid to Afghanistan, 80 percent of US aid in 2010–11 was directed to Pashtun regions in the south and east, and US-AID has been transparent about its policy of identifying villages to receive support for schools based on their location in insecure Pashtun areas. This regional imbalance has reportedly created resentment along ethnic lines, for example, among Tajiks toward Pashtuns (Fishstein and Wilder 2012).

At the same time, stabilization projects appear to undermine stability at the local level by stirring up fears that one village may be receiving more aid than a neighboring one. Perceptions of inequality appear to be very high across the country, but in places that are already volatile, they may have especially adverse effects. As one interviewee describes the project in a Pashtun-dominated area:

> There are villages that get stuff and then villages right next door that don't get stuff. Some schools do and some schools don't. There is so much politicking that goes on around these decisions with MoE, the PED [Provincial Education Director], and the governor since we have to liaise and get approval for the works from them. Who knows why one school got a boundary wall and another school didn't. There is a really high level of inequality, whether the inequality is perceived or is actually and objectively there or not.

Although the program staff did not consider any incidents of violent conflict to be a direct result of the uneven distribution of the education project, they reported frustration, and in some cases, increased resentment, among communities that did not receive benefits from the program. If such feelings have not led to open revolt, this does not mean that they may not prolong conflict. Such grievances are more likely to sway a community to cooperate with or harbor insurgents, who may promise to deliver services.

Since in Afghanistan the US is supporting a weak central government against an insurgency, aid is intended to enhance the legitimacy of the government. Unlike in many other countries, where USAID projects are intended, among other things, to build positive feelings toward the US, in Afghanistan the goal is to make the local government look good in the eyes of aid recipients, in addition to achieving its humanitarian and development aims. Given this goal, an inherent design flaw is that by providing unequal access to services, these programs may in fact undercut government legitimacy. One program staff member describes the dilemma like this:

> The government—provincial governors and PRRD [Provincial Rural Rehabilitation and Development] directors—are having a really hard time with us constantly harping on this. They try to identify what are the real issues that are causing conflict in their areas . . . and it would be natural to concentrate program interventions mostly there, as op-

posed to district centers, where things are going well. However, the district authorities cannot approve of strategic plans of that sort because they themselves are actually creating more inequality. And they [local government] believe that this kind of unequal distribution of resources and development is not only going to cause conflicts, but it's also going to create problems for them, because they would also like to be somewhat accountable [to the communities].

The premise that these projects would improve the legitimacy of the government may be either inherently flawed or based on a mistaken understanding of the way government resources are distributed. Perhaps planners envisioned stabilization programs on the model of extra support for struggling communities in the US. But conflict-affected communities in Afghanistan do not typically have fewer resources than more stable communities nearby. So poor communities close by also want support, and they perceive the greater resources going to hostile communities as rewarding insurgency (Fishstein and Wilder 2012; pers. interviews February-March 2013).

The way in which "sources of instability" are designated constitutes another design flaw. By limiting criteria for sources of instability to only those things that can be reasonably demonstrated to be linked to conflict, programs set up a conflict analysis that is very difficult to complete. Indeed, the original District Stability Framework was considered so complicated, requiring so many different steps, that it was deemed necessary to revise it substantially (see USAID 2011b for a presentation of this framework).

In addition, it is not clear that cutting back on humanitarian support with the intent of better targeting sources of instability has been justified. As mentioned above, many previous development and humanitarian efforts largely supported by PRTs and other military actors were considered to have been of such poor quality that they were significantly curtailed from stabilization programs. Within the new stabilization logic, community requests for development and humanitarian assistance were reframed as wish lists. It is unlikely that responding to community needs was itself problematic, as will be discussed in chapter 5. However, problems with previous stabilization efforts were attributed to having taken too unfocused an approach to stability, and revised plans mandate greater reliance on narrowly targeted aid (USAID 2011b), which may produce its own set of negative results.

According to staff currently working on a stabilization program, the primary grievances that have emerged across close to one hundred communities in several different provinces are similar. Furthermore, as discussed earlier, matters related to education are among the most common grievances. Education issues typically include requests for greater classroom space, boundary walls, latrines, assistance with university entrance exam preparation, and teacher training. Notably, requests include both software as well as hardware.

In order to try to separate activities that might reduce conflict from those not sufficiently targeted, some practitioners have begun to engage in a deep analysis of community problems with community members. One practitioner discusses this process:

> The stabilization approach says that we need to be far more analytical. People will want all sorts of services and they will come up with wish lists of projects. However, in addressing these wish lists, the underlying systemic problem will not go away. What we need is to uncover what causes the lack of services or what's driving the conflict in their areas. So, people will say, we need a clinic in our villages, we need potable water. And the purist stabilization, counterinsurgency view will say this is only a priority need, but not necessarily a driver of instability. People have never had a clinic or potable water, so it is unlikely that these issues are actually causing conflict. This view attempted to rectify the previous CERP [Commander's Emergency Response Program] impulse to indiscriminately fund community requests. People would say ok we need schools, we need uh, drinking well, and we need this, we need that, and these guys would just deliver whatever was needed and, as a result, communities were getting schools that were later filled with livestock, and where there were no teachers to teach.

This respondent astutely identified the problems with the new approach to community analysis, recognizing the way in which it may cause perceptions of deprivation:

Um, but, having said that, I have an issue with that . . . I have an issue with the whole theory of stabilization as seen that way because, again, I think that even though people didn't have something before, [the fact that] they feel that they are entitled to have it now, can actually easily create instability in their society.

Of course, these observations relate to many kinds of community griev-ances, not only those connected to education. However, practitioners note that many of the projects they implement are education related (often in the form of rehabilitating existing infrastructure or building boundary walls) and that they work hard to accommodate communities' requests even if these requests may veer toward needs whose connection to conflict is questionable. Indeed, in follow up discussions about education activities in this particular program, practitioners indicated that close to a quarter of the communities that are part of this stabilization program were receiv-ing support for education interventions (pers. interviews June 19, 2013).

However, given the importance of equitable access to education in mitigating horizontal inequalities, the tendency to view these education programs as inequitable, as described above, is worrisome. In addition, in cases where requests for support to education are passed over, denying people access to services to which they believe they have a right and which they believe their government should provide, is unlikely to en-hance perceptions of government legitimacy. In both ways these pro-grams may contribute to underlying conditions for conflict.

Community Responses to Lack of Access to Education

As I have shown throughout these pages, most Afghans place enormous value on education. In fact, even in the most volatile regions, where access to education is limited, parents will go to great lengths to send their chil-dren, particularly their boys, to school. Afghan respondents working closely with communities note that villagers demand education because they understand that access to it is enshrined in the constitution of Af-ghanistan. Yet respondents describe the limited access to both govern-ment and religious education in the most volatile regions of the country and note community members' consistent concerns about this issue. Government schools typically provide education in each district center and provincial capital. Government-supported madrassas also exist in each provincial capital, and smaller ones in each district center. But most villages do not have access to either form of education, because government schools do not exist in their villages. Mosque schools are the only remaining option for these communities.

As described above, communities often identify and hire a mullah to teach in mosque schools, but in volatile regions, the Taliban may appoint the mullah and pay his salary. Respondents report that in some cases Taliban members will even monitor the classes to ensure that the teacher shows up, thus winning the approval of parents. Some communities have reportedly created agreements with the Taliban to include a small percentage of math and science education along with the main religious subjects that the Taliban permit. Thus, in some places, communities negotiate with the Taliban to maintain at least some wider educational access for their boys.

Villagers consider maintaining access to education crucial, in part, because they attribute many social ills to a lack of education. When asked to expand on this point, several respondents surmise that rural populations are eager to educate their children in part because of the social advantages they see accruing to their better educated urban counterparts. In rural areas illiteracy is high and opportunities are scarce. In addition, rural populations are thought to be susceptible to the influence of insurgents, drug abuse, and illegal activities. Many urban, educated Afghans view villagers as lacking a basic understanding of Islam, which drives them to engage in activities that are "un-Islamic." For all of these reasons, respondents note that people are eager to educate their children and thus are willing to negotiate with Taliban to allow their children to attend mosque schools to receive at least some kind of education rather than none.

In addition to "education for the world," rural communities are also concerned about "education for the soul." Communities would like their children, especially their boys, to have access to appropriate religious education and are concerned about their moral upbringing. Since very few madrassas offer education for older youth in these areas, many youth travel to Pakistan to study in madrassas. One respondent describes parents' and boys' calculations: "[Boys] have to resort to traveling to Pakistan because all of the madrassas in Pakistan are free . . . parents are kind of caught between a rock and a hard place"—either their children do not have access to education or they have access to some education, but they do not know which kind that will be. The respondent continues, "Everyone thinks that in Pakistan there are two types of madrassas. One is the regular madrassa and the other ones are these jihadi madrassas. And parents never know where their children are actually going, but everyone believes that one of the reasons there are all these insurgents here during summertimes in Afghanistan is because all these madrassas are, you know, because madrassas have recess." Other respondents echoed these views (pers. interviews March 4, 2013).

Although extremist madrassas in Pakistan and Afghanistan are the minority, young people from Afghanistan do seek them out and attend them. As I discussed in chapter 3 and at the beginning of this chapter, a jihadist education may have a significant influence on students. It should come as no surprise, then, that some students who attend these madrassas become insurgents. While some Afghans surely seek these madrassas because they already share their religious beliefs, my interviews suggested that others attend because they have no other option if they want an education. Or they end up in an extremist madrassa because they know someone who attends. The influence of these jihadist madrassas may be significantly reduced if there were strong local education options available to the population in Afghanistan. The responses of many communities in Afghanistan show that the inability of the US or Afghan governments to provide access to education sometimes forces Afghans to look to the Taliban to provide it. An effective response to these considerations, however, would highlight a humanitarian, rights-based approach that focuses on providing education anywhere that does not have a school, not only in those regions that are most volatile.

Conclusion: Education, Stabilization and Instability

My interviews in Afghanistan reveal concerns about US stabilization efforts. In particular, some believe that the fact that stabilization projects have fostered unequal access to education has decreased the government's legitimacy in the eyes of many. Some of the problems with the provision of education aid can probably be traced to the US government's internalization of conventional humanitarian priorities, such that aid is more understood primarily as emergency relief. As a result, inadequate attention has been paid to education interventions and their potentially adverse, if well-intentioned, effects.

Moreover, the evidence presented here suggests that many humanitarians were right to fear the politicization of aid and its subordination to military goals. Although I argue that providing aid is an inherently political endeavor, the rights and desires of the local population rather than the strategic goals of strong states should be the guiding consideration when designing aid interventions. In contrast to strategic stabilization programs, such an approach should be less likely to feed perceptions of unequal access. Even if a fairer distribution of education aid fails to enhance government legitimacy in the same way that emergency aid in Pakistan following the 2005 earthquake or the NSP in Afghanistan did, it will not lead to a deterioration in support for the government. My research suggests that such a distribution of aid would have a greater likelihood of increasing perceptions of government legitimacy and thus of reducing conflict—which is, after all, the ultimate goal of counterinsurgency. However, stabilization interventions in Afghanistan have yet to be implemented in ways that can achieve these objectives. And while a more equitable approach to aid may improve security throughout much of the country, it is not a panacea: even effective development programs do not appear to have this effect in the most volatile provinces.

In this chapter I have sought to extend our understanding of possible pathways to conflict. The evidence presented suggests that there is a strong likelihood that stabilization programs will exacerbate underlying conditions for conflict. Understanding the relationship between education and the dynamic balance between stability and instability enhances our understanding of the relationship between education and the underlying conditions for conflict. The interviewees I have cited describe numerous ways in which programs that attempt to promote stabilization through education produce perceptions of unequal access and, consequently, of relative deprivation. Stabilization aid provided under these circumstances is likely to exacerbate existing rivalries, tensions, and resentments. People are more likely to think that others got more, or at a minimum, that they have not received what the international community has promised.

While this chapter has focused on the role of education in stabilization programs, it is important to note that this is only one type of service provided as part of counterinsurgency efforts. Admittedly, funds for education stabilization programs are relatively small compared to budget allocations for other types of projects. However, this should not be taken as implying that the effects of education interventions are unimportant. As I have argued throughout, education is critical to state formation and thus also to perceptions of government legitimacy. At the very least, these data raise questions regarding the effects of poorly implemented education projects on perceived government legitimacy and resentments between communities. Although additional research is necessary to isolate education from other forms of aid and to quantify the impact these programs have on the goals of stabilization, preliminary qualitative evidence shows unintended, negative effects. Thus, even if education constitutes only a small portion of US stabilization programs, it has the potential to create disproportionate setbacks that undermine confidence in other projects and overall progress towards peace.

In contrast to the negative views of stabilization described in this chapter, two studies provide a more positive assessment of better-implemented aid programs. One is the study of the NSP by Beath et al. (2012) described above; the other is my own (with Leigh Linden), which I will discuss at length in chapter 5. Beath et al. suggest that aid may be more effective in decreasing conflict when it does not focus on the most unstable regions, thus contributing to unequal access.

One of the fundamental flaws in stabilization programs and, by extension, counterinsurgency operations is that they are designed neither to resolve horizontal inequalities in society nor to address a community's perceived rights, the denial of which constitutes a significant grievance. Such grievances stoke resentment and discontent among the local population. Although this may not necessarily lead to an increase in insurgent violence, it exacerbates underlying conditions for conflict, likely increasing sympathy for insurgents along with resentment toward foreign forces and the government. Unequal access decreases governmental legitimacy in two ways. The population is unlikely to support a government that denies it access to education, but a government that fosters horizontal inequalities is also unlikely to be perceived as legitimate. Overlooking these two forms of grievance is likely to hobble stabilization programs as they are currently administered and, in the long term, undermine efforts to stabilize Afghanistan and resolve the conflict.

5

Education for the World

I LEFT HERAT ON A HOT EARLY MORNING in June 2007 and drove east with my research manager and a team of enumerators toward Ghor Province, one of the most remote regions in Afghanistan. The land was pancake flat and dusty, and heat mirages rose from the road. I had been sick the previous two days and was just beginning to recover, so although it probably was only a few hours before we began climbing onto the plateau that constitutes most of Ghor, it seemed much longer. When we finally made it out of the valley, the temperature dropped and we were surrounded by rolling hills covered in a light spring green. We passed few villages, but the ones we saw were beautiful—low mud-brick houses that resemble the adobe of the US Southwest clustered around a stream or spring, interspersed with patches of trees and crops that add color and variation to the landscape. But for these occasional villages, the land was strikingly empty, and it felt like we were driving to the end of the world. Despite my illness, I was elated, because the research project that I had worked for more than two years to set up was finally underway.

Security in Ghor was better in those days, but Catholic Relief Services (CRS), the nongovernmental organization (NGO) whose work we were studying, had incorporated us into their security network and required us to phone their radio room at regular intervals to let them know that all was well and nothing untoward had befallen us on our way. We were equipped with satellite phones, since regular cell phones did not work in these areas. By evening we had pulled into the CRS compound in Dar-e-Takht, a bucolic village similar to the others we had passed along the way.

In the morning we set out for the first village that was to be included in our study. To get there we drove an hour through the rolling hills on a small dirt road. The road followed a river valley, and at some point our local guide told us our target village was close, but there was no bridge across the river to get to it. We stopped our trucks next to a small sandy beach and waited for our guide to come back. While the drivers prepared lunch—beans and bread—some of the men in the team went swimming. The women sat in the cars. The day turned into afternoon, and eventually our guide returned with a horse. He explained that the river was shallow enough for the men to wade across, but the women would have to ride since it would not be culturally appropriate for them to do otherwise. I had spent many days inside compounds in Herat and Kabul and was happy to be outdoors; if being outdoors included fording rivers and riding horses, so much the better.

When we arrived in the village, the headman (*arbab*) greeted us and explained the community's circumstances. They had never had a government-supported school, and the village was too remote and isolated for the children to reach the nearest formal school. Yet some families were connected to the outside world. He showed us the turbine that generated electricity for some in the village and from which one or two fortunate families could power their satellite phones and run their satellite televisions. Even this village at the outer reaches of rural Afghan life had been penetrated by Indian soap operas and the fledging Afghan television programs from Kabul.[1]

Roughly 90 percent of the 657,000 people in Ghor Province live in similarly remote rural villages (MRRD n.d.). Few of these villages have government schools. This is not exclusively a consequence of Afghanistan's multiple conflicts—these villages have *never* been reached by the government education system. Yet parents consider education critical to the development and socialization of their children and go to great lengths to enroll them in school. With the exception of study outside the villages, parents support education for boys and girls nearly equally. A small minority of villagers cope with the geographic barriers by sending their children, almost exclusively their boys, to walk long distances to the closest government school. On average these children walk two hours to get to school for a school day that typically lasts only two and a half hours. After school, the children return home, again on foot. A larger number, perhaps 40 percent, of children study the Qur'an in the village mosque. These lessons may include Persian poetry, but they do not teach numeracy (Burde and Linden 2012).[2]

Villagers consider religious and science education equally important. In our study, 93 percent of approximately 1,200 heads of households surveyed across these remote Afghan villages agreed that "it is important to teach math and science along with the Qur'an as part of children's studies" (Burde and Linden 2012). In the eyes of parents and children, religious education and formal school do not compete, but rather complement each other. "Education for the soul" (religious education) is considered equally important as "education for the world" (science education). Afghan villagers may live in one of the most remote corners of the world, but global ideas and norms reach them even there. They want their children to become doctors, teachers, and engineers (typically listed in that order), and they know that science education is required to participate in the world beyond their village. The ability to satisfy these desires, fulfill this universal right, and provide equitable access to education to villagers across Afghanistan is within the government's reach, given the right approach.

The most common present efforts toward these goals are not adequate. Although the Afghan Ministry of Education (MoE) has made huge strides in increasing access, the ongoing conflict has nonetheless diminished the government's ability to provide access equally across the country, thereby undermining its legitimacy. Reportedly, in keeping with the long tradition of struggle against urban elites and the perceived forces of modernization, the Taliban have launched hundreds of attacks on schools, particularly across the south and east of the country. The government and international forces' inability to protect these schools has reduced these actors' legitimacy among Afghan citizens. In addition, when the Taliban are able to prevent their children from attending an existing school, parents appear willing to submit to Taliban demands to change the content of education. Many parents view limited education for boys—all the Taliban would permit—as better than none at all, which is what they are currently getting in some places because the Afghan government and US and NATO forces struggle to create an environment safe for education.

In this chapter I show that community-based schools, distinct from the formal government schools but receiving government support and using the same curriculum, increase equitable access to education because of their location and structure. They are easier to implement in hard-to-reach communities because they use existing infrastructure: a home or mosque. Because they eliminate the need for separate school buildings and reduce distance to school, they appear less likely to be targeted by insurgents and make getting to school safer. I argue as well that a proliferation of community-based schools may lower the likelihood of conflict, because it reduces horizontal inequalities and increases the fulfillment of a universal right, as villagers demand. Broader, more equitable access to government-affiliated education[3] in Afghanistan is also likely to reduce conflict because the MoE curriculum is characterized by neutral, tolerant content. Flooding the countryside with community-based education would be conducive to promoting underlying conditions for peace—tolerance, national unity, and social cohesion.

This chapter proceeds as follows. First, it reviews how outside support to education can work toward peace by ensuring positive curricular content and providing more equitable access. Second, it provides an overview of the current state of education in Afghanistan, focusing on the conditions that limit access (attacks on schools, inadequate resources). Third, I discuss how limited access may increase grievances against the government or foreign forces and also undermine the government's ability to promote social cohesion through a shared curriculum. Fourth, I show how community-based schools increase equitable access to neutral education and thereby contribute to the underlying conditions for peace across the country. I review the content of the curriculum currently used in MoE-supported schools in Afghanistan, including in community-based schools. I also show the ways in which community-based schools are likely to be less vulnerable to the types of attacks that occur in Afghanistan.

Education for Peace

Although the three previous chapters have elaborated on ways that the international aid community has failed to provide education to support peace, here I want to demonstrate that it is nevertheless possible for education interventions to have a positive effect. Just as University of Nebraska at Omaha's discriminatory, violent education texts inculcated conflict, so curricula stressing peaceful values of diversity, tolerance, and critical thinking can influence populations positively. And just as inequitable access to education can stoke hostilities and undermine government legitimacy, equitable access can eliminate some of the grievances driving conflict.

Quality, Positive Curricula

Surprisingly, the research assessing the power of positive textbooks is nearly as scarce as the opposite, research that directly assesses the power of negative textbooks. Although "peace education" is a healthy, active subfield among practitioners and academics, the work that falls under this label typically includes supplemental out-of-school or after school programs that bring together groups of young people from different ethnic groups at risk of conflict. Many of these programs are rooted in intergroup contact theory (Allport 1954), which suggests that, under certain conditions, structured contact between opposing groups can improve relations. These conditions include, for example, equal status and equal representation in the setting in which the contact occurs, activities that require intergroup cooperation to achieve common goals, and support for the contact by authorities, law, or custom (Allport 1954). Seeds of Peace, begun to foster ties between Israeli and Palestinian youth, is among the oldest and most widely known of such programs, but there are many others based on the same premise—that bringing young people together to spend time in constructive ways can help repair and strengthen ties across groups that hold animosities toward each other. Although these programs often use supplementary educational materials, they do not employ a standard curriculum, nor are they typically state sponsored. Their benefit appears to arise from direct contact with others (Salomon 2004; Kupermintz and Salomon 2005), but most analyses do not consider the relevance of the instructional materials used to support this contact.[4]

Instructional materials in some noncontact peace-education programs, however, show promising results, providing some evidence for the influence of positive curricula on attitudes and beliefs. For example, Israeli students who studied the distant conflict in Northern Ireland were more likely to give a balanced description of the Palestinian perspective than those who had not (Lustig 2002, cited in Kupermintz and Salomon 2005). Materials that teach critical thinking (especially as regards social relations) and basic democratic values by examining layers of "otherness," such as awareness of self, of others within one's community, and of the distant other (e.g. from an opposing group), also show positive effects (Biton and Salomon 2006).

Civic-education programs that are incorporated into a full-time, public-school system are perhaps most analogous to the type of education intervention described in this chapter. However, there are few assessments or evaluations of citizenship or civic-education programs in conflict-affected societies. The majority of research focuses instead on civic education in Western democratic contexts. For the most part, this work is descriptive, examining the characteristics of civic education programs and finding that they typically teach tolerance, respect for others, human rights, and conflict-resolution skills and cultivate critical thinking—thought to be a key mechanism to enhance the ability of potential supporters of militancy to consider alternative forms of political participation (Rowe 2000; Bickmore 2001).

In contrast to the pathways to conflict through violent curricula and inequitable allocation of education support, equitable access to education and a neutral, tolerant curriculum can contribute to conditions that are likely to promote peace. This conclusion is based on available knowledge of the power of negative curricula, as well as studies that demonstrate the effects of positive curricula. I show that in Afghanistan the current MoE textbooks are relatively neutral and tolerant. While they successfully and systematically reach large numbers of children through the MoE's formal schools, their use in an expanded network of community-based schools would make them available also in areas that are most at risk of submitting to Taliban demands on education.

Equal Access to Education

Community-based schools—classes outside of dedicated school buildings and within an existing community structure like a home or mosque, employing a teacher from the community—offer a clear way to distribute access to education equally across rural Afghanistan. In addition, they appear to protect education from attack (Glad 2009; Burde 2010; Rowell forthcoming), thus further enhancing access and likely increasing government legitimacy.

They work because of their size, structure, and location. Unlike traditional government schools, each community-based school is housed in an existing local building and serves only its village; schools are widely dispersed, making attendance feasible for children—both boys and girls—whose homes are scattered across remote regions. Schools that are not community-based, in contrast, are large concrete structures, often built in central locations and intended to serve multiple villages. Children who do not live very close by—particularly girls, whose movements are restricted, and young boys—have a difficult time accessing them. These buildings are less likely to be protected (or protectable) and more subject to attack. Educators have long favored community-based schools because they are quick and inexpensive to set up and because communities develop a sense of ownership of them. They are closely coordinated with the MoE and use the current government curriculum, which has been screened for violent images, extreme bias, and intolerance.

Thus, community-based schools increase equitable access to reasonably good-quality education across the country, enhancing the likelihood for peace while mitigating the effects of conflict. Despite their promise, and the multiplier effect that their development would likely have, any initiative to promote them would confront the challenges that all interventions in education in Afghanistan contend with: the poor state of schooling generally, the current conflict, and uncertainty over the impending US-NATO withdrawal.

Challenges to Education in Afghanistan Today

Security in Afghanistan deteriorated steadily after 2005 and dramatically after 2007 when the Taliban reinvigorated their fight against foreign and Afghan-government forces (ANSO 2007). In 2008 the United Nations recorded 2,100 civilian deaths, up 40 percent from the year before. Although there was a slight decline in civilian casualties in 2012, the UN still considers the majority of the country unsafe for road travel because of insecurity (UN 2012). Education personnel and students, as well as school infrastructure, are particularly popular civilian targets of threats and attacks.

Violence against Education

As they do with any actions against allied forces, civilians, or nonmilitary institutions, the Taliban use an array of asymmetrical tactics to prevent the population from pursuing education. However, the Taliban are not the only ones perpetrating attacks on education. Antigovernment forces including the Taliban, conservative mullahs, common criminals, and local warlords launch violent attacks against schools, students, teachers, and administrators (Giustozzi and Franco 2011; Rowell forthcoming). Typical attacks include bombing of buildings, arson, and targeted killings of students and teachers (HRW 2007, 2009; Glad 2009). Although data are difficult to collect and track, these attacks appear to have a significant impact. According to President Hamid Karzai, in 2008, violence in southern Afghanistan forced 300,000 schoolchildren to stay home, an increase of 50 percent from 2007 (BBC News 2008, cited in ICG 2009). Hundreds of teachers and students have been killed, and hundreds of schools have been forced to close. Girls are severely intimidated, and in Zabul, Uruzgan, and Paktika Provinces the number of girls attending lower secondary school, already low, has dropped to less than 1 percent of the provincial population (HRW 2009).

Although such attacks appear to have started to decline, in 2011 there were still at least 185 documented instances of attacks on schools in Afghanistan (UN 2012).[5] Analysts attribute the decline in part to a shift in the Taliban position on education and increased negotiations at the local level between villages and Taliban and at the national level between the minister of education and the Taliban leadership (Giustozzi and Franco 2011).[6] At least some members of the Taliban issued a statement (quoted below) requesting that their followers stop attacking schools (Semple et al. 2012), and there have been reports that Taliban members at the provincial level have publicly spoken out against attacks on schools (UN 2012). In addition, according to one BBC report, militants and village elders across Afghanistan have made local-level agreements to allow girls and female teachers to go to school. However, some government officials have expressed skepticism that the Taliban have actually agreed to this (BBC News 2011). As I will make clear, the Taliban remain strictly opposed to any foreign influence in education and often to the enrollment of girls. While their attacks do appear to have declined, this likely reflects a tactical decision; by most reports, they remain opposed to nonreligious education (pers. interviews March 4, 2013).

The Taliban efforts to limit access to education combine with other constraints. For example, increased criminality contributes to the hostile environment, further decreasing accessibility of schools. If criminal or communal violence is not necessarily initiated with the express purpose of disrupting education or preventing children from going to school,[7] the resulting instability nevertheless has a dramatic effect. Since the majority of Afghans live in sparsely populated rural areas, providing services to them is difficult, and many children walk long distances to reach schools. The walk is perilous enough, but it is even more worrisome when every minute of the journey provides an opportunity for militants or criminals to target unprotected children. Parents, education personnel, and NGO workers repeatedly cite distance as one of the biggest barriers to boys and girls attending school. Even if a school is closer, the area in which it is situated may be problematic, particularly for girls. For example, as discussed in chapter 4, it is not considered appropriate for girls to walk through busy public places to get to school. Further, attacks have destroyed hundreds of school buildings, particularly in the south and east, straining an infrastructure that, despite construction by the Afghan government and foreign forces, was already inadequate.

Community-based schools present an alternative that addresses some of these challenges. However, to understand why community-based schools are the best solution among limited options, it is first necessary to present a brief overview of the state of the education system in Afghanistan today and the logic behind attacking schools.

The State of Public Education in Afghanistan and in Ghor Province

In Afghanistan, attacks on education are likely to have a disproportionate impact because of the poor state of the educational infrastructure. In other words, despite progress the number of schools available is insufficient and the system is overburdened. According to the MoE, school enrollment increased from 900,000 to 5.4 million between 2001 and 2007, with girls benefiting significantly (UNDP 2007). The MoE schools survey recorded 800,000 new students, 40 percent of whom were girls, enrolled in 2007 alone (MoE 2007). Still, as of 2007, over half of the school-age population was not in school, and only 37 percent of children between the ages of six and thirteen attended school. By 2012, total enrollment had reportedly increased to close to 8 million, but urban areas, as well as the north and west, largely accounted for this expansion.[8]

A 2011 report from the MoE notes a number of difficulties the country has in accommodating the influx.[9] First, there are simply not enough qualified teachers even for current students. Increases in teaching staff have not been sufficient to match increases in enrollment. Furthermore, two-thirds of teachers do not meet the government certification requirements (two years of training after twelfth grade). Of a total of 412 urban and rural districts nationwide, 230 have no qualified teachers in their schools. Such problems are compounded by the fact that insecurity has caused 502 schools in 10 provinces (Farah, Kandahar, Zabul, Uruzgan, Paktika, Helmand, Khost, Paktia, Badghis and Nimroz) to be or remain closed (MoE 2011).

Education is also unevenly distributed by gender. Across the country, males make up about two-thirds of the student population in government schools. The number of females attending school drops even more after third grade. The biggest drop occurs between grades 6 and 7, and by grade 12 only 25 percent of the student population is female (MoE 2011).[10] In urban areas nearly as many girls as boys attend primary school, but the ratio is much more uneven in rural areas (UNDP 2007). A 2011 UNICEF report notes that although the gender disparity in education is being reduced in urban environments, there are still close to twice as many boys as girls enrolled in urban secondary schools. Meanwhile, there are about twice as many boys enrolled in rural primary schools.

There is also a more general urban-rural disparity, with 53 percent enrollment in urban areas and 36 percent in rural (UNICEF 2011). In Ghor Province the number of children between the ages of six and thirteen who are actually in school reaches only 28 percent. Again, this distribution is uneven between the genders. Boys make up 77.5 percent of the population attending Ghor's 385 primary and secondary schools. Distance is a problem for school enrollment. Only 29 percent of the population lives within 5 km of a primary school, only 13 percent lives within 5 km of a middle school, and only 4.2 percent lives within 5 km of a high school (MRRD n.d.).

Despite limited access, government schools serve as the principal source of education for the Afghan children who can reach them. According to the MoE in 2007, approximately 95 percent of the roughly 6 million registered students attend government schools. Approximately 1.5 percent of the total number of registered students attend Islamic schools (government-registered madrassas), and close to 3 percent attend community-based schools (MoE 2007). Government schools in Afghanistan are very similar in form and function to conventional schools elsewhere.[11] They have, or are intended to have, an educational structure similar to that found in most countries around the world, including classes, grades, certified teachers, administrators, and school buildings. Throughout the country, most classes meet for two and one-half or three hours per day, Saturday through Thursday.[12] In urban areas, many schools hold double and sometimes triple shifts to accommodate the number of pupils. Winter and summer schedules vary depending on the location, with cold areas taking long breaks in the winter months, and hot areas scheduling their long breaks during the summer. Most government schools in rural areas are located in a relatively accessible and dense population center. Because there are not enough government school buildings to cater to each community individually, rural schools often function the way rural schools do elsewhere: one central school is intended to serve the surrounding villages. However, in Afghanistan this strategy does not address the access problem for girls, who typically cannot leave their villages to walk to school. Additionally, with the deterioration in security around the country, parents are understandably reluctant to allow any of their children to walk long distances outside of their villages.

Attacks on Education and their Effect on Government Legitimacy

Effectively addressing violence against education requires a nuanced understanding of the phenomenon. In many conflicts, attacking schools is a way for a disenfranchised or belligerent group to register its complaints against a government (HRW 2006). In remote rural areas or marginalized communities, school buildings are often the only local manifestation of the state. Given that social stability and security are primary goals of the international community and the foreign-backed Afghan government, any activity that is likely to hamper or thwart these goals is useful to antigovernment forces. Attacks on schools, students, and education personnel undermine security and serve as critical indicators of social instability (Burde 2010).

In Afghanistan, motives behind these attacks are difficult to document. Official responses to the attacks on education were initially slow and lackluster. Government and multinational agencies were reluctant to recognize the problem for fear of creating a perception of failure in reaching project goals and jeopardizing progress toward development (pers. interview October 2009). Agencies collected data in a limited and unsystematic way. Although key international agencies and the MoE have begun to monitor attacks on education, there is no shared definition of what constitutes such an attack, and such definitions as there are are inconsistently applied (ICRC n.d.). Complicating the problem, once they started to make more systematic efforts to collect data, agencies faced significant obstacles, given that attacks take place in volatile and hard-to-reach places. Correspondingly, governmental and international organizations only recently learned of the extent of the damage to the education system and the ripple effect this has had on social stability and the morale of Afghan civilians.

It seems clear that disrupting provision of and access to education is critical to the Taliban's strategy. Indeed, the campaign against state schools was codified by the Taliban as an element of their strategy at the end of 2006 (Giustozzi and Franco 2011). Using two complementary approaches— targeted attacks on personnel and obstruction of access to services—the Taliban aim to demoralize civilians and undermine their support of foreign and national forces (ICG 2009). Insurgent attacks aim to reduce the numbers of schools and the educational resources available to children, as well as the number of students whose parents are willing to send them to school. In addition, as described in chapter 4, the construction of schools is a conspicuous and highly publicized process, often involving foreign donors and sometimes the military. These aspects also make them targets (Rowell forthcoming).

Judging by Taliban statements, motives for attacks appear to include opposition to the state, to the curriculum in government schools, to the type of education provided to girls, and to foreign influences (HRW 2006; O'Malley 2007, 2010). When the Taliban communicate their reasons for attacking schools, they do so via a spokesperson or through "night letters"—notes left at the site of an attack warning parents, for example, not to send their girls to school.

Yet the Taliban appear to have realized that, given the importance parents place on education, their strategy has been unpopular, and they have attempted to modify it (Giustozzi and Franco 2011). Some portion of the Taliban released a statement in March 2012 that provides a sense of their present goals, as well as their ostensibly revised position toward education. It reads in part:

> Vigilant countrymen and the people of the world are fully aware that the invading forces in Afghanistan and their domestic stooges have inflicted heavy losses on the education system of the state and have misused this phenomenon as negative propaganda against the Islamic Emirate. . . . As the policy of the Islamic Emirate is based on the rules

and regulations of Sharia; and the Holy Prophet of Islam says that seeking of knowledge is the duty of every Muslim. So the Islamic Emirate in general does not resist education in the whole country. Of course the Islamic Emirate will not support that curriculum which is the filthy gift of the colonialists. It is a phenomenon by which the transgressors and their in-house agents want to wipe away our Islamic and national values and to replace it by Western culture. Obviously it does not mean the opposition of education and educational institutions. It is a just demand for the replacement of this kind of curriculum.

(Islamic Emirate of Afghanistan 2012)

Beyond blaming foreigners for the (Taliban-sponsored) attacks on schools, the statement evinces several recurrent themes in the struggles over Afghan education: that Islam mandates education, that foreigners meddle in education, and that opposition is not to education per se, but to Western values. It is important to note that the statement makes no reference to gender. Since this statement, attacks have continued, albeit somewhat less frequently.

The Taliban's apparent need to backpedal—at least rhetorically—on their opposition to education demonstrates that they gain no legitimacy from perpetrating attacks on schools. However, they do benefit from the perception these attacks create that the government and its allies are unable to provide enough protection or public services, which not only decreases US and Afghan legitimacy but may also lead to greater local compliance—albeit reluctant—with Taliban demands, as described in chapter 4. Often locals caught in a civil war have no strong ideological commitment to either side. Rather, their main goal is to survive the violence and continue living as normal a life as possible (Kalyvas 2006:45). For these reasons, locals are likely to collaborate with whoever can exert the most control in their area (Kalyvas 2006:118–32). If the Taliban can prevent children from going to school with highly publicized and destructive attacks on education, the population will see the US and the Afghan government as unable to control or protect certain areas. They may come to see the Taliban as the only emerging power that can. That such realizations have already happened in some parts of the country is evident by the fact that some villages have struck deals with Taliban concerning compliance with their education demands (pers. interviews March 4, 2013). This does not mean that locals do not highly value education, only that they have lost hope in US or Afghan ability to protect them or provide these services.

Community-Based Schools

Community-based schools offer the most effective way to support education in the midst of the challenges described and to prevent the Taliban from gaining strength and legitimacy at the expense of Afghan education. Community-based education, a common aid program in developing countries, is slowly gaining ground as a humanitarian intervention in countries emerging from conflict. In countries where the education system has collapsed or government capacity is weak, community-based schools can provide education services quickly. Governments and international agencies use them as a way to move toward universal primary enrollment in the context of limited budgets (Bray 2000; Rose 2003) or system breakdowns (Burde 2004).

In Afghanistan, community-based schools are intrinsically local institutions, in this way similar to mosque schools, but also different, because generally they are fostered by NGOs. The sponsoring NGO asks participating communities to provide classroom space, a local teacher, and administrative support from community associations. Community members identify an existing space in the village where they can host the school, usually a room in a home or mosque. They may also provide some support to the teacher, usually through in-kind donations (e.g., labor, food). The NGO, in turn, provides training to these teachers, materials for the classroom (textbooks supplied by the MoE, notebooks, writing utensils), and regular monitoring to track progress. Although many community-based schools hold classes in a room in a private house, the community-based schools in the study discussed here held classes in the village mosque. Such local, private settings are key to ensuring access to both boys and girls and likely a critical reason for their reduced vulnerability.

In addition, their proximity decreases the danger associated with traveling to school—not only of Taliban attacks but also of criminal and internecine violence. The fact that community-based schools use existing infrastructure can make them more secure. The lack of a large, public, and clearly foreign-supported brick and mortar school building decreases the probability of Taliban attacks. Even if Taliban can easily identify the location of a community-based school, it would make for a less visible and less symbolic—and therefore also less attractive—target. This can have a secondary effect on criminal and internecine violence, since these are no doubt abetted by the general atmosphere of insecurity created by the Taliban. If Taliban attacks cease, that may facilitate more effective governance, which would allow better policing of these other forms of violence.

Beyond matters of physical setting, international agencies believe that working through community associations (e.g., parent-teacher associations, school management committees) not only provides administrative support but also increases the indirect benefits for children and their families by embedding schools socially in their communities. In countries recovering from conflict, international and national agencies consider community associations an important element in enhancing civic participation among marginalized groups, strengthening commitment to education, and increasing community cohesion. In their words, international aid agencies such as Save the Children, CARE, and CRS support these education programs to enhance stability in communities recovering from conflict, to improve child welfare, to increase girls' enrollment, to protect children (Bush and Saltarelli 2000; Machel 2001; CIDA 2001; Sinclair 2002; Nicolai and Triplehorn 2003), and to prevent "backward development"—also known as "development in reverse" (Collier 2003; World Bank 2005).

Creating Community-Based Schools

The Partnership for Advancing Community Education in Afghanistan (PACE-A) was a five-year, $26 million USAID-funded program that began in June 2006 and was meant to "expand quality learning and life opportunities for marginalized communities and their children in Afghanistan" (PACE-A 2007:1) via a consortium of NGOs tasked with providing thousands of community-based schools for children between the ages of six and eleven in seventeen provinces across Afghanistan. In establishing community schools in remote areas where children have not previously had access to education, the consortium—of which CRS was a member—intended to increase access to education equitably, particularly for girls; to strengthen community-based associations such as parent-teacher associations and community education committees; to provide education that meets a certain standard of quality; and to avoid the pitfalls that have hindered community-based schools programs in the past by developing close and careful coordination with the Afghanistan MoE. Beyond these goals, CRS and other humanitarian organizations expect that community associations will enhance parents' engagement in education, and that the program will provide indirect benefits such as protection and improved life chances for children (Nicolai and Triplehorn 2003; Burde and Linden 2012).

Prior to establishing schools, CRS surveys communities to assess their level of need, interest, and ability to commit to the terms required. CRS selects districts according to a variety of factors. Assessments consider how limited is the district's access to government primary schools (villages must be at least a three-kilometer distance from government schools), gender gaps in primary enrollment, security concerns, and other NGO projects in the vicinity. They also gauge the amount of community and MoE interest, as well as the cost-effectiveness and long-term sustainability of the undertaking. After a pool of districts that are secure enough for staff to work in without excessive risk is identified,[13] highest-priority communities are chosen based on the availability of potential teachers—especially women—as well as level of interest expressed by the community and the community willingness to mobilize resources, such as teachers' salaries and classroom space.[14] Support from the MoE is also considered. Once a community is selected, CRS first mobilizes community support to promote the project. Community members identify a space to host the school (room in a home or mosque) and help support the teacher, who usually comes from the community. CRS provides training to these teachers, materials for the classroom (textbooks supplied by MoE, notebooks, writing utensils), and regular monitoring to track progress (PACE-A 2007).

Evaluating Community-Based Schools

This holistic, local process employed to get a community-based school started ensures its success once classes are underway. Three studies are presented below to show how community-based schools allay underlying conditions for conflict. The first illustrates the ability of community-based schools to reach a wider cohort of students. The second compares the vulnerability to attack of formal government schools and community-based schools. Finally, the third analyzes MoE textbooks currently in use both in formal government schools and community-based schools to demonstrate that the improved access provided by community-based schools exposed more students to a curriculum that is better able to ameliorate intergroup tensions and teach peace.

Access to Education

In the first study described below, I used extensive quantitative and qualitative data collected in a field experiment—referred to in the story that opens this chapter—to assess the impact of community-based schools on children, households, and villages across Ghor Province. I briefly review the methods and data analysis here to clarify their explanatory power for my current argument (for a detailed description of methods see Burde 2012 and Burde and Linden 2013). The research took advantage of CRS's planned expansion of community-based schools in Ghor Province to conduct a randomized evaluation of their work.[15] CRS had surveyed dozens of communities in Ghor and Herat Provinces for possible inclusion in their community-based education program. Half of the villages in Ghor Province slated to receive a CRS school were randomly designated a treatment group and received a CRS school in 2007. The rest were designated a control group and slated to receive a school in 2008, after the study had been completed. Using this method, rather than the needs assessment that NGOs at the time usually used, we could then test educational outcomes across the "treatment" and "control" villages.

The study was designed to measure the educational outcomes and attendance in villages where children were enrolled in these schools and to compare them to control villages where no schools were available but some children were walking long distances to reach government schools. The assignment of treatment or control was randomized at the level of geographically distinct clusters of villages ("cluster randomization"), so that all closely neighboring villages were either in a treatment group (and thus each had a school) or a control group (and thus each was without a school). This randomized trial aimed to test for the effects of the CRS schools on children's attendance and achievement. The quantitative part of the study was complemented by qualitative components, which included document analysis, observation, and interviewing.

There is no reason to assume the educational outcomes observed would not apply beyond the two districts in Ghor covered by the study, even though violence is not evenly distributed across the country. Although the Taliban insurgency is much stronger in Pashtun areas in the southern and eastern provinces, Ghor Province (predominantly Tajik and Aimak), has become increasingly unstable, accounting for 11 percent of Afghan civilian casualties in 2008, versus 42 percent for the south and 40 percent for the southeast (United Nations Assistance Mission in Afghanistan 2008).[16] Furthermore, the Taliban attacks that have occurred in Ghor mirror those in other parts of the country. And if in rural areas of the province, where Taliban influence has been more limited, violent incidents resulting from internecine tensions and criminal (including domestic) motivations outnumber those motivated by ideology, such incidences contribute just the same to the unwillingness of parents to send their children on lengthy journeys to school.

From a sample of thirty-one villages in northwest Afghanistan that included roughly 1,500 children between the ages of six and eleven, thirteen villages were randomly assigned to receive community-based schools one year before schools were slated to be supplied to the entire sample. This time delay allowed for an estimate of the one-year impact of the schools on girls' and boys' attendance and knowledge of math and the local language, Dari.

The quantitative survey data was complemented by qualitative case-study and interview data. A subsample of villages—both treatment and control—were selected for interviews with village leaders, mullahs, teachers, and male and female school-management committee members. The selection of these villages was based on their relative accessibility to the main road. Although all of the villages are remote, some are slightly less so. Interviews included questions regarding the educational backgrounds of respondents. The mullahs provided background concerning the ways in which they were educated and employed, and they discussed their relationships with the villagers for whom they work. These details provided insights into a foundation of Afghan society—the relationship between rural religious leaders and their communities.

This study shows that community-based schools have a stunning effect on children's academic participation and performance and have tremendous potential for reducing existing inequities in access and gender participation in rural areas in Afghanistan. Children on the whole are almost 44 percentage points more likely to attend school if there is a community-based school available, and girls are 52 percentage points more likely to attend. The girls' rate of attendance increases 17 percentage points more than that of their male counterparts (Burde and Linden 2013). *Proximity to school,* as cited by parents, teachers, and community leaders appears to be the key reason for these dramatic results. See figure 5.1 for a representation of enrollment in relation to proximity.

In the qualitative interviews that complemented the survey data, respondents repeatedly noted distance as the primary reason their children did not attend government school. Distance affected girls and very young boys more significantly than boys age nine or older. Interviewees cited insecurity and propriety as the main reasons they kept girls home from school. For the duration of our study in Ghor, although Taliban-related ideological violence was negligible, communal and criminal violence was reportedly prevalent. Parents and village leaders cited tribal and subtribal tensions between villages as sources of concern and insecurity. For example, tensions between Chesti and Palawan groups ignited clashes between local commanders and caused deaths on each side. Incidents of criminal violence—including kidnapping and abuse of girls—were also cited, although fear of exposure and retribution likely suppressed many more reports.

Program staff also cite the employment of local teachers as a key feature that encourages parents to send their boys and girls to these schools.

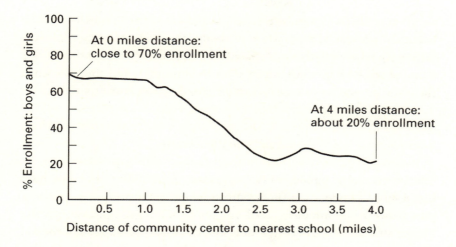

FIGURE 5.1 Enrollment and Proximity: The effect of geographic proximity of community-based schools on children's enrollment.

Results: As distance of a school from the community increases, enrollment drops dramatically, especially among girls.

Source: Reproduced from Burde and Linden 2012 (NBER paper).

Yet because levels of literacy are so low in rural Afghanistan, it is often difficult to find teachers from the immediate villages. Mullahs are typically the best-educated and frequently the only literate member of the village. In Ghor CRS relied on mullahs to teach the community-based classes, and all of the classes were conducted in mosques. Since many of the mullahs already offered religious classes (i.e., mosque schools), they often provided the government lessons in the morning for the two-and-a-half-hour official school day while continuing to provide religious classes either in the early morning hours or the afternoons.

Providing equitable access responds to parents' assertion of the right to education, reduces grievances, and thus likely reduces perceptions of horizontal inequalities and may increase government legitimacy. As noted in the opening of this chapter, these are not the remote Afghan villages of previous eras, or even of 2001, at the fall of the Taliban. If today they remain physically isolated and removed from the world in many ways, they are yet consumers of popular media. Many (if not most) villages have access to regular television broadcasts and satellite phones; these bring village life into sharp relief with the modern world. Villagers understand their rights in some ways, particularly in relation to education, and they see when the world around them appears to have access to something they lack.

Attacks on Education

While this study demonstrates the greater accessibility of community-based schools, it does not show a direct, empirical relationship with conflict. However, community-based schools should reduce the incidence of violent attacks, which in turn should decreases the overall level of conflict and reinforce accessibility. I draw on two CARE studies, conducted in 2009 and 2013 (Glad 2009 and Rowell forthcoming, respectively), to compare attacks on community-based schools versus formal government schools. The first consisted of a desk study, a field study, and school visits. CARE began with a desk study of news articles, reports from MoE, UNICEF, and ANSO (Afghanistan NGO Safety Office), and UNICEF and MoE databases. The field study included 559 focus groups in 38 districts across 8 provinces (Logar, Khost, Kunar, Wardak, Ghazni, Herat, Balkh, and Kapisa), most of which experience more Taliban violence than Ghor. Staff also carried out 455 interviews with parents, provincial education departments, NGOs, police departments, and district education departments. Finally, CARE visited schools that had experienced attacks, had not experienced attacks, and had prevented attacks, asking witnesses to describe their experiences (Glad 2009).

For the second study, CARE, in partnership with UNICEF, conducted a more rigorous assessment to learn more about types of violence against education and how school characteristics affect attacks.[17] This study found that government schools are the primary target of violence. For example, by comparing the types of schools attacked to the types not attacked while controlling for the level of conflict in an area, CARE showed that 62.5 percent of the attacked schools were in government buildings, while only 48.5 percent of the nonattacked schools were. These findings lend support to the view that the government system is structured in a way that leaves it vulnerable (Rowell forthcoming).

The study concluded that government schools appear to be vulnerable in part because of their physical infrastructure, their location, and their concentration of students and teachers. Government-supported education in Afghanistan stands apart from other types of schooling in that it is more likely to take place in conventional school buildings with multiple classrooms, desks, chairs, and chalkboards. However, attacks on government schools cannot be solely attributed to the desire to destroy educational infrastructure. Government schools attacked may be newly renovated or in various states of disrepair, and even tents may be targets (HRW 2006). Moreover, schools in private buildings and mosques are underrepresented among the attacked schools, suggesting that connection to government, not physical infrastructure per se, contributes to the increased risk of attack.

Furthermore, a school which is owned and run by the community, such as a community-based school, is far less likely to be attacked. According to observations from a focus group of Afghan educators, risks to NGO schools are linked to the administrative approach: the more the NGO integrates the community into designing and running classes, the better it is for school safety. Conversely, the farther the community is from planning and implementation, the more likely it is that the school will be attacked. Successfully implemented community-based schools are not attractive targets because they appear to be associated with the local community much more than with the government. However, they can still provide a boost to perceptions of governmental legitimacy, both because locals know the government made the school possible and because they increase local security and access to education.

The first study of community-based schools described above, in addition to providing rigorous quantitative data on children's access, offers rich descriptive and contextual information about the way in which these schools work to protect education not only in Ghor Province but across the country. A number of key attributes appear to enhance the capacity of community-based schools to curb the risks of ideological or criminally motivated violence. First, community-based schools use existing infrastructure that belongs to the community, or to a member of the community. For example, in this study, all community-based schools were housed in village mosques, and the students who attended lived in the surrounding houses. Infrastructure that is created by the community, as opposed to the government or outsiders, is typically perceived as belonging to the community.

Second, community-based schools typically are located in the center of a village. Since outsiders cannot easily arrive in villages unnoticed, threatening activity draws attention. In addition, because each community-based school serves only the village in which it is situated, students and teachers remain widely dispersed, relative to the concentration that accompanies regional schools.

Third, community-based schools have strong local ties. In this study the teachers were the village mullahs, well known to their communities. Furthermore, NGOs typically encourage parents to join school-management committees and play an active role in the schools. The school's link to community members and school management committees creates a "witnessing effect" that may reduce the likelihood of anonymous threats and attacks (Burde 2010). As the NGO staff report, communities develop a sense of ownership of their community-based schools. In the study in Ghor, many parents visited schools on a regular basis, checking attendance and observing the lessons. Although external support to community-based schools could raise questions regarding the degree of local "ownership," in the study described here neither the communities nor the NGO (in this case, CRS) publicized the foreign aid. According to interviews, most inhabitants of the villages were not aware that an international NGO supported the community-based school and believed, instead, that it was supported by the government. Although villagers believed that the government was administering the school, the classes avoided accruing negative associations with the government, for the reasons above.

Finally, proximity is critical to reducing opportunities for attack and ensuring access to services. In our study in Ghor Province, parents repeatedly cited proximity as one of the key benefits of community-based schools. Government schools often serve several villages that can be miles apart; the average distance to a community-based school for these children was only three-tenths of a mile.

Teaching Tolerant Curricula

The physical characteristics of community-based schools contribute to peace, then, not only by increasing equitable access to education, but by decreasing the ability or desire of the Taliban to carry out violent attacks on schools. But the educational materials provided to these schools also raise the prospects of contributing to conditions conducive to ending conflict in Afghanistan. To assess the content of the new national Afghan textbooks, revised in 2006, I selected and reviewed textbooks for two grades, second and fifth, using the same systematic assessment mentioned in chapter 3. This review used English translations of two subjects for second grade, math and Dari language, and the Pashto version for religious studies; for grade five, English translations of textbooks for Dari and Pashto language, social studies, and the Pashto version of religious studies were used. I did not commission the translations, rather they were completed for international organizations working in Afghanistan in 2006. They are not perfect—there are a number of grammatical and spelling mistakes—but they are reliable representations of the content of the lessons in the MoE books.[18]

To conduct this assessment systematically, I designed a tool adapted from that used by Adwan et al. (2013) in their rigorous study of Israeli and Palestinian textbooks. An advanced graduate student from New York University, my Pashtun colleague, and I used this tool to assess the books for exhortations to behave violently, exhortations to hate (minorities or foreigners), biased language, tolerant messages, human-rights information, hardened or polarized identities attributed to self or other, expressions of moral values, and appeals for national unification. The last item had two categories: inclusive and exclusive.

These textbooks are strikingly inclusive and tolerant. A representative example is this passage from the grade 5 social studies textbook lesson on education: "Each of us have responsibility in these societies which should we perform properly in order that our country develop the same as the other developed countries" (p. 13). Similarly, a lesson on agriculture from the same book emphasizes that peace is necessary for successful agriculture: "The most reliable is the need for stabilizing social peace because agricultural affairs can not go forward without peace" (p. 33).

Although there are several references to violence, they are outweighed by the number of references to peace, tolerance, human rights, and universal values, at a ratio of 11 to 1. References to violence are usually historical, describing effects of the previous years of war. Beyond this, they typically provide little specificity about actors, generally omitting names of groups and avoiding debates regarding who did what to whom. In one of the few references to specific actors, the education lesson refers to the Taliban's education policies. It contains this reference to violence (the note at the end is the translator's):

> After years and changes in the country, the education system was destroyed more than others and came under these changes. As mujahidin took over the power, a number of inactive schools restarted activities. During the era of Taliban, the name of school was changed to madrasa and girls were denied education, as it is a very black era of this time. [The last part of the sentence is dismissed with a blue pen in the Pashto version—translator] (15).

Such references to historical violence, however, pale in comparison to the exhortations to violent jihad of previous curricula, as described in chapter 3.

This post-2006 MoE curriculum, designed by Afghans with foreign support after the fall of the Taliban, is of reasonable quality, but it is not what Westerners would consider secular. Although religion is included as a separate subject, references to the Qur'an are sprinkled throughout most other subjects, as well. Curricular quality and religious content are not mutually exclusive, however. There are many powerful arguments for the separation of religion and state, but where there is an extensive history of conflict and struggle associated with efforts to impose a secular political order on a deeply religious population, it is difficult to justify an educational practice that insists on it. The more important goal for Afghan education is to teach tolerance and peace, alongside math, science, and religion. And it is crucial that religion not be used to exhort students to violence. The current Afghan textbooks go to some lengths to further these goals. Provided that educational content remains neutral, and provided that children (boys and girls) have greater access to schooling, because of proximity and greater security, this content is likely to lay the groundwork for a tolerant, peaceful society.

But textbooks are not the only element in learning. Teachers are critical to the process. Although the NGOs provide in-service training to those they hire, a number of teachers in community-based schools do not meet the government's qualifications, having never reached grade 12 and having never completed teacher training in an official teacher-training college. Indeed, most of the mullah-teachers in the qualitative portion of our study gained their literacy from study in nearby mosques. Some had never attended a government school. Some left their education when the Taliban came to power, because the Taliban recruited soldiers from mosques and they did not want to join the ranks. One interviewee had traveled to Pakistan to study in a madrassa there, but left Pakistan's tribal areas after the Taliban started to gain power. Mullahs are certainly not a monolithic group, and providing them support for more teacher training could be a fruitful initiative for the near future.

Conclusion

Optimism about the ability of community-based schools to reduce the numbers of attacks on students, teachers, and education personnel and infrastructure should be tempered by realism concerning the administrative structure required to support them and their possible drawbacks on other counts. First, when security deteriorates to the extent that it has in many parts of Afghanistan, and hostility is directed toward foreigners and the national government, it becomes difficult for NGOs or Afghan government staff to access the affected regions. Any aid delivery program, be it food aid or support to education, that requires a foreign presence faces increased challenges. Humanitarian agencies have been resourceful in devising ways to continue to support schools in the event that they cannot access them. Starting new community-based schools in conflict-ridden areas will require continued insightful planning and perhaps enhanced "remote management"—a term often used by international NGOs working in Kabul and managing education programs in remote or insecure regions.

Second, because community-based schools often employ as teachers village mullahs with limited training and education, it is important to keep in mind mullahs' historical role in conflicts. Most recently, for example, during the 1990s the Taliban relied on local mullahs to enforce their rule. But many mullahs do not share the extreme views of the Taliban, Islamic education has a rich and varied history, and mosque schools as a form of early childhood education are underappreciated by Westerners. Nonetheless, relying extensively on undereducated religious leaders as teachers of the Afghan national curriculum could bring unforeseen costs along with the expected benefits. Finally, some have suggested that requiring poor, marginalized communities to support their own schools could allow the state to abdicate its responsibility to provide education to its citizens, thus effectively revising the social contract in the process (Botchway 2000; Burde 2004). Widespread use of community-based schools may threaten to shift the burden of education to those least able to afford it. In a country with such high rates of poverty, this could have a negative impact on already struggling communities.

Nevertheless, community-based schools have characteristics that should serve to deter violence, particularly the kind of violence—disrupting access to services—that is a cornerstone of Taliban strategy. Community-based education appears to eliminate schools as a target of ideological violence because of the schools' links to the community, their use of nonstandard infrastructure, and their proximity to students and teachers. Above all, it appears that removing geographical distance as a barrier to school attendance has a multiplier effect, reducing opportunities for attacks on students and increasing children's access to learning. Community-based schools hold enormous promise for a rural, poor country trying to provide universal access to "education for the world."

Community-based schools currently serve only a small fraction of school-age children in Afghanistan, and they provide principally for the early primary grades. Historically NGOs have promoted them as a complement to the government system, but PACE-A and the MoE have worked closely to integrate NGO-fostered community-based schools into the government system, discussing new forms of teacher certification and providing community-based school teachers' salaries from the government payrolls.[19] Effective expansion of community-based schools will require a more detailed consideration of their relationship to government administration, which should in turn allay concerns that they may undermine the social contract. Such considerations must include whether community-based schools are intended as a stopgap measure or are to be a permanent fixture on the educational landscape. Given the ultimate importance of school buildings as spaces for education, it may be advisable that community-based classes eventually acquire dedicated buildings, in appropriate locations and using materials appropriate to the locale. In contrast to stabilization programs that only support schools for places most at risk of violence, community-based education employs a more rights-based approach, by providing schools in places where education is hardest to access. Community-based schools do not need to serve every child, since the MoE-constructed schools reach many in urban and provincial capitals and in district centers.

In Afghanistan today, community-based schools offer an important option for school-age children, and policymakers should consider promoting them given the alternatives—no education or insurgent-supported education that cultivates intolerance. Policymakers should also consider the added benefit these schools bring in limiting attacks and thus reducing conflict. In this regard, their local character works in their favor. Reducing distance to school and ensuring access to quality education is a key factor in reducing criminal and ideological violence. Educational policy and investment should be structured accordingly.

6

Conclusion
Education as Hope

I RETURNED TO KABUL IN SEPTEMBER 2012 for the first time in nearly four years. I was nervous before boarding the plane. From all reports, conditions had deteriorated since my last trip, in January 2009, and it was difficult not to think about bombs exploding when stories about them were appearing so frequently in the international press. Like many people who work in countries affected by conflict, I had had my share of close calls. I had successfully stowed them away for a number of years, but the impending visit sparked memories. Luckily, a friend who works for an international aid organization sat next to me on the flight from Islamabad and distracted me.

When we landed, the sky was blue, but the air was dusty. Airport security had expanded. My friend had a car waiting for him inside the security perimeter, but the organization that was meeting me did not have the same access rights to the airport, so he accompanied me outside. We trekked out past the first parking lot and through a metal gate, which led into the seemingly endless second parking lot. After crossing that, we still had to pass through a large waiting area that resembled a bus terminal before we reached our destination: Parking Lot C, where the people who have only minimum security clearance wait for their friends and colleagues. Fortunately, my colleagues were already there. We put my bag in the truck and drove out through two more security barricades and into the city.

The airport was fortified to prevent easy access by would-be bombers, but new security measures were also apparent throughout the city. On my early trips to Kabul, young, scrawny, scared-looking Afghan police would occasionally stop cars and ask questions. Their uniforms were too big, and they didn't know how to hold their guns—or even a steady gaze. Foreigners would brush them off. On this trip, the police were better fed, better dressed, and more confident in their jobs. They seemed to know the rules they were enforcing; they were authoritative and did not avert their eyes. They stood next to small metal sign posts that read "Ring of Steel," which I surmised was part of the municipal effort to keep Kabul free of bombs and suicide attacks.

The additional security was not the only thing that made the city look different. There were more trees. And flowers. Roses lined the edges of government buildings and private houses, and the Ministry of Education (MoE) had a rose arboretum. Remarkably, the piles of garbage that I remember seeing everywhere—all over the streets with sheep and goats rooting through them—were gone, at least from the center of town. But what surprised me most was the number of young women I saw walking in the streets—alone. Some were dressed in fitted jeans with a long kurta[1] or a short dress over their jeans and a light head scarf. Most men I saw were wearing Western clothes.

Many of the Afghan staff who work for international organizations in Kabul were educated in Pakistan, some in the refugee camps, others in and around Peshawar, Quetta, or other cities. They speak English. They know how to use computers. Most of them earn significant wages for their families, and some are primary wage earners. They are aware of the social tensions around them. They discuss the different levels of skills between Afghans who remained in Afghanistan during the civil war and under the Taliban and those who fled to Pakistan or Iran. English and computer skills are highly sought after and often put the returned refugees at an advantage over those who stayed behind.

The larger social tension, however, remains the contrast between life in Kabul and life in a village. These urban images—women walking in jeans, using computers—provide a striking contrast to the life one still finds in the countryside in Afghanistan—young girls churning milk into butter and scant mechanization. The differences are profound and, as noted in chapters 4 and 5, villagers are acutely aware of the contrast, ever more so because some have access to television and satellite telephones. Many people have moved from the countryside to the city; the population of Kabul has surged from approximately 1.5 million in 2001 to 5 million today. Such a shift in such a short period would be significant anywhere, but is especially so in a country of roughly 30 million. It is difficult to say whether Kabul has more in common with New York City or with rural Afghan villages.

The preceding chapters have shown that education has frequently been a pawn in the recurring conflicts between Afghanistan's urban modernizers and rural traditionalists. How can the tensions between urban and rural forces be diffused? How can international aid and national policy respond to the perceptions of relative deprivation in rural communities? How should the government of Afghanistan fulfill the universal right to education that its population assumes? Answering these questions is imperative if national and foreign governments, as well as national and international aid workers, are to help Afghans fulfill some of their hopes and dreams for a peaceful future.

In the following pages I offer, first, a short epilogue to the dramatic success story of community-based schools that I described in chapter 5. Community-based schools may not remedy all of Afghanistan's problems, but they offer the promise of expanding access to education and reducing urban-rural tensions. Despite their resounding success, these schools were subsequently abandoned by USAID in order to promote—once again—a short-term political goal. To the credit of a number of dedicated educators who work for USAID, this policy shift has since been modified, but not before it had inadvertent negative effects. Second, I reiterate some of the key points that I have presented throughout the book—the importance of education to humanitarian action, the importance it holds for Afghans, and the way education can be used for conflict or for peace more generally. In doing so, I also offer several suggestions for future research. And finally, I provide several policy recommendations to international donors, nongovernmental organizations (NGOs), and the government of Afghanistan.

Epilogue: Community-Based Education Supported by the US Government

When Richard Holbrooke took up his position as envoy to Afghanistan and Pakistan, he helped to push through a new strategy for USAID in the region. Aid had previously been granted to international NGOs who would both implement programs themselves and subcontract local NGOs as partners. This process was meant to help decentralize services in formerly highly centralized systems and build the capacity of civil society. There was a flaw in this design, however, that Holbrooke and others pointed out. Providing funding for government services through international NGOs,[2] or even through local NGOs, could have the unintended consequence of undermining the local government. As noted in the previous chapter, if provision of services by an NGO meant that local government would be seen as weak or unable to fulfill its responsibilities, it would have trouble garnering support from the population. Moreover, circumventing the government in the provision of services could weaken the government's capacity to assume these tasks itself, thus making what had been erroneous perceptions of weakness come true (Rogin 2010). In countries where the government is particularly weak or fragile to begin with, such as in war-affected countries like Afghanistan, the consequences would be greater than in more stable places.

In keeping with the new strategy, the US began encouraging and enabling the Afghan government to take hold of development projects itself. This process of shifting funds from NGOs and contractors to government ministries was referred to as going "on budget"—in other words, channeling the funds through ministry accounts.

The community-based schools project Partnership for Advancing Community Education in Afghanistan (PACE-A), described in the previous chapter was in the unfortunate position of coming to a close around the same time that this shift in USAID policy took place. However, in the spring and summer of 2010, the NGOs running the project had received a verbal commitment from USAID that their funding would continue. Foreign and local educators working in Afghanistan, as well as development workers more broadly, recognized the project as having had a dramatic impact after the findings of its internal evaluations had been affirmed by the independent, external, randomized-controlled trial described in chapter 5 (see for example, J-PAL 2012). While PACE-A recognized the concern that its long-term provision of education might undermine government capabilities and legitimacy, it attempted to address these concerns by placing staff within MoE provincial offices, and it planned to negotiate the full integration or transition of community-based schools into Afghan government-run programs. In the fall of 2010, however, US-AID decided to move the project "on budget," thus ending the NGO program and shifting the funds and management to the MoE. The NGOs protested this move, declaring that because they had been led to believe that the program would continue, they had not had time to lay the groundwork for the Afghan government's assumption of management of the schools. The MoE, for its part, also protested the change, arguing that it was not ready to administer the schools (pers. interview April 28, 2011). The USAID policy was set, however, and the change went forward as planned.

As predicted, the MoE did not have the staff available to monitor schools in remote locations. To compensate, when it took up responsibility for the classes in Ghor Province, for example, in some cases it informed villagers who lived in remote locations that, going forward, their education would be provided by a central "hub school" serving several outlying villages and that their children should walk to the nearest hub school for their education. (In other cases, CRS used private funds to continue to support the community-based schools.) Unfortunately for those in remote villages, some of the community-based schools closed, and children returned to the circumstances they had faced before—walking long distances to get to the nearest government school. This appears to have had predictable effects: some older boys could continue their educations, but girls and younger boys were no longer able to attend.

While "Afghan ownership" of education programs is important—even critical—the dissatisfaction and confusion that resulted when the government was forced to discontinue the community-based schools project on short notice highlights the problems with sacrificing program effectiveness for short-term political goals—in this case, for the appearance of greater local ownership and foreign retrenchment in the region. The sudden deprivation of education risks reigniting popular grievances that were prevalent in the past, potentially undermining government legitimacy—the very goal that "Afghan ownership" seeks to achieve—once again. This highlights the problem with tailoring aid programs for the purpose of pursuing political goals: in reality, political goals are more likely to be achieved through effectively implementing projects. Aid projects that are designed specifically to achieve political goals tend to focus resources in the wrong places, undermining their own efforts. While community-based education is likely to boost government legitimacy, as described in the previous chapter, this is not the goal of the project; the primary goal is fulfilling a key human right—access to education—and the positive political effects are second-order.

The Senate Committee on Foreign Relations specifically defended the continuation of NGO involvement in PACE-A during its review of US aid to Afghanistan, acknowledging the dilemma of balancing government capabilities with the goal of government ownership:

> To support the sustainability of these efforts, the NGOs work closely with the MoE to integrate classes into the formal education system and strengthen the MoE's ability to assume responsibility for these classes. Turning this program over to the MoE prematurely could end access to education for many students, particularly girls, and jeopardize the relationships built in these communities with village mullahs that defied the Taliban to allow their girls to attend school. (SCFR 2011:24)

Unfortunately, a policy change that was designed to enhance government capacity and improve government legitimacy was apparently having the opposite effect.

There is a more optimistic post-postscript to this story, however. The Canadian International Development Agency (CIDA) resumed sponsorship of the community-based education program about a year after the USAID funding ended. And in 2013, USAID indicated a renewed interest in providing additional support to community-based education and is now poised to become a champion of this effort, through MoE. It is easy to forget that organizations are not monolithic. Many educators who work for USAID have worked hard to promote education in countries affected by conflict. They work just as hard to keep the best projects going, even when political considerations make this difficult.

And yet aid interventions are still affected by the wider, often unpredictable, twists and turns of conflict. As this book was going to press, additional details emerged about the state of conflict and education in Ghor Province. A recent report describes increasing lawlessness, criminality, and violence between local warlords and shows the education system rife with corruption. Although schools are not the primary focus of tensions, opposing sides in Ghor's internecine violence appear to view government school buildings as a resource and fight to control them (Ali 2013). Community-based schools are not mentioned in this report, but according to local NGO staff, they appear to have fared much better than government schools in the face of deteriorating conditions. Even villages with community-based schools, however, are not so isolated from the rest of the province as to be immune to the surrounding violence. Several of the control villages described in chapter 5 have not received schools to date, and several other villages with community-based schools have been affected by the violence. Yet despite these setbacks, a number of these schools continue to function and remain accessible to both boys and girls, because of their location and their teachers.

Education as Humanitarian Action

Despite the good intentions and belief in neutrality of many individuals who do aid work within government and international agencies, education was used as a tool by the US government to advance its strategic aims in Afghanistan and Pakistan. The government was able to do this, in part, because effective education programming has been often closed out of aid projects by the dominant humanitarian paradigm that privileges approaches to suffering determined by the emergency imaginary, as I described in chapter 2. When education has been included by humanitarians, it has often been undervalued and poorly understood. Because the entrenched needs-based protocol necessarily muffles aid recipients' voices, humanitarians have inadvertently tuned out the demands for education from those who benefit from aid. Further, the powerful myth of an apolitical humanitarianism has prevented humanitarians from acknowledging both the positive ways in which aid work *is* political, and should continue to be, and the ways that clinging to this notion of apolitical action hobbles their efforts, particularly in education.

The dominant humanitarian narrative concerning political actors has it partially right—using aid exclusively for strategic aims is a bad idea. The fundamental problem with strong states' using aid to further their short-term political objectives is that, first, it does not work—it neither accomplishes the strategic goal nor provides effective aid. Even if it initially appears to work, it may create unintended and enduring negative consequences. In the case of stabilization examined in chapter 4, I showed that focusing aid on narrow strategic outcomes may win a tactical advantage but loses when it comes to overall strategy. In other words, providing aid to restive communities that are at risk of insurgency and denying it to more peaceful areas is inherently inequitable, and therefore unsustainable in the long term. Both the communities that are passed over and the Afghan government recognize it as such. Furthermore, it is likely to undermine government legitimacy—exactly the opposite of its intended effect.

Second, even in cases where using aid to accomplish a strategic goal appears to have worked (e.g., ousting the Soviets from Afghanistan), strategic goals ultimately come into conflict with development goals, undermining both in the process. When a political strategy is deemed to have been a success, or when the conflict has run its course, and the strategic approach is no longer warranted, projects are terminated. When the Soviet Union pulled out of Afghanistan, the US abruptly halted its aid to the region, leaving an enormous amount of resentment in its wake.[3] This resentment is compounded by an understanding among the population that the US cultivated jihadists, abandoned the region, and then was surprised when the jihadists continued to cause trouble.

The abuses of aid in Afghan refugee camps were among the events that prompted a season of reflection and reform in the humanitarian community, as described in chapter 2. Calls to protect humanitarian space, however, are insufficient to avoid the kinds of political abuses and missteps I recounted. Humanitarians must revise their concept of "emergency" so that it no longer constrains the programs they implement. They must move from a "needs-based" to a "rights-based" approach to aid and restructure their organizations accordingly, which means also moving away from the "humanitarian" versus "development" dichotomy in categorizations of aid. Many organizations have already made these changes and claim to be operating within a rights-based framework, but they still neglect education in their emergency responses.

The urgent requests for access to education recounted in the preceding chapters, from some of the most marginalized, remote, and conflict-affected communities in the world, should convince remaining skeptics that education is a real priority even in conditions that would be characterized as war (in military terms) or humanitarian emergency (in aid workers' terms). People in these communities may be occupied with immediate survival, but that does not preclude them from looking toward a better day and a better future with equal urgency. Such a view toward the future is otherwise known as hope, and children's education is an embodiment of hope. Humanitarians should embrace the politics of solidarity and support and defend the communities with whom and for whom they work.

Educational Pathways to Conflict and Peace

In their efforts to help realize these hopes, humanitarians must pay greater attention to the design of education interventions, which should of course be undertaken in conjunction with local partners. In this book, I have explored two pathways that may lead to conflict or peace. In keeping with the primary questions that underpin education research generally, I have focused on access and content (quality). Although worldwide access to education has increased dramatically over the past two decades, more needs to be done. As I have shown, however, simply promoting more education without considering content does a disservice to the enrolled children, the countries they live in, and the larger world. Accessibility and content must both be considered when designing education interventions that are intended—as they all should be—to reduce violent conflict.

Violent Content or Positive Messages?

Promoting conflict and violence through textbooks likely aggravates underlying conditions for conflict. Allying the message with religion—for example, distorting Islam and tying violence to religious obligation—is likely to have even greater effect, and especially in an already deeply religious society. Yet it is clear that not all children exposed to violent content

162

will take up arms. A huge number of Afghan children were exposed to the US-sponsored jihad curriculum. In fact, given that no other curriculum was available at the time, it appears that the vast majority of children enrolled in a rebel-supported or international aid-sponsored Afghan school in Afghanistan or Pakistan from 1986 to 1996 used these textbooks. These books were also reportedly used in madrassas in Pakistan along the border with Afghanistan, where it appears they are still in use today. In addition, these books—modified only to remove images of faces—were the designated curriculum under the Taliban, and only slightly revised versions of the original books were used until 2005. It is very likely that most Afghan children who attended either government-supported or private religious schools in the region were exposed to these jihadist textbooks.

Despite the widespread availability of and exposure to these books, the majority of children did not become militants. Yet clearly many children did join, first the mujahideen groups and later the Taliban. Studying from textbooks that teach acceptance of violence and militant jihad with teachers and other students who reinforce the message likely facilitated the path to resorting to violence to resolve disputes. These books helped create a climate of violence and intolerance. Political leaders in Afghanistan, from the mujahideen to the Taliban to madrassa leaders, have found these textbooks a useful recruitment tool in cultivating insurgency. Indeed, this was the purpose for which the US originally sponsored them. It is difficult to imagine that the same number of children would have grown up to embrace militancy had their education not inundated them with images encouraging and glorifying violence.

Still, it is not clear to what extent exposure to violent images influences children's behavior. Recent studies of the effects of violent video games and movies on children appear to show limited impact (Ferguson 2012). Yet these same images, taught by teachers and in schoolbooks, could have greater effect, precisely because most children recognize video games as imaginary. The glorification of violence in schoolbooks and in schooling is more significant because instructional materials are endowed with an authority and legitimacy that movies and video games do not have. A measure of authority accompanies anything on a printed page, especially in print-poor communities. The elevated status of textbooks is further reinforced by the reverence with which Islam treats both education and books, as well as by the fact that the Qur'an and other religious texts are often the only other printed materials in rural Afghan communities. Nonetheless, it would be helpful to learn more about how, and to what degree, the content of education—especially textbooks—promotes violence or peace. And although textbooks are an important aspect of education, particularly in print-poor communities, teachers are also very influential. Research is necessary to delineate the relative importance of teaching versus textbooks in cultivating particular kinds of attitudes and behaviors.

That said, curricula that promote positive messages of peace, tolerance, and critical thinking are likely to contribute to underlying conditions for peace for all of the same reasons that negative messages are likely to contribute to the opposite—messages are powerful when delivered early and children are able to absorb them more deeply (Davies 2005; Paulson and Rappleye 2007; Paluck and Green 2009; King 2011; Paulson 2011). Indeed, research in developmental psychology shows that peer groups initially become significant for children around the age of nine or ten and that in-group identification and peer exclusion intensifies around the age of thirteen or fourteen, as children begin to organize themselves into social cliques (Brechwald and Prinstein 2011; Hitti et al. 2011, cited in Killen et al. 2012). Reaching children before or at the beginning of this process may be critically important. At the same time, it is likely that even a preponderance of positive messages in a curriculum cannot overcome exposure to ongoing violence, humiliation, and conflict in the immediate environment. In such a setting, it is important at least to ensure that textbooks do not reinforce negative messages but rather promote critical thinking skills and offer neutral content, so as to encourage the open-mindedness that can help break-down the "us versus them" mentality that frequently fuels violence.

It is also possible that positive messages do not simply work in the opposite way that violent messages do. In fact, it is possible that teaching violent messages from textbooks and in school lessons is more powerful than the positive counterpart. Recent research in computer science and communications seems to suggest that this might be the case (A. A. Anderson et al. 2013; Brossard and Scheufele 2013). If it is not clear how directly applicable this research is to school settings, it nonetheless suggests that the relative weights of positive and negative messages in education is an open and important area for research.

There should be no room for religious—or for that matter, secular—education that promotes violence and intolerance anywhere in the world. That said, although religious education may not be palatable to many in the West, it is not by definition extremist or militant, and it should not be viewed as such. Hostility to religious education may actually empower supporters of more extremist views in some countries, thereby ceding control of education to them. Provided that education with religious references also teaches tolerance, it may offer a middle ground to secularists and religious traditionalists. Whatever the curricular outcome, it is important that the humanitarian community take a more nuanced approach to religious education.

Unequal or Equal Access?

Unequal access to education can arise in a variety of ways. It may be the intentional product of program goals and design, as for example, when aid is delivered as a component of a stabilization program, as examined in chapter 4. Or it may be unintended and virtually unavoidable, as comes with, in some settings, corruption and poor delivery of services. Regardless, unequal access is likely to contribute to underlying conditions for conflict in the multiple ways described throughout this book. Denied access to education, even when inadvertent, can produce profound grievances. In their understanding of human rights, villagers in Afghanistan perceive inequalities in relation to both real neighbors and imagined communities. They see that a nearby village received educational support but they did not; they see that young people living in urban areas have access to education. They may have relatives or tribal connections who live in Pakistan or Iran and have had access to relatively good education. Thus, within the many circles of people with whom they are in contact, they see that some have markedly more advantages. Understandably, villagers often attribute successes in business and social standing to education. Beyond the circles with which they are personally acquainted, there is a broad imagined community to which they feel they belong. Messages from this community, which bring measures of relative deprivation, are broadcast by media, but also appear in social-justice campaigns such as Education for All and national rights campaigns. Many Afghan villagers are aware of their national constitution, and they know that it enshrines education as a right to which they have access. They know, also, that their government is the guarantor of this right. For all of these reasons, uneven access to education is likely to aggravate instability in an already unstable country.

As with questions of content, equal access to education is unlikely to mirror exactly the effects of unequal access on underlying conditions for conflict. The positive effects of equal access may be more powerful than the negative effects of inequitable access, provided that environmental conditions are conducive to meaningful political participation and employment. Education is so highly valued in part because it is perceived as being key to many opportunities, but if opportunities are blocked even after attaining education, the promise and appeal of schooling may decline. Unfortunately, in many cases expectations for the benefits of education are stratospheric, while reality is typically far more prosaic.

While this can be a problem in developed countries, it is typically less so. Developed countries often have varied ways of effectively satisfying their citizens' aspirations. As noted in chapter 1, in developed countries with education systems designed to incorporate youth, higher levels of educational attainment do not necessarily increase the support for militancy (Brockhoff et al. 2012).

In developing countries, however, the evidence to date is less clear. The phrase "youth bulge" refers to a generation of youth, usually described as between fifteen and twenty-four years old, that is disproportionately large compared to the adult population (Urdal 2006). Scholars argue that an unusually large cohort of youth is associated with a number of social ills, including revolution (Goldstone 1991), political extremism (Huntington 1996), and increased likelihood of civil conflict (Urdal 2006). Some research suggests that education mitigates many of these ills (Urdal 2006; Ostby and Urdal 2010), but others raise questions about the ability of developing countries to absorb educated youth into political, social, and economic systems that may be weak or corrupt (Brockhoff et al. 2012; UNESCO 2012). Clearly, populations will continue to demand education and the benefits they expect it to bring. Some argue that in developing countries higher levels of education may yet contribute to militancy if the population's aspirations are not met. This is an important area for research.

Despite the apparent importance of education and the role that un-even access appears to play in conflict, research that specifies and tests the mechanisms through which the effect manifests itself is scarce. This is partly due to the neglect within academia of international education beyond a talented but small circle of international and comparative education specialists. As noted in chapter 1, the political-science subfield of international relations has, until very recently, virtually ignored education. Likewise, among educators, most research conducted by US and other Western scholars is domestic and focuses largely on outcomes—enrollment and achievement. Few empirical studies explore the relationship between education and conflict, beyond the literature on peace-education programs mentioned in chapter 5. Economists who have plunged into assessing development through randomized evaluations do look at education, but not at possible links to violence. And to date there are very few field experiments concerning questions related to education in countries affected by conflict. Thus, broadly speaking, scholars who study violence and politics do not consider education, while scholars who study education typically do not analyze its possible relation to violence. Finally, scholars of international education have produced a number of studies on education in countries affected by conflict, but these have been largely theoretical and qualitative (Davies 2005; Kagawa 2005; Smith 2005; Mundy and Dryden-Peterson 2011; Paulson 2011). They offer critical insights and important steps for refining research questions, but it is now necessary to build on this work and conduct targeted, systematic analyses of causal mechanisms and relationships. Questions related to both access and content offer important points of departure.

Policy Recommendations

Despite the fact that research on the intersection of education and peace and conflict is still an emerging field, it points to several clear recommendations for policymakers and practitioners. Humanitarians, policymakers, and academics have a significant role to play in improving the quality of foreign aid to education.

First, humanitarians must abandon the restrictive concepts of "needs-based," "life-saving," and "emergency" aid and disabuse themselves of the myth of "apolitical" humanitarian action, so that they can embrace a rights-based approach. Support for education should be included along with any other forms of relief.

Humanitarians who work on education projects in countries affected by conflict have defined procedures and systems for providing support in these circumstances. The Inter-Agency Network for Education in Emergencies has made enormous progress in this regard. Many humanitarian organizations make use of its resources, but education is still often sidelined within many of these organizations. That must change. In addition, humanitarians should listen to aid recipients and consider adopting an approach to aid that is rooted in the politics of solidarity—a politics, after all, from which many of these organizations emerged.

Second, policymakers should provide adequate funding to education from beginning to end of a program, in this way taking as a model the successful program that Teachers College, Columbia University, implemented in Afghanistan in the 1950s and 60s. Commitments to education should be long-term and undertaken in close partnership with local educators and appropriate government counterparts. For hard-to-reach communities, it is important that policymakers explore nontraditional methods of providing services, such as community-based schools.

Specifically in relation to Afghanistan, it is important that aid workers and foreign-policy makers have a better understanding of religious content in mainstream education and religious education. It is critical that the West better understand and refrain from eliding the difference between religious education and extremist education. Misunderstanding this distinction is counterproductive and reinforces stereotypes in the Muslim world about Western hostility, ignorance, and insensitivity.

Finally, although the US-sponsored jihadist books are still available in Afghanistan and Pakistan, they do not appear to be popular with parents and students. Books of any kind are powerful in communities where literacy is low and printed material scarce, but the current MoE books are generally much more appealing than the old jihadist textbooks. Most parents want their children to have better lives than their own, and they see quality education as the path toward this goal. The jihadist books are stuck in the past. The current MoE books are much more appealing to children. They are better designed and laid out and more interesting. The Afghan government with support from international organizations committed to helping Afghanistan should flood the countryside with the current MoE books. The jihadist books will not be able to compete.

These recommendations are all the more important given that the current US war effort in Afghanistan is winding down. The 2014 transition is likely to signal a decline in attention to Afghanistan—if not from the US administration, then at least from aid workers and the general public. Such a shift would be a serious mistake. Memories of US abandonment after the Soviet withdrawal more than two decades ago are still fresh for many Afghans. It is important that current effective aid programs—especially those devoted toward expanding access to good education—are seen through to completion.

The withdrawal of most US troops in 2014 will not bring about an end of violence in Afghanistan. Even assuming the increasingly improbable scenario of a complete victory over the Taliban or a negotiated settlement, the country faces many additional potentially destabilizing forces. The raging proxy war between Saudi Arabia and Iran, alluded to in chapter 3, has already wreaked havoc in Pakistan, Iraq, and Syria. There are worrying signs that it could spill over into Afghanistan.

Good education interventions cannot prevent such violence. However, they can limit its effectiveness and appeal. And, at the very least, well-designed interventions can avoid complicity in perpetuating existing conflicts or creating new ones.

Notes

1. Introduction

1. For example, Jackie Kirk worked for the International Rescue Committee (IRC) providing support to education programs in Afghanistan in the 2000s. In August 2008, Jackie and three of her IRC colleagues were killed in their car as they were returning to Kabul from Logar Province. The Taliban claimed responsibility (Gall 2008).

2. The seven journals surveyed in the study cited include two devoted to peace and conflict studies (*Journal of Peace Research* and *Journal of Conflict Resolution*) and five from the International Studies Association (*International Studies Quarterly, International Studies Review, International Studies Perspectives, Foreign Policy Analysis,* and *International Political Sociology*) (King 2014).

3. Despite some recent advances (e.g., Dalrymple 2013), Afghan history in English is nascent, and there are few monographs. Gregorian (1969; revised and reissued in 2013) is a standard text. Anthropology (e.g., Barfield 2010) and political science (e.g., Rubin 1995; Dorronsorro 2005) have contributed significant insights into the period but do not offer a specialized view into education. Thus I have included analyses from doctoral dissertations on education in Afghanistan written during the 1970s. This work, although somewhat limited by the modernization ideology then dominant, nevertheless offers interesting details regarding both the state of education in Afghanistan at the time and the West's attitudes toward the system.

4. Mosque schools should not be confused with madrassas. In Afghanistan, madrassas typically cater to older students as well as younger ones, offer longer and more varied classes, and are sometimes boarding schools. Some madrassas are public (i.e., part of the government educational system), but the majority in Afghanistan is private. Although no statistics are available, most qualitative and anecdotal

reports indicate that while there may be several madrassas in cities, provinces often have only one per district (as was true of Ghor Province, the locale of my study of community-based education discussed below). Madrassas in Afghanistan appear to play a negligible role in rural children's religious education.

5. However, even most mullahs do not speak or understand much Arabic, despite the fact that most can read and recite the Qur'an in Arabic.

6. Though mosque schools were instrumental in the expansion of Afghan education, accounts of Afghan history and education have either ignored them altogether or minimized their role. Thus, it is not clear from when to date their prevalence.

7. "Clergy" usually refers to both ulema (higher order, educated religious leaders) and mullahs.

8. Tribal leaders and landlords maintained their importance in politics, but religious clergy reigned in the social realm (Roy 1990).

9. Writing in 1815, the Scottish explorer and diplomat Mountstuart Elphinstone describes mullahs tutoring the sons of elite families in religious texts as a common practice. He also remarks on the prevalence in villages of mullahs teaching basic prayers (cited in Ekanayake 2004).

10. The paper was *Saraj-ol-Akhbar-Afghaniyeh* (The lamp of news of Afghanistan), and it lasted for eight years, from October 1911 until December 1918.

11. This tension between urban Islamists and rural clergy—with urban Islamists declaring that rural clergy mixed un-Islamic practices with true religion—persisted through the decades and into the struggle against the Soviet occupation, the civil war, and today's Taliban insurgency. See Brown and Rassler (2013), for an excellent discussion of these tensions.

12. Habibia College (named after King Habibullah, its founder) was based on the Anglo-Indian system, with Turkish and French influences, but most of the teaching faculty were from India and taught their classes in English. The first public library in the country was included in this school.

13. The first government schools for girls in Afghanistan were founded in 1921.

14. Indeed, increasing rural unrest in response to the Afghan communist government's secularization programs was a key factor in the Soviet Union's decision to invade and attempt to stabilize its neighbor in late 1979 (Gibbs 1987).

15. While grievance theories emphasize "*motives* for groups to change their situation," greed theories favor explanations about "opportunities to organize a rebellion" (Ostby 2008:145).

16. See also G. K. Brown (2011) for a review of quantitative literature showing "when differences in the absolute levels of educational attainment between different ethno-religious groups overlap with different returns to education" (196).

17 . It is interesting to note that Hezbollah is well known for their successful provision of social services, especially education (see, e.g., Berman and Laitin 2009), but the authors of this study do not consider this relationship in their analysis.

18. For example, Lall (2008:104) concludes that the education systems in India under the Baharatiya Janata Party (BJP) and Pakistan under General Zia-ul-Haq

led to "increasingly nationalistic views of self and antagonistic views of the other, which "could lead to heightened tension."

19. Berrebi (2007) relies instead on descriptive information reported by the Center for Monitoring the Impact of Peace (CMIP), which has been heavily criticized for bias—for example, for using different methods for analyzing Palestinian and Israeli textbooks. In addition, although CMIP claimed to be critiquing Palestinian Authority textbooks, it cited incendiary statements that actually came from Jordanian and Egyptian textbooks used in the West Bank and Gaza Strip, not Palestinian Authority books (Brown 2001).

2. Humanitarian Action and the Neglect of Education

1. "Bilateral aid" refers to government-to-government assistance. Hence, donors that represent a single government such as USAID or the Danish International Development Agency are referred to as "bilateral agencies," and the UN is referred to as a "multilateral agency."

2. In fact, the Inter-Agency Network for Education in Emergencies recently launched "Guiding Principles on Integrating Conflict Sensitivity in Education Policy and Programming in Conflict-Affected and Fragile Contexts" (April 2013). These principles are accompanied by extensive "guidance notes" and other tools to put the principles to use. See http://www.ineesite.org/en/education-fragility/conflict-sensitive-education for these principles and tools.

3. A handful of academics in comparative and international education have started writing about "education in emergencies" or education and humanitarian aid (e.g., Burde 2005; Davies 2005; Smith 2005; Paulson and Rappleye 2007; Burde et al. 2011; Mundy and Dryden-Peterson 2011a, b; Novelli 2011; Karpinska 2012).

4. I use the term "relief" interchangeably with "humanitarian assistance," and unless otherwise noted, "aid" refers to humanitarian aid, not development aid. The type of relief I address here is exclusively that provided to populations affected by conflict.

5. The old proverb "Give a man a fish and you feed him for a day; teach a man to fish and you feed him for a lifetime" embodies the distinction between these two strands of international assistance.

6. Most humanitarians today consider Henry Dunant, who in the early 1860s proposed the development of charitable societies to care for those wounded or killed regardless of their nation, the founding father of modern humanitarianism.

7. By the late 1980s, international organizations began to identify a gap in services between the time when short term humanitarian relief stopped and longer term development support began. This ushered in a discussion of the "relief-to-development continuum," which was soon followed by a critique of this linear notion of progress given the cyclical, durable, and uneven nature of most conflicts. However, as I discuss later, this critique did not significantly alter the perception of education's role in humanitarian aid.

8. It is important to note that this understanding of aid to education as political is particular to the humanitarian community. In contrast to the humanitarian position, many people in the US donate money—charity—to fund schools (often buildings and materials) explicitly because it appeals as an "apolitical activity."

9. This figure incorporates official and private giving (Barnett 2011: 3), which explains the difference between it and OCHA's figure for 2012 (fig. 2.2) which incorporates only official development assistance.

10. "Official development assistance" is an umbrella term that includes development and humanitarian aid.

11. Although education fares better within development budgets, it still tends to receive less than sectors such as health, economy, and security.

12. Education is not included in this list, although "women, health, and HIV" are (USAID 2005a:6).

13. For more information, see www.sphereproject.org/.

14. UNICEF, UNESCO, UNHCR, and many international NGOs now include education systematically in their humanitarian responses. This kind of attention to education as part of a humanitarian response was unthinkable even fifteen years ago.

15. For more information on innovative mechanisms for disbursing aid to education, see Schmidt and Taylor (2010).

16. UNRWA holds responsibilities similar to those of the United Nations High Commission for Refugees (UNHCR), but was established before UNHCR and is dedicated to working exclusively with Palestinians.

17. In fairness, at this time the aid community did not seem particularly concerned with the subordination of aid to military goals in Afghanistan, but in the case of education, the subordination was particularly problematic because of the durability of the interventions.

18. The idea of apolitical humanitarian aid has been widely debunked among academics, but it persists in many aid circles.

3. Jihad Literacy

1. The movie depicts Charlie Wilson, a US Congressman played by Tom Hanks, successfully persuading Congress to provide covert funds to the Afghan mujahideen in the 1980s; it is based on a nonfiction book of the same title (Crile 2003).

2. Additional funds to support the distribution of these books may have also come from Saudi Arabia, but, as will be detailed later in the chapter, the US provided all of the funds to design and print them and was responsible for the direction of the project.

3. It is important to point out that tribal leaders also played and continue to play a large role in perpetuating these tensions, in fact, often assuming more political power than the clergy (Roy 1990). However, because the clergy have historically monopolized education, I discuss them here.

4. In 1991, the United States Court of Appeals for the Second Circuit found that the establishment clause of the First Amendment to the US Constitution applied to USAID grants, meaning that the agency can only finance those programs that are secular in nature and do not promote or hinder religion (USIP 2009:7). The decision was not appealed to the Supreme Court.

5. The reputation of the project was so strong and its results considered so compelling, in fact, that after the fall of the Taliban in 2001, Teachers College was invited back to Afghanistan to conduct another textbook reform project.

6. The accuracy of these statistics is unclear, and the reliability of more recent education statistics continues to be questioned.

7. Ashraf Ghani is a well-known politician and public intellectual in Afghanistan. He served as finance minister in Karzai's first administration from 2002 to 2004, as chancellor of Kabul University from 2004 to 2008, and today heads a policy institute concerned with state-building, called the Institute for State Effectiveness. In October 2013 he declared his candidacy for the presidency of Afghanistan.

8. UNHCR puts the number at 6.2 million, split evenly between Pakistan and Iran. Dupree (1988) notes that the estimated number of refugees in Pakistan varied between 1 million and 3 million, depending on the source. Part of the reason for this wide discrepancy was that up to 40 percent of refugees were unregistered.

9. In 2010, the official name of the province changed to Khyber-Pakhtunkhwa, often referred to simply as KP.

10. The Saudis used this income in part to print Qur'ans, fund mosque construction, distribute Wahhabi texts, and support Wahhabi-influenced education across the region from Southeast Asia to the Maghreb. Afghan Islamists began seeking refuge from the political turmoil in Afghanistan as early as 1973 (Roy 1990).

11. It is beyond the scope of this study to discuss the Shia-Sunni rivalry, but it has escalated dramatically in the past several years, wreaking havoc in Pakistan's Balochistan Province and spilling over into Afghanistan. Some Afghans in government institutions report Saudi and Iranian government representatives lobbying them to choose allegiances (pers. interview October 1, 2012).

12. Deobandism is a subsect of the Hanafi school of Islam.

13. CAR is the Pakistani government body that was established to handle Afghan refugee affairs in the 1980s. It still serves this purpose.

14. Either the figure for school-age children (5–6 million) or that for the total estimated number of refugees in Pakistan (3.2 million) must be incorrect. Although the number for total refugees may be low, and many families had children in the camps, it is unlikely that the number of school-age children was so large in 1987–88, the approximate year when these figures were recorded.

15. See Coll (2004) and Rubin (1995) for a clear and thorough description of these seven political parties, their members, and their growth and cultivation by the CIA and Saudis via the Pakistani ISI (Inter-Services Intelligence). Pakistan favored the most conservative among the Afghan mujahideen, setting the stage for the emergence and later dominance of the Taliban. The US favored them too, because the Islamists were considered the best fighters.

16. In fact, the total aid (including military) to the Afghan resistance movement coordinated by the Central Intelligence Agency (CIA) and USAID from 1980 to 1992 is estimated to have reached $4–5 billion (Turton and Marsden 2002).

17. It appears that the *Alphabet of Jihad Literacy* referred to a text developed for older students who had never had access to education and were enrolled in literacy classes as they took their military training and between periods of fighting at the front. Afghans today refer to the 1–12 grade textbooks either as "J is for Jihad," the "Mujahideen books," or "Muslim Afghanistan." The first two names appear to be from the mujahideen period; the latter appears to be the Taliban name for them. Aid workers simply refer to them as the "UNO books."

18. It appears that USAID issued a consultancy contract to a team of representatives from AED (Academy for Educational Development), Teachers College, and UNO to conduct the preliminary assessment on which the project was later based (AED 1985). It is not clear from the publicly available records at USAID how the funding for this project was awarded in 1986 to UNO—whether or not through a competitive bidding process, for example. Either way, the original team that conducted the needs assessment would have an advantage in landing the funding for the project since they built relationships and designed the future project during the needs assessment.

19. Mohammad Najibullah Ahmadzai was the last communist president of Afghanistan and served from 1987 to 1992.

20. These textbooks were available in both Dari and Pashto—the two most commonly spoken languages in Afghanistan.

21. These reports were collected by using the USAID Development Clearinghouse database to locate progress reports from the 1980s and early 1990s issued by the universities and organizations responsible for carrying out the ESSP education intervention.

22. Tracing which schools had received kits proved difficult in some areas. For example, kits were sent to Ghor Province, but monitoring teams were unable to reach schools there at the time of this activity report. The report does, however, include a list of receiving schools by name and province.

23. The Basic Competencies project included seventy Afghan educators and twenty-four private aid agencies (Stephens and Ottaway 2002).

24. At the time, JUI, headed by Maulana Fazlur Rehman, was a strong coalition partner in Benazir Bhutto's government (Nojumi 2008).

4. Education for Stability

1. Marja (also spelled Marjah) is a subdistrict in Afghanistan's Helmand Province in the southern poppy-growing area of the country, with a population of approximately 100,000.

2. Humanitarians make a distinction between nonprofit NGOs, which typically try to take a principled approach to aid work, adhering to the professional

standards and ethics discussed in chapter 2, and for-profit companies, which may be guided less by humanitarian norms and more by contractual relationships with a government agency. Tensions exist between these two types of aid organizations.

3. As noted above, US aid flows through multiple channels, each with distinct administrative and management structures. Aid to education in Afghanistan is included in US humanitarian, stabilization, military, and development efforts. Although the individual mechanisms may differ in their goals, aid recipients are not privy to these differences, so I discuss the combined effects of these efforts here.

4. *Ilm* means "knowledge" in Pashto, Dari, Urdu, and Arabic.

5. Pakistani regional foreign policy is nearly single-minded in its focus on India, its archrival. Ensuring a friendly neighbor to the northwest is a key element in Pakistan's strategy toward India.

6. The Northern Alliance is the English name for what was called in Afghanistan the United Front for the Salvation of Afghanistan and refers to opposition factions including the Jamiat-e Islami, Junbish-i Milli, Eastern Shura, Harakat-e Isalmi, and Hezb-e Wahadat.

7. Although Massoud was killed by a suicide bomber posing as a journalist on September 9, 2001, many of the educated Islamists are still active in Afghan politics. For example, Hekmatyar opposes US and NATO troops, and Sayyaf has been an active member of the Afghan parliament.

8. Pashtunwali consists of an elaborate set of rules governing Pashtun men and women's behavior. Its most well-known features relate to honor, hospitality, and revenge. The British colonizers relied on aspects of Pashtunwali to create customary law in South Asia, and it continues to govern behavior in many Pashtun regions today (Strickland 2007; Khan 2009; Lieven 2011).

9. Private violence against women (and children) is another matter, as is true in many societies.

10. Women and adolescent girls are also subjected to severe restrictions on their mobility in India, as well as throughout Afghanistan in areas dominated by Tajiks and other ethnicities.

11. Indeed, defending honor, known collectively as *namus: zan, zar, zamin* (woman, gold, land), is considered a man's most important duty (B. R. Rubin 1995:24).

12. These numbers are rough estimates given the state of data collection in the country at the time.

13. Assessments of the Taliban relationship to girls' education during the time of their rule differ. According to Dorronsoro (2005:301), "The Taliban was not formally opposed in principle to the education of women, but wanted to set up an 'Islamic' system whose details were never clarified, although it was to be based on the separation of men and women."

14. The Taliban are famous in the West for having successfully banned poppy cultivation, but there are indications that maintaining the ban, which started in summer 2000, for another year would have been difficult (pers. comm. July 27, 2013).

15. It is important to note that some branches of the US government—particularly the military and many sections of the State Department—do not make the distinction between development and humanitarian activities that most aid workers and aid organizations do. Instead, they commonly refer to both development and humanitarian work as development. Hence, the policy document that is intended to unite three branches of government work refers to these as "Defense, Diplomacy, and Development" or the "3Ds" (Burde 2005; see also USAID 2012)

16. In contrast to nonprofit NGOs such as, for example, CARE, Catholic Relief Services, and Save the Children, Louis Berger Group Inc. and Development Alternatives Inc. are for-profit companies that are contracted by the US government to carry out large-scale projects that often focus on infrastructure in Afghanistan and many other countries.

17. PRTs may also provide classroom materials but do not appear to train teachers in how to use them.

18. As noted above, many of the earlier stabilization initiatives were accused of responding to supposed community desires that may not in fact have been representative of broad community interests, or of having been implemented rapidly without sufficient planning or understanding of the local context.

19. In keeping with US government 3D terminology, most academics assessing the effects of civilian aid on insurgency use the word "development" to refer to programs that may include humanitarian activities.

20. Dube and Naidu's (2010) study of US military aid to Colombia is an exception. They note the pervasive lack of specificity in the analysis of aid programs and address it by isolating the effects of military aid from other forms of development.

21. I conducted interviews with ten key staff members (foreign and Afghan) of two projects over several months in person and via Skype and e-mail. I also reviewed program documents and reports. Seven of the ten respondents were interviewed twice, and each interview lasted between one to two hours. The interviews were recorded and transcribed. Before publication, respondents read their quotes along with the paragraphs preceding and following to verify accuracy of meaning. Because direct access to local communities was impossible, I relied on the experiences and observations of these key program staff, all of whom had been working in Afghanistan in relevant capacities for a number of years (four years was the shortest stint among the foreigners).

22. Because of these problems historically, some interviewees report exceedingly careful planning to ensure transparency and community inclusion in more recent projects (pers. interview February 15, 2013).

23. Boundary walls are extremely important for the level of privacy that parents require for their children, especially their daughters. Schools without boundary walls will be much less likely to enroll girls.

24. There are other forms of aid to education that support soft investments, as I discuss in the next chapter, but these are not part of stabilization programs.

5. Education for the World

1. Most families with televisions watch Tolo TV (the Afghan national station), which broadcasts foreign programs and movies from India, Turkey, and the US. Certain programs, like *Afghan Star* (similar to *American Idol*) and *Ganjina* (similar to *Who Wants to be a Millionaire?*), are thought to be the most watched across the nation (pers. comm. March 6, 2013).

2. To learn Islamic morals, in Dari-speaking areas children in mosque schools study the *Panj kitab* (Five books). The same books may be used to some extent in Pashto-speaking areas as well, but little data is available from English-language sources on the mosque-school curricula in these regions.

3. Community-based schools are typically considered part of the government system (but managed by NGOs) because they deliver the same curriculum as the government schools.

4. For more information about these programs and evidence of their effectiveness, see Bar-Tal and Rosen (2009).

5. The figure 185 refers only to the number of documented cases in which the UN had enough confidence to say there was a Taliban attack. There were about 100 other cases reported over the same period that are either unattributable or sectarian, communitarian, or criminal in nature (pers. interview February 25, 2013).

6. These negotiations between the MoE and the Taliban are widely believed to have taken place, but it is unclear when they began (Semple et al. 2012).

7. I use "internecine" or "communal" for what people in Ghor Province typically describe as "intertribal" or "interethnic" when referring to violence among subgroups or "clans" who may share the same ethnicity, language, and religious beliefs but differentiate themselves according to clan or tribe.

8. Many organizations and educators in Kabul are concerned about the impending transition and how enrollment trends might be affected. Several factors are important to consider: (1) conflict might increase, which could involve schools either directly or indirectly, but regardless the resulting environment of fear will likely affect attendance rates; (2) if regional civil war breaks out and government access to certain areas of the country suddenly or systematically drops, so too will delivery of essential services such as education, potentially producing more school closures; and (3) many Afghans whose employment has been tied to the international presence (working on bases, as translators, or as staff in internationally-funded projects) might lose their jobs, perhaps destabilizing families' abilities to send their children to school (J. Rowell, pers. comm. February 20, 2013). In all cases, the result could contribute to renewed grievances concerning unequal access to education.

9. In 2010, 16,781,000 people, or approximately 56 percent of the population of Afghanistan, were under the age of 18 (UNICEF 2010).

10. Some say this figure is too optimistic and the real figure is lower (pers. interview March 3, 2013).

11. Although many scholars, practitioners, and policymakers take for granted the structure and organization of mass education found in most countries today, the fact that many mass-education systems evolved simultaneously and in ways that are remarkably similar has been the subject of much scholarly inquiry. See for example Ramirez and Boli (1987) and Meyer et al. (1992).

12. The typical work week in Afghanistan, as in many Muslim countries, runs from Sunday through Thursday.

13. It is important to point out that, although when the PACE-A program began most of the community-based schools were established in relatively stable areas, many of these areas became unstable as the conflict wore on and the Taliban gained ground. That said, there was a minimal Taliban presence in Ghor at the time of our study. In this chapter I use these data to provide descriptive information on community-based schools and show how they eliminate disparity in gender enrollment and attendance. I use data from another study, collected in more volatile parts of the country, to show that community-based schools are less likely than official government schools to come under attack. I explain this in more detail under "Attacks on Education," below.

14. Although across Afghanistan communities are overwhelmingly interested in education, not all communities would like to have a community-based school; some may perceive such schools as second-rate, since no construction is involved.

15. Randomized controlled trials, or field experiments, are considered among the most rigorous ways to test the impact of program interventions.

> By establishing statistically similar "treatment" and "control" groups, randomized trials allow researchers to vary one element of interest at a time and thus provide "'internally' valid estimates of the causal effect" of a particular factor on a program participant....Proponents of randomized trials argue that any difference in the two groups subsequent to treatment can be attributed to the intervention, allowing researchers to estimate the average impact on study participants. (Duflo and Kremer 2003:4; in Burde 2012:451).

16. The population in Afghanistan is approximately 30 million; roughly 657,200 live in Ghor, while a total of 9,585,500 live in the south and east of the country (Islamic Republic of Afghanistan, Central Statistics Organization, 2012–13).

17. I served as an advisor to this study. A database of schools was created for each stratum by randomly selecting formal schools from two lists: the government's comprehensive list of schools (including NGO-supported community-based schools) and a compiled incident database that records attacks on schools (14,700 government-listed schools including 6,000 community-based schools and 1,600 schools that reported incidents of violence). The lists were stratified by regional level of conflict—low, medium, or high—and a stratified random sample of schools was drawn from each list. A standardized questionnaire asked schools about attack incidents. Because of difficulties traveling to and working in the villages in the samples, school headmasters served as primary respondents and were typically contacted by phone. Since headmasters are closely connected to MoE and may be

partial in their representation of events (favoring one group over another), where possible their responses were validated against those of members of the community unconnected to the headmaster or the government. To complement these data further, qualitative data were collected from focus-group interviews with education practitioners (Rowell forthcoming).

18. For the convenience of the reviewers, all of whom speak English, we used the English translations where available. Because we also wanted to review religious studies and these texts were only available in Pashto and Dari, the member of the team who is a native speaker reviewed the Pashto text.

19. For a thorough discussion of integrating community-based schools into the government system, see Guyot (2007).

6. Conclusion: Education as Hope

1. A kurta is a typical South Asian shirt or top that extends at least to the knees and sometimes below the knee. It usually has one slit on each side. Women wear them as blouses or dresses throughout Pakistan and India.

2. Holbrooke also argued that overhead costs paid to international NGOs and contractors created waste and that that money would be better spent if given directly to national governments, provided that appropriate systems were in place to monitor the funds. It is important to remember that while most organizations referred to as "international NGOs" are not-for-profit organizations, and therefore their overhead reflects the costs of running the agency, "contractors" usually refers to for-profit organizations that profit from the aid work they carry out on behalf of a government.

3. In this case, once the strategic goals were met and funding decreased, local and international educators were freer to clean up the curriculum, which they tried to do in the late 1990s. But progress was slow, since funding was scarce, and when the project was finally completed, it was usurped, as noted in chapter 3.

References

AED (Academy for Educational Development, Univ. of Nebraska at Omaha and Teachers College, Columbia Univ.). 1985. "Afghanistan Education Activity, Final Report." Submitted to United States Agency for International Development (ANE-0290-C-00–60–16–00), December.

Afzal, M. 2012. "Are the Better Educated Less Likely to Support Militancy and Terrorism? Women Are: Evidence from a Public Opinion Survey in Pakistan." Paper presented at the Annual Meeting of American Political Science Association.

Alexander, J., N. Boothby, and M. Wessels. 2010. "Education and Protection of Children and Youth Affected by Armed Conflict: An Essential Link." In *Protecting Education from Attack: A State of the Art Review*, edited by UNESCO, 55–70. Paris: UNESCO.

Ali, O. 2013. "Pupils as Pawns: Plundered Education in Ghor." Kabul: Afghanistan Analysts Network. August 27. http://www.afghanistan-analysts.org/pupils-as -pawns-plundered-education-in-ghor.

Allport, G. 1954. *The Nature of Prejudice*. Reading, MA: Addison-Wesley.

ALNAP (Active Learning Network for Accountability and Performance). 2012. *The State of the Humanitarian System*. London: Overseas Development Institute. http://www.alnap.org/pool/files/alnap-sohs-2012-lo-res.pdf .

Anderson, A. A., D. Brossard, D. A. Scheufele, M. A. Xenos, and P. Ladwig. 2013. "The 'Nasty Effect': Online Incivility and Risk Perceptions of Emerging Technologies." *Journal of Computer-Mediated Communication* (February 19). doi:10.1111 /jcc4.12009.

Anderson, B. 1983. *Imagined Communities: Reflections on the Origin and Spread of Nationalism*. London: Verso.

Anderson, J. W. 1985. "Sentimental Ambivalence and the Exegesis of 'Self' in Afghanistan." *Anthropological Quarterly* 58, no 4: 203–11.

Anderson, M. B. 1999. *Do No Harm: How Aid Can Support Peace—or War*. Boulder, CO: Lynne Rienner.

Anderson-Levitt, K., ed. 2003. *Local Meanings, Global Schooling: Anthropology and World Culture Theory.* New York: Palgrave Macmillan.

Andrabi, T., and J. Das. 2010. "In Aid We Trust: Hearts and Minds and the Pakistan Earthquake of 2005." World Bank Policy Research Working Paper no. 5440.

Andrabi, T., J. Das, A. I. Khwaja, and T. Zajonc. 2006. "Religious School Enrollment in Pakistan: A Look at the Data." *Comparative Education Review* 50, no. 3: 446–77.

ANSO (Afghanistan NGO Safety Office). 2007. "ANSO Quarterly Data Report Q. 4 2007." Kabul: Afghanistan NGO Safety Office.

Baitenmann, H. 1990. "NGOs and the Afghan war: The Politicisation of Humanitarian Aid." *Third World Quarterly* 12, no. 1: 62–85.

Baiza, Y. 2013. *Education in Afghanistan: Developments, Influences and Legacies since 1901.* London: Routledge.

Barakat, B., Z. Karpinska, and J. Paulson. 2008. "Desk Study: Education and Fragility." Paper presented by the Conflict and Education Research Group to the International Network for Education in Emergencies Working Group on Education and Fragility, Paris.

Barakat, B., and H. Urdal. 2009. "Breaking the Waves? Does Education Mediate the Relationship Between Youth Bulges and Political Violence?" World Bank Policy Research Working Paper no. 5114.

Barfield, T. 2010. *Afghanistan: A Cultural and Political History.* Princeton, NJ: Princeton Univ. Press.

Barnett, M. 2002. *Eyewitness to a Genocide: The United Nations and Rwanda.* Ithaca, NY: Cornell Univ. Press.

——. 2005. "Humanitarianism Transformed." *Perspectives on Politics* 3, no. 4: 723–40.

——. 2009. "Evolution without Progress? Humanitarianism in a World of Hurt." *International Organization* 63, no. 4: 621–63.

——. 2011. *Empire of Humanity: A History of Humanitarianism.* Ithaca, NY: Cornell Univ. Press.

Barnett, M., and J. Snyder. 2008. "The Grand Strategies of Humanitarianism." In *Humanitarianism in Question: Politics, Power, Ethics,* edited by M. Barnett and T. G. Weiss, 143–71. Ithaca, NY: Cornell Univ. Press.

Barnett, M., and T. G. Weiss. 2008. "Humanitarianism: A Brief history of the Present." In *Humanitarianism in Question: Politics, Power, Ethics,* edited by M. Barnett and T. G. Weiss, 1–48. Ithaca, NY: Cornell Univ. Press.

Bar-Tal, D. 1998. "The Rocky Road Toward Peace: Beliefs on Conflict in Israeli Textbooks." *Journal of Peace Research* 35, no. 6: 723–42.

Bar-Tal, D., and Y. Rosen. 2009. "Peace Education in Societies Involved in Intractable Conflicts: Direct and Indirect Models." *Review of Educational Research* 79, no. 2: 557–75.

BBC News. 2008. "Afghan Strife Keeps Children Home." January 21. http://news.bbc.co.uk/2/hi/south_asia/7200935.stm.

——. 2011. "Afghan Taliban 'End' Opposition to Educating Girls." January 14. http://www.bbc.co.uk/news/uk-12188517.

Beath, A., F. Christia, and R. Enikolopov. 2012. "Winning Hearts and Minds through Development? Evidence from a Field Experiment in Afghanistan." World Bank Policy Research Working Paper no. 6129.

Berdal, M., and D. M. Malone. 2000. "Introduction." In *Greed and Grievance: Economic Agendas in Civil Wars*, edited by M. Berdal and D. M. Malone, 1–18. Boulder, CO: Lynne Rienner.

Bergan, P. L., and S. Pandey. 2006. "The Madrassa Scapegoat." *Washington Quarterly* 21, no. 2: 117–25.

Berman, E., M. Callen, J. H. Felter, and J. N. Shapiro. 2011. "Do Working Men Rebel? Insurgency and Unemployment in Afghanistan, Iraq, and the Philippines." *Journal of Conflict Resolution* 55, no. 4: 496–528.

Berman, E., and D. D. Laitin. 2008. "Religion, Terrorism and Public Goods: Testing the Club Model." *Journal of Public Economics* 92: 1942–67.

Berman, E., J. N. Shapiro, and J. H. Felter. 2011. "Can Hearts and Minds Be Bought? The Economics of Counterinsurgency in Iraq." *Journal of Political Economy* 119, no. 4: 766–819.

Berrebi, C. 2007. "Evidence About the Link Between Education, Poverty and Terrorism Among Palestinians." *Peace Economics, Peace Science and Public Policy* 13, no. 1: 1–36.

Bickmore, K. 2001. "Student Conflict Resolution, Power 'Sharing' in Schools, and Citizenship Education." *Curriculum Inquiry* 31, no. 2: 137–62.

Biton, Y., and G. Salomon. 2006. "Peace in the Eyes of Israeli and Palestinian Youths: Effects of Collective Narratives and Peace Education Program." *Journal of Peace Research* 43, no. 2: 167–80.

Blattman, C., and E. Miguel. 2010. "Civil War." *Journal of Economic Literature* 48, no. 1: 3–57.

Bohnke, J., and C. Zurcher. 2013. "Aid, Minds and Hearts: The Impact of Aid in Conflict Zones." *Conflict Management and Peace Science* 30, no. 5: 411–32.

Boltanski, L. 1999. *Distant Suffering: Morality, Media and Politics*. Cambridge: Cambridge Univ. Press.

Botchway, K. 2000. "Paradox of Empowerment: Reflections on a Case Study from Northern Ghana." *World Development* 29, no. 1: 135–53.

Boyle, H. 2006. "Memorization and Learning in Islamic Schools." *Comparative Education Review* 50, no. 3: 478–95.

Bray, M. 2000. *Community Partnerships in Education: Dimensions, Variations and Implications*. Paris: UNESCO.

Brechwald, W. A., and M. J. Prinstein. 2011. "Beyond Homophily: A Decade of Advances in Understanding Peer Influence Processes." *Journal of Research on Adolescence* 21, no. 1: 166–79.

Brett, R., and I. Specht. 2004. *Young Soldiers: Why They Choose to Fight*. Boulder, CO: Lynne Rienner.

Brockhoff, S., T. Krieger, and D. Meierrieks. 2012. "Great Expectations and Hard Times: The (Nontrivial) Impact of Education on Domestic Terrorism." CEB Working Paper no. 12/004, Centre Emile Bernheim, Research Institute in

Management Sciences, Solvay Brussels School, Université Libre de Bruxelles, Brussels.

Brossard, D., and D. A. Scheufele. 2013. "This Story Stinks." *New York Times*, March 2.

Brown, G. K. 2011. "The Influence of Education on Violent Conflict and Peace: Inequality, Opportunity and the Management of Diversity." *Prospects* 41, no. 2: 191–204.

Brown, N. 2001. "Democracy, History, and the Contest over the Palestinian Curriculum." Paper presented to the Adam Institute for Democarcy and Peace, Jerusalem. http://home.gwu.edu/~nbrown/Adam_Institute_Palestinian_textbooks .htm.

Brown, V. and D. Rassler. 2013. *Fountainhead of Jihad: The Haqqani Nexus, 1973–2012*. London: Hurst and Company.

Buchanan-Smith, M., and S. Maxwell. 1994. "Linking Relief and Development: An Introduction and Overview." *Ids Bulletin* 25, no. 4: 2–16.

Bumiller, E. 2010. "Unlikely Tutor Giving Military Afghan Advice." *New York Times*, July 18.

Burde, D. 2004. "Weak State, Strong Community: Promoting Community Partnerships in Post-Conflict Countries." *Current Issues in Comparative Education* 6, no. 2: 73–87.

——. 2005. *Education in Crisis Situations: Mapping the Field*. Washington, DC: USAID.

——. 2008. "Protecting Children from War and Ensuring their Prospects for the Future: Pilot Study Preliminary Findings." Report to the Spencer Foundation. New York.

——. 2010. "Preventing Violent Attacks on Education in Afghanistan: Considering the Role of Community-Based Schools." In *Protecting Education from Attack: A State of the Art Review*, edited by UNESCO. Paris: UNESCO.

——. 2011. "NGOs." In *Key Words in Youth Studies: Tracing Affects, Movements, Knowledges*, edited by S. Talburt and N. Lesko. New York: Routledge.

——. 2012. "Assessing Impact and Bridging Methodological Divides: Randomized Trials in Countries Affected by Conflict." *Comparative Education Review* 56, no. 3: 448–73.

Burde, D., A. Kapit-Spitalny, R. Wahl, and O. Guven. 2011. *Education and Conflict Mitigation: What the Aid Workers Say*. Washington, DC: USAID.

Burde, D., and L. L. Linden. 2012. "The Effect of Village-Based Schools: Evidence from a Randomized Controlled Trial in Afghanistan." NBER Working Paper 18039, National Bureau of Economic Research, Cambridge, MA.

——. 2013. "Bringing Education to Afghan Girls: A Randomized Controlled Trial of Village-Based Schools." *American Economic Journal, Applied Economics*. 5, no. 3: 27–40.

Bush, K., and D. Saltarelli, eds. 2000. *The Two Faces of Education in Ethnic Conflict*. Florence, Italy: UNICEF Innocenti Research Center.

Bush, L. 2001. "George W. Bush: Radio Address by Mrs. Bush" (Nov. 17). Available through the American Presidency Project, Univ. of California Santa Barbara.

Calhoun, C. 2004 "A World of Emergencies: Fear, Intervention, and the Limits of Cosmopolitan Order." *Canadian Review of Sociology/Revue Canadienne de Sociologie* 41, no. 4: 373–95.

———. 2008. "The Imperative to Reduce Suffering: Charity, Progress and Emergencies in the Field of Humanitarian Action." In *Humanitarianism in Question: Politics, Power, Ethics*, edited by M. Barnett and T. G. Weiss, 50–72. Ithaca, NY: Cornell Univ. Press.

———. 2010. "The Idea of Emergency: Humanitarian Action and Global (Dis) Order." In *Contemporary States of Emergency: The Politics of Military and Humanitarian Interventions*, edited by D. Fassin and M. Pandolfi, 29–58. New York: Zone Books.

Centlivres, P., and M. Centlivres-Demont. 1988. "The Afghan Refugees in Pakistan: A Nation in Exile." *Current Sociology* 36, no. 2: 71–92.

Central Intelligence Agency, Directorate of Intelligence. 1985. "The Soviet Invasion of Afghanistan: Five Years After." CIA Historical Review Program Release, as Sanitized 1999. http://216.12.139.91/docs/DOC_0000496704/DOC_0000496704.pdf.

Christia, F., and M. Semple. 2009. "Flipping the Taliban: How to Win in Afghanistan." *Foreign Affairs* 88: 34.

CIDA (Canadian International Development Agency). 2001. *CIDA's Action Plan for Child Protection: Promoting the Rights of Children Who Need Special Protection Measures*. Ottawa: Canadian International Development Agency, 2001.

Colenso, P. 2012. "Donor Policies: The Evolution and Development of DFID's Commitment to Education in Fragile States (2000–10)." In *Education as a Humanitarian Response: Education, Aid and Aid Agencies*, edited by Z. Karpinska, 51–70. New York: Continuum.

Coll, S. 2004. *Ghost Wars: The Secret History of the CIA, Afghanistan, and Bin Laden, from the Soviet Invasion to September 10, 2001*. New York: Penguin.

Collier, P., ed. 2003. *Breaking the Conflict Trap: Civil War and Development Policy*. Washington DC: Oxford Univ. Press/World Bank.

Collier, P., and A. Hoeffler. 2004. "Greed and Grievance in Civil War." *Oxford Economic Papers* 56, no. 4: 563–95.

Collier, P., A. Hoeffler, and M. Soderbom. 2004. "On the Duration of Civil War." *Journal of Peace Research* 41, no. 3: 252–73.

Collinson, S., and S. Elhawary. 2012. *Humanitarian Space: A Review of Trends and Issues*. HPG Report 32, Humanitarian Policy Group, Overseas Development Institute, London, April. http://www.odi.org.uk/sites/odi.org.uk/files/odi-assets/publications-opinion-files/7643.pdf.

Colucci, C.C. 2007. "Committing to Afghanistan: The Case for Increasing US Reconstruction and Stabilization Aid." *Military Review* 87, no. 3: 38.

Coulson, A. 2004. "Education and Indoctrination in the Muslim World: Is There a Problem? What Can We do About It?" Policy Analysis 511, Cato Institute, Washington, DC.

Crile, G. 2003. *Charlie Wilson's War: The Extraordinary Story of How the Wildest Man in Congress and a Rogue CIA Agent Changed the History of Our Times*. New York: Grove.

Crost, B., and P. B. Johnston. 2010. *Aid Under Fire: Development Projects and Civil Conflict*. Cambridge, MA: Harvard Kennedy School, Belfer Center for Science and International Affairs.

Dalrymple, W. 2013. *Return of a King: The Battle for Afghanistan, 1839–42*. New York: Knopf.

Davies, L. 2004. *Education and Conflict: Complexity and Chaos*. London: Routledge Falmer.

——. 2005. "Schools and War: Urgent Agendas for Comparative and International Education." *Compare* 35, no. 5: 357–71.

Davis, C. 2002. "A is for Allah, J is for Jihad." *World Policy Journal* 19, no. 1: 90–94.

De Waal, A. 1997. *Famine Crimes: Politics and the Disaster Relief Industry in Africa*. Bloomington: Indiana Univ. Press.

Dicum, J. 2008. "Learning, War, and Emergencies: A Study of the Learner's Perspective." *Comparative Education Review* 52, no. 4: 619–38.

DOD (US Department of Defense). 1983. "The Economic Impact of Soviet Involvement in Afghanistan (U)." DDB-1900–32–83, Resources Division, Directorate for Research, Defense Intelligence Agency, April.

——. 2005. "DOD, Directive 3000.05: Military Support for Stability, Security, Transition, and Reconstruction (SSTR) Operations." November 28.

——. 2009. "Stability Operations." Instruction no. 3000.0, September 16. http://www.dtic.mil/whs/directives/corres/pdf/300005p.pdf.

Dorronsoro, G. 2005. *Revolution Unending: Afghanistan, 1979 to the Present*. Translated by J. King. New York: Columbia Univ. Press.

DOS (US Department of State). 1996. "Afghanistan: Taliban Biodata," Cable, Confidential, October 4. Available through George Washington University: http://www2.gwu.edu/~nsarchiv/NSAEBB/NSAEBB295/doc01.pdf.

——. 2002. "Terrorism Finance: Updating the Taliban Names Designated Under UNSCR 1267," Secret, May 22. Available through George Washington University: http://www2.gwu.edu/~nsarchiv/NSAEBB/NSAEBB295/doc17.pdf.

DOS (United States Department of State) and USAID. 2010. "Leading Through Civilian Power: The First Quadrennial Diplomacy and Development Review." http://www.state.gov/documents/organization/153108.pdf.

Dryden-Peterson, S. 2011. *Refugee Education: A Global Review*. Geneva: UNHCR.

Dube, O., and S. Naidu. 2010. "Bases, Bullets and Ballots: The Effect of US Military Aid on Political Conflict in Colombia." Working Paper no. 197, Center for Global Development, Washington, DC.

Duffield, M. 1994. "Complex Emergencies and the Crisis of Developmentalism." *IDS Bulletin* 25, no. 4: 37–45.

——. 2002. "Governing the Borderlands: Decoding the Power of Aid." *Disasters* 25, no. 4: 308–20.

——. 2005. "The New Development-Security Terrain." In *Perspectives on World Politics*, edited by R. Little and M. Smith, 325–32. New York, Routledge.

Duflo, E., and M. Kremer. 2003. "Use of Randomization in the Evaluation of Development Effectiveness." Paper prepared for the World Bank Operations Evaluation Department Conference on Evaluation and Development Effectiveness, Washington, DC, July 15–16. http://econ-www.mit.edu/files/765.

Dupree, N. H. 1988. "Demographic Reporting on Afghan Refugees in Pakistan." *Modern Asian Studies* 22, no. 4: 845–65.

Dupuy, K. 2008. *Education for Peace: Building Peace and Transforming Armed Conflict through Education Systems.* Oslo: Save the Children Norway.

Easterly, E. M. 1974. "Impact of the Afghanistan Ministry of Education Curriculum and Textbook Project." PhD diss., Teachers College, Columbia Univ.

Ekanayake, S. B. 2004. *Afghan Tragedy: Education in the Doldrums.* Peshawar, Pakistan: Al-Azeem Printing Concern.

El Edroos, S. N. 2011. "Learn to be Taliban: K is for Kalashnikov." *The Verdict* (blog), March 12, 2011. http://blogs.tribune.com.pk/story/4877/learn-to-be-taliban-k-is -for-kalashinkov/.

Elias, B., ed. 2013. "The Taliban Biography: Documents on the Structure and Leadership of the Taliban 1996–2002." Available through George Washington University: http://www.gwu.edu/~nsarchiv/NSAEBB/NSAEBB295/Taliban_Structure -1.jpg.

Fair, C. 2007. "Who Are Pakistan's Militants and their Families?" *Terrorism and Political Violence* 20, no. 1: 49–65.

Fearon, J. D. 2008. "The Rise of Emergency Relief Aid." In *Humanitarianism in Question: Politics, Power, Ethics*, edited by M. Barnett and T.G. Weiss, 49–72. Ithaca, NY: Cornell Univ. Press.

Feifer, G. 2010. *The Great Gamble: The Soviet War in Afghanistan.* New York: Harper Collins.

Ferguson, C. J. 2012. "Violent Video Games and the Supreme Court: Lessons for the Scientific Community in the Wake of Brown v. Entertainment Merchants Association." *American Psychologist* 68, no. 2: 57–74.

Fishstein, P. 2010. *Winning Hearts and Minds? Examining the Relationships Between Aid and Security in Afghanistan's Balkh Province.* Boston, MA: Tufts Univ., Feinstein International Center.

Fishstein, P., and A. Wilder. 2012. *Winning Hearts and Minds? Examining the Relationships between Aid and Security in Afghanistan.* Boston, MA: Tufts Univ., Feinstein International Center.

Freedman, S. W., H. M. Weinstein, K. Murphy, and T. Longman. 2008. "Teaching History After Identity-Based Conflicts: The Rwanda Experience." *Comparative Education Review*, 52, no. 4: 663–90.

Frye, M. 2012. "Bright Futures in Malawi's New Dawn: Educational Aspirations as Assertions of Identity." *American Journal of Sociology* 117, no. 6: 1565–1624.

Fuller, B. 1987. "What School Factors Raise Achievement in the Third World?" *Review of Educational Research* 57, no. 3: 255–92.

Gall, C. 2008. "3 Western Aid Workers and an Afghan Driver Killed in Attack." *New York Times*, August 13.

Galster, S. 2001. "Afghanistan: The Making of U.S. Policy, 1973–1990." *The September 11th Sourcebooks. Volume II: Afghanistan: Lessons from the Last War.* George

Washington Univ., National Security Archive, October 9. http://www.gwu.edu/
~nsarchiv/NSAEBB/NSAEBB57/essay.html.

Getler, M. 1980. "Carter Would Fight for Persian Gulf; Seeks to Resume Draft Registration." *Washington Post*, January 24.

Ghani, A. 1993. Gulab: An Afghan Schoolteacher. In *Struggle and Survival in the Modern Middle East*, edited by E. Burke III, 336–50. Berkeley: Univ. of California Press. Gibb, H. A. R. *Studies on the Civilization of Islam*. Princeton, NJ: Princeton Univ. Press, 1982.

Gibbs, D. N. 1987. "Does the USSR Have a 'Grand Strategy'? Reinterpreting the Invasion of Afghanistan." *Journal of Peace Research* 24, no. 4: 365–79.

——. 2000. "Afghanistan: The Soviet Invasion in Retrospect." *International Politics* 37, no. 2: 233–45.

Girardet, E. R. 1985. *Afghanistan: The Soviet War*. New York: St. Martin's.

Giustozzi, A. 2000. *War, Politics and Society in Afghanistan, 1978–1992*. Washington, D.C.: Georgetown Univ. Press.

Giustozzi, A., and C. Franco. 2011. "The Battle for the Schools: The Taleban and State Education." Kabul, Afghanistan: Afghanistan Analysts Network.

Glad, M. 2009. *Knowledge on Fire: Attacks on Education in Afghanistan—Risks and Measures for Successful Mitigation*. Kabul, Afghanistan: CARE, World Bank, and the Ministry of Education.

Glewwe, P., M. Kremer, and S. Moulin. 2007. "Many Children Left Behind? Textbooks and Test Scores in Kenya." *American Economic Journal: Applied Economics* 1, no. 1: 112–35.

Goldman, M. I. 1967. *Soviet Foreign Aid*. New York: Praeger.

Goldstone, J. 1991. *Revolution and Rebellion in the Early Modern World*. Berkeley: Univ. of California Press.

Graff, C., and R. Winthrop. 2010. "Beyond Madrasas: Assessing the Links Between Education and Militancy in Pakistan." Working paper, Center for Universal Education, Brookings Institution, Washington, DC.

Grare, F., and Maley, W. 2011. "The Afghan Refugees in Pakistan." Research paper, Refugee Cooperation, June 30. http://www.refugeecooperation.org/publications/Afghanistan/09_grare.php.

Gregorian, V. 1964. "The Emergence of Modern Afghanistan: Politics of Modernization, 1880–1930." PhD diss., Stanford University.

——. 1969. *The Emergence of Modern Afghanistan: Politics of Modernization, 1880–1930*. Stanford, CA: Stanford Univ. Press.

Gurr, T. R. 1970. *Why Men Rebel*. Princeton, NJ: Princeton Univ. Press.

——. 2000. *Peoples Versus States: Minorities at Risk in the New Century*. Washington, DC: United States Institute of Peace Press.

Guyot, W. 2007. "Transition from Community Based Education to the Ministry of Education System in Afghanistan: An Investigation of the Integration Process for Students and Teachers in Selected Districts of the PACE-A Partnership." PACE-A Integration Study, Partnership for Advancing Community Education in Afghanistan, Kabul, Afghanistan.

Hehir, A., and N. Robinson, eds. 2007. *State Building: Theory and Practice.* New York: Routledge.

Heyneman, S. P. 2000. "From the Party/State to Multiethnic Democracy: Education and Social Cohesion in Europe and Central Asia." *Educational Evaluation and Policy Analysis* 22, no. 2: 173–91.

———. 2003. "Education and Social Cohesion and the Future Role of International Organizations. *Peabody Journal of Education* 78: 25–38.

———. 2004. "Education and Corruption." *International Journal of Educational Development* 24, no. 6: 637–48.

Hitti, A., K. L. Mulvey, and M. Killen. 2011. "Exclusion in Adolescent Peer Relationships." In *Encyclopedia of Adolescence*, edited by R. Levesque, 2783–92. New York: Springer.

Hojman, D. 1996. "Poverty and Inequality in Chile: Are Democratic Politics and Neoliberal Economics Good for You?" Journal of Inter-American Studies and World Affairs 38: 73–96.

HRW (Human Rights Watch). 2006. *Lessons in Terror: Attacks on Education in Afghanistan.* New York: Human Rights Watch.

———. 2007. *The Human Cost: The Consequences of Insurgent Attacks in Afghanistan.* New York: Human Rights Watch.

———. 2009. "Letter to President Barack Obama on Afghanistan." New York: Human Rights Watch, March 26.

Humphreys, M., and J. Weinstein. 2008. "Who Fights? The Determinants of Participation in Civil War." *American Journal of Political Science* 52, no. 2: 436–55.

Huntington, S. 1996. *The Clash of Civilizations and the Remaking of World Order.* New York: Simon & Schuster.

ICG (International Crisis Group). 2009. "Afghanistan: New U.S. Administration, New Directions." Asia Briefing no. 89, March 13.

ICRC (International Committee of the Red Cross). n.d. "International Humanitarian Law." http://www.icrc.org/Eng/ihl.

INEE (Inter-Agency Network for Education in Emergencies). n.d. *Minimum Standards for Education: Preparedness, Response, Recovery—A Commitment to Access, Quality and Accountability.* New York: Inter-Agency Network for Education in Emergencies.

Islamic Emirate of Afghanistan (the Taliban). 2012. "Promotion of Education Inside the Country a Main Objective of the Islamic Emirate" (March 7). Translated by FlashPoint. https://flashpoint-intel.com/inteldocument/flashpoint_talibano 30712.pdf .

Islamic Republic of Afghanistan Central Statistics Organization. 2012–13. "Population Estimation 2012–13." http://cso.gov.af/en/page/6449.

Johnson, L. 2010. "Towards a Framework for Critical Citizenship Education. *Curriculum Journal* 21, no. 1: 77–96.

Jones, A. 2009. "Curriculum and Civil Society in Afghanistan." *Harvard Educational Review* 79, no. 1: 113–22.

Jones, S. 2009. "Going Local: The Key to Afghanistan," *Wall Street Journal*, August 7.

——. 2010. *In the Graveyard of Empires: America's War in Afghanistan.* New York: W. W. Norton.

J-PAL (Abdul Latif Jameel Poverty Action Lab). 2012. "The Effect of Village-Based Schools: Evidence from an RCT in Afghanistan." J-PAL Evaluation Summary, J-PAL, Massachusetts Institute of Technology, Cambridge. http://www.poverty actionlab.org/evaluation/effect-village-based-schools-evidence-rct-afghanistan.

Kagawa, F. 2005. "Emergency Education: A Critical Review of the Field." *Comparative Education* 41, no. 4: 487–503.

Kakar, M. H. 1995. *Afghanistan: The Soviet Invasion and the Afghan Response, 1979–1982.* Los Angeles: Univ. of California Press.

Kalyvas, S. 2006. *The Logic of Violence in Civil War.* New York: Cambridge Univ. Press.

Karlsson, P., and A. Mansoory. 2008. "Islamic and Modern Education in Afghanistan: Conflictual or Complementary?" Institute of International Education, Stockholm Univ., and World Bank. http://ddp-ext.worldbank.org/EdStats/AFGstu08.pdf.

Karpinska, Z. 2012. "Education, Aid and Agencies: A Global Overview." In *Education as a Humanitarian Response: Education, Aid and Aid Agencies,* edited by Z. Karpinska. New York: Continuum.

Keen, D. 2000. "Incentives and Disincentives for Violence." In *Greed and Grievance: Economic Agendas in Civil Wars,* edited by M. Berdal and D. M. Malone, 19–42. Boulder, CO: Lynne Rienner.

Kershner, I. 2013. "Academic Study Weakens Israeli Claim That Palestinian School Texts Teach Hate." *New York Times,* February 3.

Kifner, J. 2001. "A Nation Challenged: Changing Sides—As Alliance Deals With a Warlord, Taliban Fighters Slip Away." *New York Times,* November 24.

Killen, M., A. Rutland, D. Abrams, K. L. Mulvey, and A. Hitti. 2012. "Development of Intra-and Intergroup Judgments in the Context of Moral and Social-Conventional Norms." *Child Development* 84, no. 3: 1063–80.

King, E. 2011. "The Multiple Relationships Between Education and Conflict: Reflections of Rwandan Teachers and Students." In *Educating Children in Conflict Zones: Research, Policy, and Practice for Systemic Change—A Tribute to Jackie Kirk,* edited by K. Mundy and S. Dryden-Peterson, 137–52. New York: Teachers College Press.

——. 2014. *From Classrooms to Conflict in Rwanda.* New York: Cambridge Univ. Press.

Khan, J. 2009. "Masculinity in *Pashtunwali*: Beliefs, Practices, Symbols, and Discourses." Working paper, New York Univ.

——. 2012. "School or Madrassa? Parents' Choice and the Failure of State-run Education in Pakistan." PhD diss., New York Univ.

Krueger, A. B., and J. Maleckova. 2003. "Education, Poverty and Terrorism: Is There a Causal Connection?" NBER Working Paper no. 9074, National Bureau of Economic Research, Cambridge, MA.

Kupermintz, H., and G. Salomon. 2005. "Lessons to Be Learned From Research on Peace Education in the Context of Intractable Conflict." *Theory Into Practice* 44, no. 4: 293–302.

Lall, M. 2008. "Educate to Hate: The Use of Education in the Creation of Antagonistic National Identities in India and Pakistan." *Compare* 38, no. 1: 103–19.

Le Billon, P. 2003. "Buying Peace or Fuelling War: The Role of Corruption in Armed Conflicts." *Journal of International Development* 15, no. 4: 413–26.

Lieven, A. 2011. *Pakistan: A Hard Country.* New York: Public Affairs.

——. 2012. "Afghanistan: The Best way to Peace." *New York Review of Books,* February 9.

Londono, J. L. 1996. *Poverty, Inequality, and Human Capital Development in Latin America, 1950–2025.* Washington, DC: World Bank.

Lustig, I. 2002. "The Effects of Studying Distal Conflicts on the Perception of a Proximal One." Master's thesis, Univ. of Haifa, Israel (Hebrew).

Machel, G. 2001. *The Impact of War on Children.* London: UNICEF.

Macrae, J., and N. Leader. 2001. "Apples, Pears and Porridge: The Origins and Impact of the Search for 'Coherence' Between Humanitarian and Political Responses to Chronic Political Emergencies." *Disasters* 25, no. 4: 290–307.

Maley, W., and F. H. Saikal. 1986. "Afghan Refugee Relief in Pakistan: Political Context and Practical Problems." Working paper, Department of Politics, Univ. College, Univ. of New South Wales.

Mass, P. 2001. "Why Peshawar's Youth are Tinder for Islamic Extremism." *New York Times,* October 21.

McManus, D. 2010. "Key to Success Lies with Afghan Officials Coming Through." *Los Angeles Times,* April 18.

Meyer, J., F. O. Ramirez, and Y. Soysal.1992. "World Expansion of Mass Education, 1870–1980." *Sociology of Education* 65, no. 2: 128–49.

Minear, L. 2002. *The Humanitarian Enterprise: Dilemmas and Discoveries.* Sterling, VA: Kumarian Press.

Mir Munshi Sultan Muhamed Kahn, ed. 1900. *The Life of Abdur Rahman, Amir of Afghanistan.* Vol. 2. London.

MoE (Islamic Republic of Afghanistan Ministry of Education). 2007. *Schools Survey Summary Report.* Kabul: Ministry of Education EMIS Department.

——. 2011. *1390/2011 Annual Progress Report.* Kabul: Ministry of Education General Planning and Evaluation Department EMIS Directorate.

MRRD (Islamic Republic of Afghanistan Ministry of Rural Rehabilitation and Development). n.d. *Ghor Provincial Profile.* Kabul: Afghanistan Ministry of Rural Rehabilitation and Development. http://www.mrrd.gov.af/NABDP/Provincial%20Profiles/Ghor%20PDP%20Provincial%20profile.pdf.

Muller, G. 2011. *Designing History in East Asian Textbooks: Identity Politics and Transnational Aspirations.* New York: Routledge.

Mundy, K., and S. Dryden-Peterson, eds. 2011a. *Educating Children in Conflict Zones: Research, Policy, and Practice for Systemic Change—A Tribute to Jackie Kirk.* New York: Teachers College Press.

——. 2011b. "Educating Children in Zones of Conflict: An Overview and Introduction." In *Educating Children in Conflict Zones: Research, Policy, and Practice for*

Systemic Change—A Tribute to Jackie Kirk, edited by K. Mundy and S. Dryden-Peterson. New York: Teachers College Press, 2011.

Murshed, S. M., and S. Gates. 2005. "Spatial–Horizontal Inequality and the Maoist Insurgency in Nepal." *Review of Development Economics* 9, no. 1: 121–34.

Nasr, V. 2007. *The Shia Revival: How Conflicts Within Islam Will Shape the Future.* New York: W. W. Norton.

Nawid, S. 1999. *Religious Response to Social Change in Afghanistan, 1919–29.* Costa Mesa, CA: Mazda.

Nelles, W., ed. 2004. *Comparative Education, Terrorism and Human Security: From Critical Pedagogy to Peace Building?* New York, Palgrave Macmillan.

Nicolai. S., and C. Triplehorn. 2003. "The Role of Education in Protecting Children in Conflict." HPN Paper no. 42, Overseas Development Institute, London.

Niens, U., and M. Chastenay. 2008. "Educating for Peace? Citizenship Education in Quebec and Northern Ireland." *Comparative Education Review* 52, no. 4: 519–40.

Nojumi, N. 2002. *The Rise of the Taliban in Afghanistan: Mass Mobilization, Civil War, and the Future of the Region.* New York: Palgrave.

Nojumi, N., D. E. Mazurana, and E. Stites. 2009. *After the Taliban: Life and Security in Rural Afghanistan.* New York: Rowman & Littlefield.

Novelli, M. 2011. "Are We All Soldiers Now? The Dangers of the Securitization of Education and Conflict." In *Educating Children in Conflict Zones: Research, Policy, and Practice for Systemic Change—A Tribute to Jackie Kirk,* edited by K. Mundy and S. Dryden-Peterson. New York: Teachers College Press.

NSC (United States National Security Council). 1952. "United States Objectives and Policies with Respect to the Arab States and Israel." Executive Secretary Report to the National Security Council, April 7. Annex to NSC 129, National Archives, Washington, DC.

O'Malley, B. 2007. *Education Under Attack: A Global Study on Targeted Political and Military Violence Against Education Staff, Students, Teachers, Union and Government Officials, and Institutions.* Paris: UNESCO.

——. 2010. *Education Under Attack 2010.* Paris: UNESCO.

Ostby, G. 2008. "Polarization, Horizontal Inequalities and Violent Civil Conflict." *Journal of Peace Research* 45 no. 2: 143–62.

Ostby, G., R. Nordas, and J. K. Rod. 2009. "Regional Inequalities and Civil Conflict in Sub-Saharan Africa." *International Studies Quarterly* 53: 301–24.

Ostby, G., and H. Urdal. 2010. "Education and Civil Conflict: A Review of the Quantitative, Empirical Literature." Paper commissioned for the Education For All Global Monitoring Report 2011, UNESCO.

Oxfam. 2010. "Quick Impact, Quick Collapse: The Dangers of Militarized Aid in Afghanistan." http://www.oxfam.org/sites/www.oxfam.org/files/quick-impact-quick-collapse-jan-2010.pdf.

PACE-A (Partnership for Advancing Community Education in Afghanistan). 2007. PACE-A Summary. Kabul, Afghanistan: USAID Afghanistan/CARE International.

Paluck, E. L., and D. P. Green. 2009. "Deference, Dissent, and Dispute Resolution: An Experimental Intervention Using Mass Media to Change Norms and Behavior in Rwanda." *American Political Science Review* 103, no. 4: 622.

Paris, R. 2004. *At War's End: Building Peace After Civil Conflict.* New York: Cambridge Univ. Press.

Paris, R., and T. D. Sisk. 2009. *The Dilemmas of Statebuilding: Confronting the Contradictions of Postwar Peace Operations.* New York, Routledge.

Paulson, J. 2011. *Education, Conflict, and Development.* Oxford, UK: Symposium.

Paulson, J., and J. Rappleye. 2007. "Education and Conflict: Essay Review." *International Journal of Educational Development* 27: 340–47.

Peters, K., and P. Richards. 1998. "Why We Fight: Voices of Youth Ex-Combatants in Sierra Leone." *Africa* 68, no. 1: 183–210.

Pillsbury, K., and A. M. Nashef. 1964. "The UNRWA-UNESCO School System for Palestine (Arab) Refugees." *Comparative Education Review* 8, no. 3: 285–89.

Ramirez, F., and J. Boli. 1987. "The Political Construction of Mass Schooling: European Origins and Worldwide Institutionalization." *Sociology of Education* 60, no. 1: 2–17.

Rashid, A. 2000. *Taliban: Militant Islam, Oil, and Fundamentalism in Central Asia.* New Haven: Yale University Press.

——. 2012. "Why Are We Abandoning the Afghans?" *New York Review of Books,* May 22.

Richards, P. 2003. "The Political Economy of Internal Conflict in Sierra Leone." 'Clingendael' Conflict Research Unit Working Paper, Netherlands Institute of International Relations, The Hague.

Rieff, D. 1995. "The Humanitarian Trap." *World Policy Journal* 12, no. 4: 1–11.

Rogin, J. 2010. "Holbrooke Wins the War . . . Against USAID." *Foreign Policy, the Cable,* July 19.

Rose, P. 2003. "Community Partnerships in School Policy and Practice in Malawi: Balancing Local Knowledge, National Policies and International Agency Priorities." *Compare* 33, no. 1: 47–64.

Rose, P., and M. Greeley. 2006. "Education in Fragile States: Capturing Lessons and Identifying Good Practices." Prepared for the Fragile States Group, Development Assistance Committee, Organization for Security and Cooperation in Europe.

Rowe, D. 2000. "Value Pluralism, Democracy, and Education for Citizenship." In *Developing Pedagogy,* edited by J. Collins, K. Insley, and J. Soler, 173–86. New York: Sage.

Rowell, J. Forthcoming. *Learning Resilience: A Study of Vulnerability and Protection in Afghan Schools.* Kabul: CARE Afghanistan.

Roy, O. 1990. *Islam and Resistance in Afghanistan.* 2nd ed. New York: Cambridge Univ. Press.

Rubin, A. J. 2010. "Reports Say Afghan Official in Showcase City May Have Criminal Background." *New York Times,* March 6.

——. 2013. "In Old Taliban Strongholds, Qualms About What Lies Ahead." *New York Times,* January 8.

Rubin, B. R. 1995. *The Fragmentation of Afghanistan.* New Haven, CT: Yale Univ. Press.

——. 2002. *The Fragmentation of Afghanistan.* 2nd ed. New Haven, CT: Yale Univ. Press.

Rugh, A. B. 2012. *Education Assistance in Egypt, Pakistan, and Afghanistan.* New York: Palgrave Connect.

Salomon, G. 2004. "Does Peace Education Make a Difference in the Context of an Intractable Conflict?" *Peace and Conflict: Journal of Peace Psychology* 10, no. 3: 257–74.

Samady, S. R. 2001. *Education and Afghan Society in the Twentieth Century.* Paris: UNESCO.

Sassani, A. H. K. 1961. *Education in Afghanistan.* Washington DC: US Department of Health, Education, and Welfare, Office of Education, 1961.

Save the Children. 2013. *Attacks on Education: The Impact of Conflict and Grave Violations on Children's Futures.* London: Save the Children.

SCFR (Senate Committee on Foreign Relations). 2011. *Evaluating U.S. Foreign Assistance to Afghanistan: A Majority Staff Report Prepared for the Use of the Committee on Foreign Relations.* United States Senate, 112th Congress, S. Rep. 112–21, June 8.

Schmidt, C., and A. Taylor. 2010. "Liberia's Education Pooled Fund: A Case for Private Foundation Engagement in Post Conflict Education Recovery." Paper presented at conference "Leveraging the Private Sector for Results in Education," World Bank, Washington, DC.

SCHR (Steering Committee for Humanitarian Response). 2010. "SCHR Position Paper on Humanitarian-Military Relations." Geneva: Steering Committee for Humanitarian Response.

Semple, M., T. Farrell, A. Lieven, and R. Chaudhuri. 2012. "Taliban Perspectives on Reconciliation." Briefing paper, Royal United Services Institute, London.

Shafi, A., and N. Sharifi. 2013. "The Myth of the American Superman." *Foreign Policy,* August 7. http://afpak.foreignpolicy.com/posts/2013/08/07/the_myth_of_the _american_superman.

Shafiq, M. N., and A. H. Sinno. 2010. "Education, Income, and Support for Suicide Bombings: Evidence from Six Muslim Countries." *Journal of Conflict Resolution* 54, no. 1: 146–78.

SIGAR (Special Investigator General on Afghanistan Reconstruction). 2011. *Audit of USAID/Afghanistan's Afghanistan Stabilization Initiative for the Southern Region.* Report no. F-306–12–001-P, Office of Inspector General, Kabul, Afghanistan, November 13.

——. 2012a. *Audit of USAID/Afghanistan's Afghanistan Stabilization Initiative for the Southern Region.* Report no. F-306–12–001-P, Office of the Inspector General, Kabul, Afghanistan, April 25.

——. 2012b. *Progress Made Toward Increased Stability under USAID's Afghanistan Stabilization Initiative-East Program but Transition to Long Term Development*

Efforts Not Yet Achieved. Office of the Inspector General, Kabul, Afghanistan, June 29.

Sinclair, M. 2002. *Planning Education in and After Emergencies*. Paris: UNESCO -IIEP.

Smith, A. 2005. "Education in the Twenty-First Century: Conflict, Reconstruction and Reconciliation." *Compare* 35, no. 4: 373–91.

Sobe, N. 2009. "Educational Reconstruction 'By the Dawn's Early Light': Violent Political Conflict and American Overseas Education Reform." *Harvard Educational Review* 79, no 1: 123–31.

Spink, J. 2005. "Education and Politics in Afghanistan: The Importance of an Educational System to Peacebuilding and Reconstruction." *Journal of Peace Education* 2, no. 2: 195–207.

Stein, M. 2011. "Lawmakers Question CERP Funds in Afghanistan." *Marine Corps News*, August 4.

Stephens, J., and D. B. Ottaway. 2002. "From US the ABCs of Jihad: Violent Soviet-Era Textbooks Complicate Afghan Education Efforts." *Washington Post*, March 23.

Stewart, F. 2000. "The Root Causes of Humanitarian Emergencies." In *War, Hunger, and Displacement: The Origins of Humanitarian Emergencies*, edited by E. Nafziger, F. Stewart, and R. Vayrynen, 1–42. New York: Oxford Univ. Press.

——. 2002. "Horizontal Inequalities: A Neglected Dimension of Development." Univ. of Oxford Working Paper Series no. 81, Queen Elizabeth House, Univ. of Oxford.

Stewart, F., G. Brown, and L. Mancini. 2005. "Why Horizontal Inequalities Matter: Some Implications for Measurement." Working Paper no. 19, Centre for Research on Inequality, Human Security and Ethnicity, Univ. of Oxford.

Stoddard, A. 2009. "Humanitarian NGOS: Challenges and Trends." Humanitarian Policy Group Briefing No. 12. London: Overseas Development Institute.

Strickland, R. T. 2007. "The Way of the Pashtun: Pashtunwali." *Canadian Army Journal* 10, no. 3: 44–55.

Sullivan, M. G. 1973. "Schooling and National Integration in Afghanistan: A Study of Students in the Faculty of Education, Kabul University." PhD diss., Univ. of Pittsburgh.

Sustainable Development Policy Institute. 2004. *The Subtle Subversion: The State of Curicula and Textbooks in Pakistan*. Islamabad, Pakistan: Sustainable Development Policy Institute.

Tarnoff, C. 2010. "Afghanistan: U.S. Foreign Assistance." Washington, DC: Congressional Research Service, August 12.

Terry, F. 2002. *Condemned to Repeat? The Paradox of Humanitarian Action*. Ithaca, NY: Cornell Univ. Press.

Thier, J. A. 2008. As quoted in M. Gordon. "Afghan Strategy Poses Stiff Challenges for Obama." *New York Times*, December 2.

Thyne, C. 2006. "ABC's, 123's and the Golden Rule: The Pacifying Effect of Education on Civil Conflict, 1980–1999." *International Studies Quarterly* 50: 733–54.

Turton, D., and P. Marsden. 2002. "Taking Refugees for a Ride: The Politics of Refugee Return to Afghanistan." Issue Paper Series, Afghanistan Research and Evaluation Unit, Kabul, December.

UN (United Nations). 2012. *Children and Armed Conflict: Report of the Secretary-General.* A/66/782–S/2012/261. New York: United Nations.

UNDP (United Nations Development Program). 2007. *Afghan Human Development Report 2007.* Kabul: Center for Policy and Human Development, Kabul Univ.

UNESCO (United Nations Educational Scientific and Cultural Organization). 2004. *Education, Conflict, and Social Cohesion.* Geneva: UNESCO International Bureau of Education.

——. 2011. *Global Monitoring Report: The Hidden Crisis: Armed Conflict and Education.* Paris: UNESCO Publishing.

——. 2012. *Global Monitoring Report: Youth and Skills: Putting Education to Work.* Paris: UNESCO Publishing.

UNICEF (United Nations Children's Fund). 2009. *Humanitarian Action Report: Mid-Year Review.* New York: UNICEF.

——. 2010. "Afghanistan: Statistics." http://www.unicef.org/infobycountry/afghanistan_statistics.html#91.

——. 2011. *Education in Emergencies and Post Crisis Transition: 2010 Report Evaluation.* New York: UNICEF.

——. n.d. "Convention of the Rights of the Child: Frequently Asked Questions" http://www.unicef.org/crc/index_30229.html (March 4, 2013).

United Nations Assistance Mission in Afghanistan. 2008. *Armed Conflict and Civilian Casualties, Afghanistan: Trends and Developments, 01 January 2008–31 August 2008.* Kabul, Afghanistan: United Nations Assistance Mission in Afghanistan.

UNO (Univ. of Nebraska, Omaha). 1987. "Sovietization of Afghan Education." Education Support Sector Project.

——. n.d. "Thomas E. Gouttierre." http://world.unomaha.edu/cas/img/teg_bio_poem.pdf .

Urdal, H. 2006. "A Clash of Generations? Youth Bulges and Political Violence." *International Studies Quarterly* 50, no. 3: 607–29.

USAID (United States Agency for International Development). 1988. *Education Support Sector Project, Quarterly Report for Sept. 1, 1987–January 31, 1988.* Order no. PD-ABU-427. Office of Afghan Field Operations, January.

——. 1994a. *Project Assistance Completion Report: Education Sector Support Project.* Order no. PD-ABJ-201. Office of Afghan Field Operations, June.

——. 1994b. *End of Project Report, Education Sector Support Project.* Order no. PD-ABK-618. Office of Afghan Field Operations, June.

——. 2005a. *Conflict Mitigation and Management Policy.* Washington DC: USAID.

——. 2005b. *Youth and Extremism.* Washington, DC: USAID.

——. 2006a. *Education and Fragility: An Assessment Tool.* Washington, DC: USAID.

——. 2006b. *Provincial Reconstruction Teams in Afghanistan: An Interagency Assessment.* Washington DC: USAID.

——. 2009. *Religion, Conflict, and Peacebuilding.* Washington, DC: USAID.

——. 2011a. *The Development Response to Violence Extremism and Insurgency: Putting Principles into Practice.* Washington, DC: USAID.

——. 2011b. "District Stability Framework." Paper presented at the Social Science Underpinnings of Complex Operations MORS Mini-Symposium, George Mason Univ., Arlington, VA, October 18–21, 2010.

——. 2011c. "Stabilization." USAID Afghanistan, June. http://afghanistan.usaid.gov/en/programs/stabilization#Tab=Description (March 5, 2013).

——. 2011d. "Text Descriptions for U.S. Official Development Assistance (ODA) Fast Facts: CY2011." http://usoda.eads.usaidallnet.gov/data/fast_facts_text_descriptions .html#chart6 (February 11, 2013).

——. 2011e. "U.S. Official Development Assistance (ODA) Fast Facts: CY2011." http://usoda.eads.usaidallnet.gov/data/fast_facts.html (February 11, 2013).

——. 2012. "3D Planning Guide: Diplomacy, Development, Defense." 31 July. http://www.usaid.gov/sites/default/files/documents/1866/3D%20Planning%20Guide _Update_FINAL%20%2831%20Jul%2012%29.pdf.

US Army. 2008. "Stability Operations." US Army FM 3–07. Ann Arbor, MI: Univ. of Michigan Press.

US Army Combined Arms Center. 2011. *Afghanistan Provincial Reconstruction Teams: Observations, Insights, and Lessons.* Fort Leavenworth, KS: US Army Combined Arms Center.

US Army/Marine Corps. 2006. *Counterinsurgency Field Manual.* US Army FM 3–24 and Marine Corps Warfighting Publication no. 3–33.5.

USG (United States Government [agency not indicated]). 1962. "Elements of US Policy Toward Afghanistan." DD (1978, 65B), March 27.

——. 1980. "The Soviets and the Tribes of Southwest Asia." DD (1985, 000834).

——. 2002. *The National Security Strategy of the United States of America.* Washington, DC: US Department of State. http://www.state.gov/documents/organization/63562 .pdf

USIP (United States Institute of Peace). 2009. *Religion, Conflict, and Peacebuilding.* Washington, DC: United States Institute of Peace, 2009.

USIP and US ARMY (United States Institute of Peace and United States Army Peacekeeping and Stability Operations Institute). 2009. *Guiding Principles for Stabilization and Reconstruction.* Washington, DC: United States Institute of Peace.

Van Linschoten, A. S., and F. Kuehn. 2012. *An Enemy We Created: The Myth of the Taliban-Al Qaeda Merger in Afghanistan.* New York: Oxford Univ. Press.

Voreacos, D. 2011. "Berger Group Pays $69.3 Million for Iraq Overbilling," *Bloomberg Businessweek,* May 5.

Ward, F. B., III. 1978. "Education for National Allegiance in Afghanistan: A Study of the Development of a New Elementary School Social Studies Curriculum as a Means of Encouraging National Unity in a Developing Country." PhD diss., Columbia Univ.

Weiss, T. G. 1999. "Principles, Politics, and Humanitarian Action." *Ethics and International Affairs* 13, no. 1: 1–22.

Williams, B. 2003. *Windfalls of War.* Washington, DC: Center for Public Integrity.

Winthrop, R., S. Ndaruhutse, J. Dolan, and A. Adams. 2010. *Education's Hardest Test: Scaling up Aid in Fragile and Conflict-Affected States.* Washington, DC: Center for Universal Education, Brookings Institute.

Woo, Y. Y. J., and J. A. Simmons. 2008. "Paved with Good Intentions: Images of Textbook Developments in Afghanistan." *Asia Pacific Journal of Education.* 3: 291–304.

Woodward, S. L. 2001. "Humanitarian War: A New Consensus?" *Disasters* 25, no. 4: 331–44.

World Bank. 2005. *Reshaping the Future: Education and Post-Conflict Reconstruction.* Washington DC: World Bank Group.

Wray, H. 1991. "Change and Continuity in Modern Japanese Educational History: Allied Occupational Reforms Forty Years Later." *Comparative Education Review* 35, no. 3, 447–75.

Wright, L. 2006. "The Master Plan." *New Yorker,* September 11.

Zaeef, A. S. 2010. *My Life with the Taliban.* Translated by A. S. Van Linschoten and F. Kuehn. New York: Columbia Univ. Press.

Zelikow, P. D., E. R. May, and B. Jenkins. 2004. *The 9/11 Commission Report.* New York: W. W. Norton.

Index

jihad/jihadist curriculum, 21–22, 163
jihad literacy: Cold-War education
strategy and its influence on US
invasion, 81–84; education as part
of war effort, 72–80; geopolitical
context, 67–72; modernization and
continuing struggle over education,
60–64; power of negative curricula,
57–59; relationship between
textbooks and violence, 84–85;
religious education in Afghanistan,
60–61; scope and reach of, 79–80;
Soviet invasion of Afghanistan,
64–67; textbook analysis, 75–79; as
US education policy in Afghanistan
in 1980s, 5

Kandahar, 3, 95
Karmal, B., 66
Karzai, H., 17, 99, 132
KhAD, 66
Khalilzad, Z., 84
Khalq, 78
King, E., 15
Kosovar Albanians, 32
Krueger, A. B., 18
Kuehn, F., 70

*Leading with Civilian Power: The First
Quadrennial Diplomacy and
Development Review*, 37
Lebanon, 107
life-saving aid, 168
Louis Berger Group Inc., 100, 114
Loya Jirga, 96

madrassas, 56, 59, 60–61, 64, 69, 73, 79,
86, 87, 95, 96, 120, 121, 163
Maleckova, J., 18
Marja, 89
Massoud, A. S., 95, 96
maulawis, 64
maximalist paradigm, 26, 27, 40–42,
43, 46, 47

Mazar-i-Sharif, 95
McChrystal, S., 13, 89
Médecins San Frontières (MSF)
(Doctors Without Borders), 36,
42, 47
media coverage, 39, 49, 166
metaphor of light, moving from
illiteracy to literacy, 8
militancy: correlation between
education and support for, 58,
85; and education, 18–20;
indoctrination into, 75; madrassas
and, 59; UNO educators approach
to fostering, 80
militarization, of humanitarian aid,
37–39, 40
minimalist paradigm, 26, 27, 39, 40–42,
46, 47, 48
Ministry of Education (MoE), 62, 63,
67, 83, 127, 128, 130, 131, 134, 135, 139,
141, 146, 150, 152, 155, 157, 158, 160,
168, 169
mixed gender classes, 66
modernists/traditionalists tensions,
12, 156
modernization, and education, 11, 13,
60–64, 97, 112
Morocco, 19
Mortenson, G., 3, 4, 13
mosque schools, 9, 11, 12, 60–61, 62, 64,
96, 120, 139, 145, 152
MSF (Médecins San Frontières)
(Doctors Without Borders), 36,
42, 47
mujahideen, 12, 56, 59, 68, 69, 70, 71, 72,
73, 74, 75, 78–79, 80, 86, 87, 94, 95,
163
mujahideen textbooks, 55, 73, 87
Mullah Mohammad Omar, 86
mullahs, 9, 10, 12, 60, 61, 64, 65, 120,
145, 151, 152

Nadir Shah, 60
Najibullah, M., 74, 94

Index

US aid, stabilization and counterinsurgency, 98–107, 121

stabilization programs, 7, 16, 18, 38, 90, 91, 92, 93, 100, 103, 104–119, 122, 123, 124, 153, 165

standards, for aid to education into humanitarian reforms, 28

state-building, 4, 5, 24, 41, 55

state-controlled school system, 61

Stones into Schools (Mortenson), 3

suicide bombings, 18, 19, 20, 58, 85

Sunnis, 69

Sunni-Shia tensions, 69

Syria, 52

Tajiks, 115

Taliban: attacks on schools, 127, 133; attempting to modify attitude toward education, 137, 138; demands for curriculum changes, 127; disrupting provision of and access to education, 137, 152; educational access for boys, 120; education policy during rule of, 94–98; efforts to limit access to education, 133; on girls' education, 2, 96, 97, 98, 133, 137, 150; shift in position on education, 133; tactics to prevent pursuit of education, 132; and US-sponsored jihadist books, 56

taliban, meaning of word, 94–95

Tarzi, M., 11

teachers: difficulty in finding local teachers, 145; female, 19, 80, 133; lack of qualified teachers, 134, 151

Teachers College, Columbia University (TC), 62, 168

Terry, F., 36, 37, 41

textbook analysis, 75–79

textbooks: current MoE textbooks, 130, 142, 168; Israeli textbooks, 58, 149; jihadi/jihadist textbooks, 20, 55, 56, 57, 59, 84, 85, 86, 87, 163, 168, 169; mujahideen textbooks, 55, 73, 87;

negative textbooks, 129; new national Afghan textbooks, 149; Palestinian textbooks, 20, 58, 149; positive textbooks, 129; relationship of with violence, 84–85; violence-infused, 81; violent content or positive messages? 162–65

Three Cups of Tea (Mortenson), 3, 13

traditionalists/modernists tensions, 12, 156

traditional school system, 61

Truman, H. S., 31

UN Consolidated Appeals, 35

unequal access: to education, 91, 92–94, 115, 122, 123, 124, 165–67; to stabilization programs, 107–112

UNESCO Global Monitoring Report, 16

UNHCR/CAR schools, 73

United Nations, 31

United Nations Children's Fund (UNICEF), 42, 44, 82, 83, 135, 146

United Nations High Commission for Refugees (UNHCR), 48, 72, 73, 79

United Nations Office for the Coordination of Humanitarian Affairs (UNOCHA), 35

United Nations Relief and Works Agency (UNRWA), 48

Universal Education (Brookings Forum on), 81

universality, 30, 41, 47

universal right, 18, 127, 128, 156, 166

University of Kabul, 61

University of Nebraska at Omaha (UNO), 56, 57, 74, 79, 80, 81, 82, 83, 84, 129

urban concerns/attitudes, 120

urban-rural contrasts, 155

urban-rural disparity, 135

urban-rural tensions, 9, 12, 60, 62–63, 97, 156

Urdal, H., 14